OBJECT RELATIONS AND
SOCIAL RELATIONS

OBJECT RELATIONS
AND
SOCIAL RELATIONS

The Implications of the Relational
Turn in Psychoanalysis

edited by

*Simon Clarke, Herbert Hahn,
and Paul Hoggett*

KARNAC

First published in 2008 by
Karnac Books Ltd
118 Finchley Road, London NW3 5HT

British Library Cataloguing in Publication Data

A C.I.P. for this book is available from the British Library

ISBN 978 1 85575 563 5

Edited, designed and produced by The Studio Publishing Services Ltd
www.publishingservicesuk.co.uk
e-mail: studio@publishingservicesuk.co.uk

Printed in Great Britain

www.karnacbooks.com

CONTENTS

Simon Clarke is Professor of Psycho-Social Studies and Director of the Centre for Psycho-Social Studies at the University of the West of England. His research interests include the interface between sociological and psychoanalytic theory; emotions; Kleinian and post-Kleinian thinking; and the social application of psychoanalytic theory and practice. He has published numerous articles, essays, and reviews on the psychoanalytic understanding of racism, ethnic hatred, and social conflict. Simon is the author of *Social Theory, Psychoanalysis and Racism* (2003, London, Palgrave); *From Enlightenment to Risk: Social Theory and Contemporary Society* (2005, London, Palgrave); and *Emotion, Politics and Society* (2006), (co-edited with Hoggett and Thompson). Simon is a member of the board of directors of the Association for the Psychoanalysis of Culture and Society and Editor of *Psychoanalysis, Culture & Society*. He has recently completed a research project that forms part of the larger £4 Million ESRC "social identities" programme. The project looks at notions of home and identity in contemporary Britain.

Lynn Froggett is Reader in Psychosocial Welfare and Director of the UCLAN Psychosocial Research Unit. Her work is strongly interdisciplinary. She has a social work background and draws on perspectives from the humanities and creative arts, social sciences, psychoanalytic theory, and gender studies. She also co-edits *The Journal of Social Work Practice*. Her wider project is to develop the theoretical and conceptual terrain on which to link social policy and social provision with day-to-day experiences of care. This approach was developed in *Love, Hate and Welfare* (2003, Policy Press), and has been supported by an empirical research programme with a particular focus on arts-based community settings and the development innovative research strategies that include narrative, biographical, visual, and performative methods. She recently completed a three-year study of integrated approaches to adult health and social care in an arts-based community setting, and is currently developing research and evaluation in a range of locations that use creative interventions. These include a children's centre and restorative youth justice and regeneration contexts. She is Executive and Founding member of the International Research Group for Psychosocietal Analysis.

Herbert Hahn is a Senior Visiting Research Fellow in the Centre for Psycho-Social Studies at the University of the West of England. He is an experienced psychotherapist, supervisor, mentor, group facilitator, and organizational consultant who has worked at the Tavistock Institute and Clinic and the European School of Management Studies. He co-founded the Severnside Institute for Psychotherapy when he moved to Bristol some years ago. Recently, he has engaged in and contributed to the development of social dreaming and its application to a variety of settings, including conflict resolution, and has discovered a keen interest in relational psychoanalysis and the place of passion in professional work.

Paul Hoggett is Professor of Politics and Director of the Centre for Psycho-Social Studies at the University of the West of England. He is a psychoanalytic psychotherapist, a member of the Severnside Institute for Psychotherapy, Associate Member of the Lincoln, and is also an experienced group relations consultant. He teaches and writes in the area of political psychology and applies psychoanalytic and other theories of the emotions to understanding the organization of civil society and the dynamics of democracy and conflict.

He has authored two books on these issues: *Partisans in an Uncertain World* (1992, Free Association Books), and *Emotional Life and the Politics of Welfare* (2000, Macmillan); and, with Simon Clarke and Simon Thompson, has edited the collection *Emotion, Politics and Society* (2006, Palgrave). He recently completed an ESRC funded project, "Negotiating ethical dilemmas in contested communities", and, with Simon Thompson, is currently organizing an ESRC-funded seminar series on "Politics and the emotions". He is a board member of the Association for Psychoanalysis, Culture and Society, and has editorial roles on *Organisational & Social Dynamics, Psychodynamic Practice*, and *Psychoanalysis Culture and Society*.

Wendy Hollway is Professor in Psychology at the Open University. She is interested in applying psychoanalytic principles to theorizing subjectivity, to methodology, and to empirical research on identity. Her current ESRC-funded research on the transition to a maternal identity uses both free association narrative interview and psychoanalytic observation methods. She has researched and published on questions to do with subjectivity, gender, sexuality, mothering, qualitative methods, psycho-social methods, history of work psychology, and fear of crime. Her books include *Changing the Subject: Psychology, Social Regulation and Subjectivity* (1984/1998, London, Routledge) (with Henriques, Urwin, Venn, and Walkerdine); *Subjectivity and Method in Psychology: Gender, Meaning and Science* (1989, London, Sage); *Mothering and Ambivalence* (1997, London, Routledge) (co-edited with Brid Featherstone); and *Doing Qualitative Research Differently: Free Association, Narrative and the Interview Method* (2000, London, Sage) (with Tony Jefferson).. Her latest book, *The Capacity to Care: Gender and Ethical Subjectivity*, was published by Routledge in 2006.

Karen Izod is an independent organizational change consultant, KIzod Consulting, and a Principal Associate at the Tavistock Institute, where she is Co-Director of their Coaching for Leadership and Professional Development course and Faculty Member for the MA in Advanced Organisational Consultation. Working across a wide range of sectors, she specializes in helping organizations and individuals create structures and positions to work to best effect. Her research interests focus on entrepreneurial leadership and the organizational dynamics of delivery. Karen's early background in is social work and public sector management.

Lynne Layton, PhD, is Assistant Clinical Professor of Psychology, Harvard Medical School. She has taught culture and psychoanalysis for Harvard's Committee on Degrees in Social Studies and teaches at the Massachusetts Institute for Psychoanalysis. She is the author of *Who's That Girl? Who's That Boy? Clinical Practice Meets Postmodern Gender Theory* (2004, Analytic Press), co-editor, with Susan Fairfield and Carolyn Stack, of *Bringing the Plague. Toward a Postmodern Psychoanalysis* (2002, Other Press), and co-editor, with Nancy Caro Hollander and Susan Gutwill, of *Psychoanalysis, Class and Politics: Encounters in the Clinical Setting* (2006, Routledge). She is editor of *Psychoanalysis, Culture & Society* and associate editor of *Studies in Gender and Sexuality*. Her private practice is in Brookline, Massachusetts, USA.

Susie Orbach is a psychotherapist and writer. She co-founded The Women's Therapy Centre in 1976 and The Women's Therapy Centre Institute, a training institute in New York, in 1981. Her books include *Fat is a Feminist Issue*; *Hunger Strike*; *On Eating*; *What's Really Going on Here*; *Towards Emotional Literacy*; and, with Luise Eichenbaum, *Understanding Women*; *Between Women*; and *What Do Women Want? The Impossibility of Sex* is a series of imagined tales from therapy told from the psychotherapist's point of view. She is a founder member of ANTIDOTE (working for emotional literacy) and Psychotherapists for Social Responsibility. She is also convenor of ANYBODY (working on body diversity) and a board member of The International Association for Relational Psychoanalysis and Psychotherapy. She is currently a Visiting Professor at the LSE, and has been a consultant to the World Bank, the NHS, and Unilever. She has a clinical practice seeing individuals and couples.

Margaret Page is a Senior Lecturer in Organisation Studies at Bristol Business School, University of the West of England. She teaches Leading and Managing Change on a variety of postgraduate and undergraduate programmes. Her current research concerns inquiry-based methodologies for leadership, learning, and change in organizations. Previously, she was an independent organizational consultant, specializing in women's equality and inter-organizational partnership working. Through her early work roles in community development and women's equality, she became interested in methods for sustaining collaborative practice and learning across differences of culture and identity. These interests continue to inform her teaching and research. Her publications are eclectic, and include consultancy reports on women's equality projects, and academic conference papers on inquiry as pedagogy and as methodology for organizational culture change.

Paul Zeal began psychoanalytic practice in 1970, worked in London until 1988, and in Taunton from 1985. He was a therapist in therapeutic households for people in extreme states of mind for twenty years. He chaired Severnside Institute for Psychotherapy for six years, and is a training therapist and supervisor for SIP and a number of other organizations. He has published little, taught a lot, and given many papers. Publications include: "Schreber's fall", *British Journal of Psychotherapy* (2006) 22(4); a dissertation on autobiographical genres (Nietzsche, Derrida, and Laing) at Dartington College of Arts; and mini-essays on R. D. Laing, Erich Fromm, and Bob Dylan in *Visionaries of the Twentieth Century* (2006, Totnes, Green Books).

Introduction

Herbert Hahn

In "How it all started" (Karnac, 2007) Harry Karnac ascribes the birth of his now famous publishing house to friendly encouragement from Donald Winnicott in the 1950s. It was also Donald Winnicott, in the 1960s during my Tavistock Child Psychotherapy Training, who opened my heart and mind to the spirit of what we, in this book, name as the "relational turn". However, apart from enlivening connections with Nina Coltart, Cecily de Monchaux, and Meg Sharpe (group analysis), the relational spirit in me remained largely dormant over the next four decades. The beginnings of a reawakening were reflected in a chapter on supervision (Hahn, 1998) but were only fully re-enlivened on 16 April 2005, when I participated in the first London teach-in on "(Trans Atlantic) relational psychoanalysis", organized by a UK steering group and focusing on a pre-circulated paper by Jody Messler Davis (2004). The day itself began in a spirit of creative dialogue between invited respondents, followed by an encouragingly facilitated group engagement. For me, the whole experience was a professional turning point, not dissimilar to that described by our contributors to this book as they began actively to engage with the relational psychoanalytic vertex.

The precursor to the book as a whole was a conference organized by the Centre for Psycho-Social Studies at the University of
the West of England, entitled "Relational thinking: connecting psychoanalysis, institutions and society". This itself stemmed from a
Centre reading group on "relational psychoanalysis". Our intention
at the conference was to encourage dialogues between academics,
researchers, and clinicians.

The emergence of what has become known as "the relational
turn" in psychoanalysis has interesting implications not just for
clinical practice, but for other psychoanalytically informed practices, such as group relations, the human service professions, and
social research. Relational forms of psychoanalysis have emerged
primarily in the USA, and as a result their core concepts and methods are less well known in other countries, including the UK. Moreover, even within the USA, few attempts have so far been made to
consider the wider implications of this development for social and
political theory, intervention in groups and organizations, and the
practice of social research. As with all new developments, there is a
tendency to deal with them in one of two ways: either to insist that
there is nothing new about them and that existing practices already
include their implied critique, or to sharpen and exaggerate the difference, thereby construing the new arrival as something that is a
counter, rather than an extension and complement, to what already
exists.

This book has two essential aims. First, to introduce some of the
key assumptions behind relational psychoanalysis to an international audience and to outline the points where this approach counters, complements, or extends existing object relations' (Kleinian
and Independent) traditions. Second, to consider some of the implications of the relational turn for the application of psychoanalytic
concepts and methods beyond the consulting room.

Coming now to the nine chapters that form the book, Lynne
Layton begins with an account of both the analytic and socio-political forbears of the relational analytic theories and practices on both
sides of the Atlantic. Describing the relational approaches broadly
as emphasizing relationships rather than drives, she focuses on
developments in the late 1980s at New York University, where
Stephen Mitchell, in collaboration with Lewis Aron, Jessica Benjamin, and other faculty colleagues, conceptualized the "co-created"

analytic task as including the emergence and resolution of "mutual enactments". Interpretations were reconstrued as interactions in support of the goal of expanded and enriched awareness. In parallel, Jay Greenberg, Darlene Ehrenberg, and their colleagues at William Alanson White developed their own relational perspective. They put more emphasis on the child being developmentally influenced by the mother than did Mitchell and his colleagues, who saw the baby as "an active weaver" from the very start, as did Jessica Benjamin when emphasizing "mutual recognition" and the baby's innate capacity for pleasurable attunement.

While this clearly positions their work alongside that of Bion, the British Independents, and Contemporary Kleinians, the relational analysts differ because the focus of their attention is *both* the analyst's tracking of the patient *and* the patient's tracking of the analyst. The second half of Layton's chapter centres on her own relationally and personally informed writings on gender and ethics, including her "negotiation model". She extrapolates her clinical findings to social and political life, and argues for a politics grounded on an understanding and recognition of complicity, mutual vulnerability, and interdependence.

In Chapter Two, "Democratizing psychoanalysis", Susie Orbach acknowledges the development of an increasing emphasis on the *actual* analyst–patient relationship in most British psychoanalytic schools, initiated by "Independents" including Fairbairn, Balint, Winnicott, and John Bowlby, and weaves in her and her colleagues' work experience at the Women's Therapy Centre. However, she also expresses serious concerns regarding lingering tendencies towards hierarchical formulaic reactions to patient enactments, rather than dynamically attuning to and engaging with each instance in its context, bearing in mind that patient and analyst "cannot not affect one another". Illustrations from her own practice include an account of the democratized fee structure she has developed to mediate clichéd responses to missed sessions that are not paid for.

In his chapter, "Staying close to the subject", Paul Zeal dialectically explores the origins, theories, practices, and dilemmas of relational psychoanalysis and its British Independent and Contemporary Freudian psychoanalytic counterparts. With regard to the intricate "overlap and underlap" between interpersonal

relationship, transference–countertransference matrix, and intersubjective relationship, he reflects that the intersubjective is both
the most inclusive and the most unnerving for the analyst. Aware
of pros and cons in both his first ("relational") and second ("analytic") analyses and in his own clinical work, he now includes both
a relational aspect and a passionate engagement with "analytic neutrality". He also engages with theory, a key narrative in the pursuit
of meaning.

He challenges relational egalitarianism by making a case for the
analyst's important symbolic order difference from the patient; the
analyst *is* "the one who is supposed to know" and has the task of
"holding" that knowing place. Recognizing that analytically
informed relational influences and initiatives have tended towards
replacing patriarchal classical psychoanalytic metaphors with
maternal equivalents in a way that has led to a much more personal, intersubjective, "authentic, analytic engagement", Zeal, quot-
ing Lacan, sees a lack of clarity around the concept of "subject".
With regard to the influence of European traditions, he researches
both conscious and implicit transgenerational and transcontinental
interconnections between Nietzsche and Socratic Greek dialectical
philosophy, via Freud and Heidegger, to Hans Loewald, Lacan, and
R. D. Laing. In a similar vein, he notes the commonality in the
underlying search for truth by close subjective observation of both
psychoanalysts, and systemic family constellationists (Bert
Hellinger), whose differences appear in how they make these observations available to those who have been observed. Two clinical
accounts illustrate his own engagement with the complexities of the
clinical task and the way in which he endeavours to walk the fine
line between being drawn in and becoming the all-knowing expert
outsider. In doing so, he draws innovatively on his experience of
Hellinger's family constellation work as a way of bridging the gap
between the exclusivity of the analytic dyad and the overwhelming,
conflict-ridden presence of internalized family members in one of
his patients.

In Chapter Four, Paul Hoggett, drawing on post-liberal theory,
widens the frame of the previous two chapters by integrating the
intrapsychic model of human frailty with the interpsychic realities
of human violence, and applies his model to both welfare services
and professional practice to propose a "truly democratic" reflexive

practice. He reviews the classical liberal "ethics of patrimonialism" and post-war social democratic and socialist theories (all of which embodied the privileging of expert knowledge), democratic models of user engagement, and the feminist ethic of care, all of which failed to recognize the complexities of subject dynamics. Advances in this direction via Foucault's post-structuralism and Kleinian internal object relations, supplemented by the UK Independent and the US relational psychoanalytic contributions, illuminate that "in dialogue, we are subjects seeking [both] understanding and to be understood rather than objects seeking to act upon or to be acted upon". Extending this understanding from the consulting room to public welfare supports a dialogic model that includes recognition and the exercise of democratic professional authority roles in a reflexive and transparent way in which all participants are recognized as dialogically and interdependently both knowing and defended. Hoggett proposes filling the gap in the dearth of research into the subjective psychical suffering implicit in current societal systems of class, race, and poverty by insightful introduction of a relational perspective that does justice to people's experiences of powerlessness and poverty. He concludes with an appeal for radical social policy to "advance beyond its formal understandings towards something that is more fully lived, suffered, enjoyed, and experienced".

Lynn Froggett, in Chapter Five, engages with Hoggett's appeal, proposing "restorative justice" as a method of drawing on *the relational* to deepen the interplay between welfare subjects, providers, and society. She conceives of the community as a symbolic third space within which to seek to restore relatedness between victim and offender by means of a practice that promotes a dynamic of mutual recognition; a recognition that includes the capacity of welfare workers to acknowledge their own destructiveness.

She offers an example from the context of a particular group of practitioners who are themselves at the precarious, though also innovative, edge of community-based provision. They draw on strategies of empowerment and inclusion in their relationships with materially and socially disadvantaged subjects who are also perceived as being "conflicted, ambivalent, and defended". From this context, she offers a vivid creative illustration of this type of intersubjective engagement drawn from video footage of sessions between burly, affable, forty-year-old poet and community worker Bob, and pale, curfewed, and electronically tagged seventeen-year-old Tom, whose dangerous reputation precedes him. Bumpily and convincingly, a resonance develops between this couple in a way that inspires Tom to co-create and proudly present a poem about himself which includes the couplet:

I'm not a yob
I'm just me.

Froggett characterizes the process as one in which Bob and Tom, by a process of surrender that transcends twoness, co-create a relational space of an "energetic third", out of which a "moral third" becomes manifest that contains the tension between the needs of self and other. Thus enabled, Tom could engage in moral self-reflection, and move towards giving up his offending and holding down a full-time job.

Froggett considers that the arts-based practice exemplified in Bob and Tom's relationship requires an "a radically embodied form of perception" (or Bollas's "aesthetic intelligence") in which the "experience of the other's experiencing" mediates the "othering" to which young offenders are vulnerable, and enables the subject to "feel real". She notes that the approach has been extrapolated to a wide range of creative activities, also in Europe and Latin America.

As with Hoggett and Froggett in the previous two chapters, the next two chapters, by Simon Clarke and Wendy Hollway, respectively, reflect a dialogic professional relationship rooted in their approaches to psychoanalytically informed psycho-social research. In Chapter Six, Clarke delineates his preferred theories and related methodology, which are finely illustrated by his account of his relationally nuanced research interviews with Billy; and Hollway, in Chapter Seven, elaborates on her psychoanalytically and relationally informed epistemology, ontology, and methodology, which she contextualizes in relation to her mother-and-baby research in a London borough.

Clarke begins by linking his approach to understandings gained from the Frankfurt School, Franz Fanon, Foucault, and Melanie Klein. For him, the Frankfurt School's insights transpose Freud's thoughts regarding the free associative clinical method in a way that enables a lessening of the ideological domination of distorted social functioning. Habermas's psychoanalytically informed self reflection illuminates and reduces the ideological domination of unconscious projective dynamics of diseased racist states of mind. Fanon's "psychoexistential" linking of Freud and Sartre leads to the inclusion of socio-historic internalizations in understanding the sociogenesis of the oppressive force of "false consciousnesses in identity". These are, in turn, further illuminated by Kleinian insights into projective identification and the oscillation between paranoid–schizoid unconscious states of mind and by relational understandings including that of the co-created dynamics in the dyad.

The implications for research practice include the use of open-ended, rather than "why", questions to elicit the subject's story, and reflexivity regarding both "the relationality of the interview environment, and the complexities of researcher–researched dynamics". Exploration of the co-created conscious and unconscious emotional life of both researcher and respondent become central. In his account of his work with Billy in relation to research into British identity, immigration, and access to resources, Clarke takes us deeply below the surface of Billy's initial self presentation as a retired tough-man, with not much going for him other than a tendency to violence, and we meet someone towards whom we can have warm feelings. However, when Clarke himself reads the transcript of their second set of more focused interviews, he is shocked by Billy's explicitly racist statements and initially provides good reasons to explain them away. Further reflection also challengingly raises the possibility of mutual relational identifications and projections and leaves the reader with much food for thought.

In Chapter Seven, Hollway describes and elaborates the ontology, epistemology, and methodology of her thoroughly and creatively psychoanalytically informed psycho-social research. She brings clinical child psychoanalytic approaches to theory and practice into relationship with methods of psycho-social research in order to engage with the individual, the interpersonal, and the social, and to create a transcending "third". Her research material includes process recordings, observer's notes, and further insights gained by the observers in their regular supervision sessions with an experienced child analytic clinician. The spoken, the observed, and transference–countertransference are all attended to and drawn on to illuminate an understanding of how mother and baby are co-created in the dynamic interaction between family, culture, and society. Drawing on the thinking of Winnicott, Ogden, Bion, and Benjamin, Hollway herself becomes a not-knowing subject, curious about the gradations of co-created identifications. The sensitive and potentially conflicting relationship between clinical ethics and research ethics is also explored.

Chapters Eight and Nine involve another collegial dialogue between organizational consultants Karen Izod and Margaret Page. Izod writes that her current, relationally-inspired consultancy has grown out of her prior trainings in general social work and clinical and organizational specializations. Her Tavistock clinical and organizational trainings immersed her in traditional Kleinian psychoanalytic, and Bionic–systemic group relations, theory and practice. She has come to consider the former too narrowly focused on the *subject* at the expense of the dyad, and the latter too concerned with unconscious "basic assumptions" to engage creatively with co-created fluid interdependencies. She currently draws on Benjamin's (2004) relational concept of thirdness, and Orbach's focus on internal structures, which develop through social interaction, to revitalize her work and creatively engage with her clients and her own tensions in our postmodern society, whose systems require both adherence to traditional tasks and identities and innovative implementation of change. She also draws on the British Independent's elaboration of a socially orientated object relations' theory, the contributions of attachment theory, and group analysis (the social unconscious).

In her work, Izod seeks to hold "a space for inner conversation and actual dialogue" that "has the capacity to create movement and to negotiate new positions from which to think". For example, in consulting to two individuals who were in a "grievance" relationship, she sees her achievement as enabling them, at least for the present, to be subjects engaged in a process that could include acknowledging their differences. An important aspect of her approach is the way in which she seeks to recognize and engage with her own proclivities and encourage all *others* to find a voice. Her over-arching intention is to promote "governance", by which she means a capacity to hold differences as complementarities in relation to tasks, their processing, their representation, and their regulation. Her chapter includes a further consultancy illustration—an outline of a proposed project on the transfer and generation of knowledge—and concludes by relationally inviting readers' ideas and associations.

In the final chapter, "Inquiry as relational practice", Margaret Page links and develops aspects of the themes explored by Karen Izod in relation to her own professional role as a university staff member working with mid-career managers on Masters-level, university-based management education programmes. She has become committed to subject-led inquiry as an enlivening educational method, and values the way in which the relational perspective bridges polarities between staff/student/client/institution desired outcomes. Jessica Benjamin's key relational concepts ("intersubjectivity", "recognition", inevitable breakdown, and "thirdness") are elaborated and their usefulness illustrated in Page's role as a "new teacher" seeking to promote co-operative inquiry in her module for managers doing an MA at a business school. Prior relational exploration of "theory *vs.* experience" polarities with her mentor led to a quality of creative interrelationship between them that, in turn, facilitated the emergence of an engaging space for new learning with the students.

She offers two further examples from a programme set in a staff culture committed to peer and experiential learning. The first details how she "stumbled upon the capacity to hold in tension two complementary realities" and then take up her role as "an educator with authority". This process included discovering an internal space for containing and valuing both a humanistic *and* a Tavistock Group Relations' model of group dynamics.

Her final example relates to a teaching session on gender in organizations, during which subject-to-subject relating was both creatively achieved and anxiously lost. Some of her students were subsequently able to introduce inquiry practices into their own workplaces, team management, and peer relationships. She cautions that relational thinking and methods of co-inquiry need to be rooted in, and held alongside, pre-existing cultures and practices.

References

Benjamin, J. (2004). Beyond doer and done-to: an intersubjective view of thirdness. *Psychoanalytic Quarterly*, LXIII(1): 5–46.

Hahn, H. (1998). Supervision: seen, sought and reviewed. In: P. Clarkson (Ed.), *Supervision: Psychoanalytic and Jungian Perspectives*. London: Whurr.

Karnac, H. (2007). Karnac Forum: How it all started. *Karnac Review, Summer*: 31.

Messler Davis, J. (2004). Whose bad objects are we anyway? *Psychoanalytic Dialogues*, 14: 711–732.

CHAPTER ONE

Relational thinking: from culture to couch and couch to culture

Lynne Layton

Introduction: history and key assumptions of relational analytic theory

At one point in my personal analysis, my analyst, whom I had chosen in part because the self psychology and object relations books on her shelf suggested that she was someone who would not bludgeon me with predictable oedipal and penis envy interpretations, told me that the reason she had forgotten to call me at the agreed upon time during her three-month maternity leave was that I appear self-sufficient and give the impression of having no needs. This touched a very sore spot in me and I went off to seek consultation—having parents whose mantra when they did something hurtful was always "You're too sensitive," the last thing I needed was an analyst who made a big blunder and blamed it on something about me. We worked it out. But I begin with this vignette because I think that it is my sensitivity to this issue that drew me to what has come to be known as relational psychoanalysis. Of the many schools of psychoanalysis, none besides relational analysis, so far as I know, holds as a central ethical principle not just awareness, but acknowledgement, of the analyst's complicity in the inevitable re-enactments that are at the heart of any treatment.

The term "relational psychoanalysis" has two common uses, one quite broad and one more narrow. In 1983, Jay Greenberg and Stephen Mitchell wrote *Object Relations in Psychoanalytic Theory*, a groundbreaking comparative analysis in which they divided the psychoanalytic terrain into drive theories, represented by Freud, and theories that posit that at the heart of psychic life are relationships, internal and external. They considered Sullivan, founder of interpersonal psychoanalysis, the primary progenitor of relational theories. Greenberg and Mitchell argued that although you cannot understand Sullivan without knowing Freud, you also cannot have it both ways: the drive model and the relational model's assumptions lead to radically different ideas about development, technique, motivation, unconscious process, and therapeutic action. As Merton Gill (1995) elaborated, "classical theory emphasizes defenses against drive, and relational theory emphasizes defenses against altering patterns of interpersonal relationships" (p. 93). Gill clarifies that the distinction here is innate *vs.* experiential, not intrapsychic *vs.* interpersonal. In fact, relational analysts are every bit as focused on dreams, fantasies, ucs process and other staples of the intrapsychic as are drive analysts. But for relational analysts, the intrapsychic is marked by the individual's idiosyncratic elaborations of actual relational experience. As a recent paper by the Boston Change Process Study Group (2007) argues, the interactive level has traditionally been seen as the mere instantiation of deeper forces and thus regarded as superficial. But, in a relational paradigm, the interactive process is primary, deep, "and generates the raw material from which we draw generalized abstractions that we term conflicts, defenses, and phantasy" (*ibid.*, p. 16).

At the time that Mitchell and Greenberg's book appeared, the dominant paradigm in psychoanalysis in the USA was ego psychology, but this paradigm was being challenged on several fronts, in particular, by the generation of interpersonalists that came after Sullivan, Horney, Fromm, and Thompson, primarily Edgar Levenson and Benjamin Wolstein, by Merton Gill; by the Balint–Winnicott wing of the British Independent Group; and by Kohut, founder of self psychology. When I trained in psychology in the 1980s, self psychology was clearly on its way to becoming the dominant paradigm, in part because increased awareness of the effects of trauma demanded theories that stressed what actually happened in one's relational history. Although Mitchell (1988) went on to develop a version of what I will call the narrow definition of relational theory, his generous and intellectually curious spirit embraced all theorists who grounded their work in the ongoing effect of relational experience. So, in the broad sense, relational theory refers to any theory whose basic assumption is that development and unconscious phenomena are marked primarily by relationships, not by drives. This includes interpersonal, intersubjective, object relations, self psychology, and relational conflict models; indeed, conferences of the International Association of Relational Psychoanalysis and Psychotherapy, the organization Mitchell and others founded, often also include versions of Jungian, Lacanian, and Kleinian theory. But, even in their early work, Greenberg and Mitchell differentiated relational theories that are drive theories from relational and interpersonal models that "view relational configurations as derivative of actual experience with others . . ." (1983, p. 102). In these models, for example, pure pleasure seeking and pure rage are seen not as manifestations of drive, but of breakdown in relationships. Interpretations are not valued merely for the content they convey, but for the relational transformations the interpretive event triggers.

Having trained at the William Alanson White Institute in New York, Mitchell was greatly influenced by the interpersonal tradition. By Mitchell's own account (2004, p. 532), Levenson was the "dominant intellectual influence at White" when Mitchell trained in the mid-1970s. Although others may not agree, I would place Levenson at the beginning of the relational tradition in its narrow sense, so I shall spend some time here elaborating the groundwork he laid. In 1972, Levenson wrote *The Fallacy of Understanding*, one thesis of which is that all concepts, including psychoanalytic ones, change in meaning over time, as does how we see patients and pathologies. Levenson calls the current age of psychoanalysis organismic, wherein the health of each part of the human system is considered to be dependent on the whole context in which we operate. Levenson uses the term perspectivism to describe the organism. In any given system, he argues, there are different realities operating and the perspective from which one sees things *always* makes sense to the person seeing it, that "within the organized totality of the other person's world, his perceptions and behavior are coherent and appropriate" (*ibid.*, p. 77). If this is the case, the analyst's job is not to show patients how they distort, and interpretation is neither the only nor even perhaps the primary tool in the analyst's toolkit; rather, understanding the sense it makes to the person is primary. On this, self psychology and the interpersonal school are in agreement. They diverge dramatically, however, on their view of the patient–analyst relationship and therapeutic action. Levenson's radicalism lies primarily in the way he elaborated on both Sullivan's idea of the analyst as participant observer and on the interpersonalist emphasis on the impact of culture. One thing that differentiates Levenson from most analysts in most schools is his view, derived from Fromm, Horney, Sullivan, and Thompson, that the family is only one of the systems that impacts the psyche; for Levenson, the culture is part of the psyche, too, and the 1972 book in fact includes an interesting study he did of adolescent dropouts. Levenson writes:

> But if we also recognize the hierarchy of systems, the organization of systems, then it must also be recognized that . . . we belong to a network of hegemonic social structures, from our businesses or professions, through national and supernational networks. [*ibid.*, p. 78]

Of course Levenson learned from Fromm, who wrote about the ways that particular social systems pull for particular kinds of social character. Levenson's focus is perhaps more indebted, however, to R. D. Laing, who tracked the way that people become part of the crazy systems in which they find themselves. "Enter a prison," Levenson says, "one is part of the prison system" (*ibid.*, p. 165). Yet, Levenson's theory is not determinist: for interpersonalists, perceptions are shaped *in* interaction with others, not *by* the reactions of others. Levenson sustains the tension between an idiosyncratic subjectivity and interacting psyches permeated by social experience.

Perhaps Levenson's most important contribution to what has now become known as relational theory, however, was his development of a constructivist two-person *vs.* a one-person psychology. He says,

As psychotherapist, I cannot be sure that what I have said is heard as I said it, I cannot be sure that the perception of the patient, if different from mine, is any less appropriate, and I cannot be sure that I did not say what *he* thinks I said, rather than what I think I said. [*ibid.*, p. 99]

Imagine, for a moment, what such a thought does to our traditional notions of transference and countertransference, projection and projective identification, neutrality and resistance. One could say, without too much exaggeration, that the pages of relational and interpersonal journals are currently filled with papers that elaborate the effects of Levenson's insight that every moment of the analytic encounter is shaped by the interaction between two unconscious minds, operating within power relations that are both symmetric and asymmetric (Aron, 1996). To return to my opening vignette, what Levenson means when he seeks a psychoanalysis that is "beyond understanding" is the acknowledgement of the analyst's complicity in what transpires in analysis. And this goes beyond postmodern and constructivist ideas of mere co-creation to the inevitability of what relational theorists call "mutual enactments". For Levenson, Freud's most important discovery has nothing to do with metapsychology or any particular contents of the mind; rather, the important discovery is that in talking, we recreate relational patterns. Levenson says,

It is not the therapist's uncoding of the dynamics that makes the therapy, not his "interpretations" of meaning and purpose, but, rather, his extended participation with the patient. It is not his ability to resist distortion by the patient (transference) or to resist his own temptation to interact irrationally with the patient (countertransference), but, rather, his ability to be trapped, immersed and participating in the system and then to work his way out. (1972, p. 183]

What distinguishes psychotherapy from psychoanalysis is that, in the latter, the continuous mutual enactments between patient and analyst are talked about and made explicit. As I shall discuss below, some of the most interesting contemporary relational and interpersonal analysts are trying to understand the nature of mutual enactments and how we get ourselves out of them.

Before leaving Levenson, I want to mention that because he sees analysis as primarily working "not because of what it says but how it proceeds" (1983, p. 111), because every interpretation is, for him, primarily an interaction, he describes the goal of analysis as "an expansion of awareness, an enrichment of pattern" (*ibid.*, p. 31)— not, as classical analysis might argue, a relinquishing of infantile wishes or a correction of distortion.

Stephen Mitchell, as I said earlier, trained at White and was a student of Levenson's. In the 1980s, some members of the interpersonal/humanistic track faculty at the New York University Postdoctoral Program in Psychotherapy and Psychoanalysis invited Mitchell to teach object relations theory (Mitchell, 2004, p. 535). As I have heard it, however, some key interpersonalists in authority were opposed to teaching object relations in that track. In 1989, after some years of political power struggles between the interpersonal/humanistic track and the Freudian track, the "quasi-independent" (*ibid.*) relational track at NYU Postdoc was born. In that track, Mitchell worked with Emmanuel Ghent, Lew Aron, Jessica Benjamin, Neil Altman, and many of the other clinicians who would become the face of relational psychoanalysis. Meanwhile, analysts such as Jay Greenberg, Darlene Ehrenberg, Phillip Bromberg, and Donnel Stern, assuming both interpersonal and relational identities, have developed their own integrated versions of interpersonal analysis at William Alanson White and in the pages of their journal, *Contemporary Psychoanalysis*. For example, *Contemporary Psychoanalysis* published Irwin Hoffman's foundational relational paper, "The patient as interpreter of the analyst's experience" in 1983, the same year Greenberg and Mitchell's book came out. In 1991, Mitchell founded *Psychoanalytic Dialogues*, the high quality of which brought relational theory into the US mainstream.

Before moving on to elaborate the way I use relational theory in my own work, I want to mention briefly four emphases of relational theory that appear to me to mark the way this school differs from other psychoanalytic schools: development, the unconscious, mutual enactments, and the pleasures of attunement. With regard to development, Hirsch (1998) has persuasively argued that a primary difference between even those who consider themselves relational in the narrow sense is whether or not they attribute psychopathology to developmental arrest (as self psychologists do) or to unconscious conflict. Mitchell disagrees with developmental models that privilege early over later experience, and he critiques the developmental arrest model because it figures the subject as a stuck baby and not as an active weaver of the loom of his/her experience (1988, p. 274). Both models tend, however, to ground human motivation in the "striving for safety and security of self and for loved others" (Hirsch, 1998, p. 518). This premise derives from Sullivan and Fromm, as well as from Fairbairnian object relations theory and attachment theory. If we recall Levenson's suggestion that all psychoanalytic theories and diagnostic categories are historical, we might wonder about the current dominance of relational theories in the USA: does their dominance suggest that we live in a historical moment in which the anxiety about security is more salient than anxiety about sex and aggression?

Personally, I am more drawn to a conflict model such as the one elaborated by Mitchell, who suggests that the way we respond to the unique relational matrices in which we develop, our relational history, makes us who we are. In his developmental theory, psychosexual stages, Oedipus complexes, dichotomies between the pre-oedipal and oedipal are subordinate to the relational contexts in which they occur. Mitchell's thesis is that what is deep in the psyche, what is intrapsychic, is a result of childhood experiences of separation, physical illness and pain, sibling comparison and competition, childhood dependency. These, he says,

> and other travails of early life are certain to make childhood at least intermittently stormy, and early relationships inevitably somewhat insecure. . . . One is always, in some ultimate sense, at the mercy of adults, [and the child has to] design himself within the spaces provided by the contours of parental character . . . [1988, pp. 275–276]

So, sources of conflict derive from the pull to mould oneself to parental and cultural demands, to negotiate union *vs.* separateness, from the demand on the child to work out how to accommodate simultaneously to mother and father when the rules for accommodation conflict. Development is not about shifting zones, but about shifting relational needs that grow in complexity and intimacy (Greenberg & Mitchell, 1983, pp. 102–103).

Most critiques of relational theory focus on what appears to other schools to be its emphasis on surface and its abandonment of unconscious process. Relational theorists are only fairly recently beginning to elaborate the theory of unconscious process that has been implicit in many of their clinical descriptions. One such elaboration grounds unconscious process in dissociation of relational experience rather than repression of unacceptable impulses. A cornerstone of Sullivan's (1953) theory, elaborated by Fromm, was the idea (borrowed from George Herbert Mead's model of self) that the slings and arrows of early relational experience lead to splits between what a person considers me and not-me. Children intuit from the beginning what self states are and are not responded to, what the parent finds acceptable and unacceptable, and often the unacceptable parts of self and modes of relating are dissociated. Bromberg (2003) writes about the undramatic but highly painful traumas of living day in and day out in a family that systematically disavows the existence of a child's subjective experience and discredits the validity of that child's emotional states. Traumas of all kinds make a person hypervigilant for a repeat, always screening for danger; the screening itself makes it very hard to have new experience that would contest the old.

A key premise of relational analysis is that mutual enactments are at the heart of treatment, not just the dramatic enactments exemplified by my opening vignette, but the sometimes hard to work out ongoing impasses that make a treatment feel dead or hostile or otherwise stuck. Like contemporary Kleinians, relational analysts follow the moment-to-moment conscious and unconscious interactions in treatment, assessing effects of interpretations and other interventions, tracking affective shifts, looking for what Betty Joseph (1985) calls the total transference: that is, the way in which what the patient talks about is enacted in the entire session. In tracking affect and patient responses, however, relational analysts, unlike contemporary Kleinians, believe that the patient is simultaneously tracking the analyst, picking up on shifts of affect, empathic failures, body language, defensiveness. Some contemporary Bionians, such as Antonino Ferro (2002), similarly track the analyst's effect on the patient and, like Bion, emphasize the importance of tolerating uncertainty, but relational analysts differ in that they not only track effects but stress the importance of being willing to be open about the way their own unconscious process may have entered into the mix. They often do not keep the data in their own heads the way Ferro does, and they do not necessarily try to "correct" their stance if the patient reacts with anxiety to an intervention. Rather, the data is considered crucial to both the patient's and the analyst's understandings of the system that they have formed. As Irwin Hirsch has put it, the interpersonal/relational idea of therapeutic action is "highlighted by becoming confused, transformed, and lost in unwitting enactments, living out old repetitions before arriving at new interactional experience" (1998, p. 512).

Donnell Stern (2004) offers a compelling interpersonal/relational view of mutual enactments, which he defines in the narrower sense of breakdowns in the relation between analyst and patient. Many relational analysts assume that we are made up of multiple and often conflicting self-states that emerge from the variety of relational experiences we have had. Stern (1997, 2004) distinguishes between bad-me and good-me states, which reveal themselves in treatment through inconsistencies and contradictions, and me and not-me states that are only available through enactment because, in his view, they have never been formulated and never been conscious. For Stern (2004), "Enactment is the interpersonalization of dissociation: the conflict that cannot be experienced within one mind is experienced between or across two minds" (p. 213, see also, Bromberg, 2003). A major difference between Kleinian views of projective identification and relational views of enactment, then, is that relational theorists see the analyst as complicit, as a co-initiator. In Stern's view, mutual enactments involve mutual or reciprocal dissociations:

> When the analyst participates in an enactment, it is because she dissociates; and when she dissociates, it is because she finds herself in circumstances that make her vulnerable in a way she can manage, for the time being, *only* by dissociating. ... The patient cannot provoke such a dissociation if the analyst is not vulnerable to it. ... The analyst's role is not defined by invulnerability ... but by a special (though inconsistent) willingness, and a practiced (though imperfect) capacity, to accept and deal forthrightly with her vulnerability. [Stern, 2004, p. 216]

Stern, following Levenson, suggests that the way out of an enactment occurs when either analyst or patient perceives what is going on in a different way and can either experience the two states that make up the enactment as an internal conflict or can suddenly see the other in an empathic rather than an adversarial light. Only then can the pair reflect on what has happened; only then can the patient experience an internal conflict rather than a dissociated state. Not all relational theorists agree with Stern (and Bromberg's) views on the primacy of dissociation; conflict models of unconscious process are more prominent for other theorists. But enactment and resolving impasse are central themes in contemporary relational theorizing.

Finally, a major premise of relational theory derives from Jessica Benjamin's (1988) elaboration of the pleasures of attunement—whereas most analytic theories did and do posit an originary merger between baby and mother, Benjamin, drawing on the infant research of Daniel Stern (1985), Louis Sander (1983), and others, posits a baby and mother system centred on mutual regulation of affect and self states. The baby, Stern argued, is never in a merged or symbiotic phase, but rather has subjectivity from the outset. Based on contemporary research, Stern and the other members of the Boston Change Process Study Group (2007) argue that humans have an innate capacity and need to intuit the intentions of others with whom they engage, and this capacity temporally precedes capacities for symbolization. By the age of ten months, co-created mutual accommodations and attunements become a source of the baby's pleasure. Benjamin counters centuries of Western philosophy and decades of analytic theory by arguing that the Other is not necessarily a hostile presence bent on limiting my freedom. Rather, by insisting on the mother's subjectivity—not the ground against which a boy baby develops but a figure in relation with boy and girl babies—Benjamin accents the pleasures of affective, verbal, and body attunement between self and other. Writing within a second wave feminist tradition, which includes, as Susie Orbach's chapter in this volume elaborates, the work of the Women's Therapy Centre Institute (see, for example, Eichenbaum & Orbach, 1983), Benjamin's developmental theory puts connection on an equal footing with autonomy, countering centuries of political, philosophical, and psychological theories that enact and ideologically enforce the split between agency and connection, and devalue connection—a split that works so well for capitalism and patriarchy.

Benjamin (2004) places the striving for mutual recognition at the heart of analysis, a developmental achievement that she erects into an ethical principle of psychoanalysis. But equally important, both for clinical work and for social theory, are her contributions on the ways that this striving inevitably breaks down into what she calls doer–done to relations. Indeed, the most intractable problems patients have, and the kind of dramatic enactments that often lead to impasse in analysis, occur when recognition fails, interactions are locked into patterns of dominance and submission, and patient and analyst treat each other as objects rather than subjects. Benjamin (1988, 1990, 2004) emphasizes a developmental line of intersubjective experience that is built from histories of mutual attunement and from surviving inevitable relational cycles of rupture and repair. We might state her psychoanalytic ethics as follows: where doer–done to relations were, there mutual recognition between subjects shall be. (In her 1990 paper, Benjamin argues that the contribution that relational theory makes to existent analytic theories and practices that elide real others with their internal representation is to insist that "where objects were, subjects must be" [p. 34].)

To conclude this section on the history and key assumptions of relational analysis, I want to emphasize that both Levenson's work and relational analytic theory have clearly been influenced not just by their analytic forebears (Sullivan, Fromm, Ferenczi, and Fairbairn), by structuralism, systems theory, and any number of other paradigms, but most profoundly by the new social movements of the 1950s through the 1970s in the USA. Even where there is no acknowledgement of the importance of the cultural surround—a regression, to my mind, from early interpersonal insights—the challenge relational theory poses to the analyst's authority and omniscience is unthinkable without taking into account the period in which US relational theorists came of age, a "question authority" era of civil rights, Marxist activism, Vietnam, Watergate, feminism, and gay liberation. The third issue of the inaugural 1991 volume of *Dialogues* highlighted a feminist relational rethinking of gender. A left flank of relational psychoanalysts has done groundbreaking work on the ways class, race, gender, and politics inflect clinical practice (see, among others, Altman, 1995; Benjamin, 1988; Corbett, 2001; Dimen, 2003; Domenici & Lesser, 1995; Goldner, 1991; Harris, 2005; Layton, 1998; Leary, 1997).

From culture to couch

My own work on gender and other identity categories is informed by Benjamin's psychoanalytic ethics. In my 1998 book, *Who's That Girl? Who's That Boy? Clinical Practice Meets Postmodern Gender Theory*, I proposed a model for thinking about gender identity that I thought could account both for the narcissistic wounds incurred from living in a sexist culture and for the kinds of gendered experience we all have that make us feel good about being men or women or something in between. I called it a negotiation model (a term elaborated by Pizer, 1998), because I wanted to capture the way we constantly negotiate gender identity both from doer–done to relations—where we are treated as objects—and from relations of intersubjective mutuality, where we are treated as subjects. Gender negotiations include those between the often conflicting gender fantasies, desires, and norms of one's parents, culture, and subculture. In my own family, for example, there were clear messages about what girls could and couldn't do, and I do not think my 1950s lower middle-class white family was unique in endorsing gender norms in which males had agency and women were to subordinate their agentic capacities to what Dorothy Dinnerstein (1976) once described as women's monstrously overdeveloped capacity for unreciprocated empathy. At the same time, those clear messages were undercut by unconscious ones and by mother messages and father messages that were in conflict. My mother, for example, was the resentful breadwinner who felt that it was men's role to be the breadwinner. Circumstances made her unable to enact the gender norms proper to her class, norms that organized her desire and whose very function was to distinguish her from white and black working-class females who *had* to work. My father was a nurturer who was rarely home because of the constraints of work. Further, I knew from playing with my girlfriends that my body could give itself over to fantastic flights of exuberance no matter what anyone said about being ladylike, and I knew, too, that I could be truly aggressive and mean. But many of these experiences went underground, split off as not-me or bad-me when the time came to be ladylike and nice enough to get adult and male approval, and when the time came to make sure my developing body would not invite dangerous assault. As Benjamin (1988) described it, my desires for agency did not disappear, but rather were projected on to the males who were to play subject to my object, and they were distorted into covert ways of getting what I wanted, for example, nagging. Towards the end of my analysis, I was describing to a friend the way that I felt I had given over my agency to men and then hated them for their selfish display, and how that was changing now that I had begun to reclaim agency and rework the way I related to others—she responded by sending me a card that showed a weeping cartoon woman and a caption that read: "Oh my God! I think I'm becoming the man I wanted to marry!"

My book was in part written "against" postmodern theories that suggest that identity categories are necessarily coercive and oppressive, that no version of racial or gender identity is healthy. I wrote about the way gender and other categories can facilitate growth and transformation, how feminism and gay liberation redeployed categories built on splitting into categories that differentiated without splitting. At the same time, I wanted to give the coercive aspect of identities their due, because so often psychoanalytic theory ignores the psychic effects of the power hierarchies in which we live. To better understand the regressive and foreclosing use of identity categories, I began elaborating the concept of "normative unconscious processes" (2002, 2004, 2006a,b). With this term, I refer to the psychological consequences of living in a culture in which many of the norms serve the dominant ideological purpose of maintaining power inequities. More particularly, I have investigated the consequences of living within particular class, race, sex, and gender hierarchies. My assumption is that these hierarchies, which confer power and exist for the benefit of those with power, tend not only to idealize certain subject positions and devalue others, but tend to do so by splitting human capacities and attributes and giving them class or race or gender assignations. To be proper subjects, members of the dominant group are pulled to split off what the norm disavows and project it on to abject subordinate groups. Thus do psychological structures such as dependency, reason, vulnerability, and emotion become gendered, raced, classed, and sexed. In my book, I noted, as have many feminists, that sexism and capitalism aligned in the nineteenth century to split the public from the private sphere and to gender the former masculine and the latter feminine. In so doing, human capacities that belong together, agentic capacities and relational capacities, were torn asunder, and we still treat the psychic consequences of that split. Indeed, I believe that this split produces two subtypes of narcissism that we have come to call traditional masculinity and femininity: in the one, embeddedness in relation is split off, which results in a version of autonomy based in grandiosity, devaluation of the other, and needs to distance. In the other, agentic capacities are split off, which results in a version of relatedness in which self-deprecation, idealization of the other, and longings for merger predominate.

As my autobiographical gender example suggests, norms are rarely internalized without conflict. Because the hierarchies split and categorize *human* attributes and capacities, we find in the clinic and in our lives unceasing conflict between those unconscious processes that seek to maintain the splits and those that refuse them. The ones that seek to maintain the splits are those that I call "normative unconscious processes". So, normative unconscious processes are those unconscious processes that pull to repeat affect/behaviour/cognition patterns that uphold the very social norms that cause psychic distress in the first place. For example, I said above that traditional gender norms split capacities for connection and dependence from capacities for agency and independence, and gender the former female and the latter male. Adherence to those norms brings about the very symptoms we treat: conforming to the norms of femininity can make and has made women feel "unfemale" and hurtful to others when they pursue their own interests, and conforming to masculine norms can make men feel "feminine" when they cry or express vulnerability. What is unconscious and conflictual is produced from the way a culture or subculture's norms psychologically constitute dependence and independence. People tend to have no idea that what they suffer from is the way they have split the two, *why* it is so difficult to feel like a man when feeling vulnerable, *why* it is so hard simultaneously to accomplish a sense of competence and a sense of connection.

Normative unconscious processes, then, are one of the psychic forces that push to consolidate the "right" kind of identity and to obfuscate the workings of unequal power hierarchies. They protect the psychic splits that cultural norms mandate, and they do so because the risk of contesting them is loss of love and social approval. But let us not forget that the result of splitting is to keep what has been split off near. Repetition compulsions are the very place where the struggle between coercive normative unconscious processes and counter-normative unconscious processes are enacted. And, since all identities are relational, these repetitions are stirred up and played out in relation. In the clinic then, we are likely to find patient and analyst engaging all the time in enactments of normative unconscious processes, enactments in which the therapist is either unconsciously pulled by the same norms as those pulling the patient, or is herself pulled by oppressive norms.

I have elsewhere discussed a range of such enactments (Layton, 2002, 2006a,b). In a psychotherapy with an Asian American gay male patient who tended to stereotype Westerners and Asians rather rigidly, I found myself unconsciously supporting dominant racial and gender norms by feminizing him (Layton, 2006a). Over time, he had described several situations in which he thought Westerners reacted differently from the way he did. In some instances, he felt superior to Westerners; in others, he felt inferior. For instance, he told me that when people were walking towards him on the street, he always stepped aside. His white Western boyfriend had pointed that out to him in a way that suggested he was not assertive enough. He was confused, because to him this felt polite. But he wondered if he was being a doormat in this and other situations. At one point, I told him I was struggling to understand this dilemma. I said that I recognized that in part what he described had to do with norms of politeness that he preferred to what he called Western rudeness, but that I also recognized in what he was describing the position of female subordination to men that feminists such as Benjamin have written about. As it turned out, the latter part of what was meant to be an empathic comment seems to have reignited wounds that undoubtedly derive from the way Asian males are feminized in white Western culture and with the way gay males are feminized in heterosexual culture. Something unconscious in my own history, an area of my own gender and

sexual vulnerability, made me humiliate him, and, towards the end
of the session, he retaliated by telling me he was thinking of ending
therapy, and then associating to the younger, more beautiful female
therapist he had seen before he began his work with me. Moments
such as these illustrate a relational perspective on identity, revealing the way that our own identity investments can consciously and
unconsciously work to repudiate the investments of others. As
Bourdieu (1984) might say, we secure our "distinction" as we
defend against vulnerability.

In another moment of the same treatment, I colluded with him
in upholding a fantasy that I, like all of the white boyfriends he
chose, held the invulnerable position of whiteness. He longed for a
position in which he would be immune from gender, racial, and
other slights, and he associated that position with whiteness. I
suppose I, too, long for a superior position in which I might be
invulnerable, so I unconsciously accepted that interpellation. Once
I realized that I was performing "whiteness" to his inferior non-
whiteness, I began to ask different questions of him than I had been
asking, trying then to deconstruct whiteness and figure out what
were the vulnerable parts of himself that he hated and how whiteness had both wounded him and become for him a fantasy guar-
antee that he would never again feel the pain of inferiority and
humiliation.

In a paper titled "Attacks on linking: the unconscious pull to
dissociate individuals from their social context" (2006b), I wrote
about the way I frequently enact in treatment professional norms
that dictate that we separate the psychic from the social. One of my
patients reported a political dream and, as we explored the dream,
I found myself struggling against reducing to family drama her
civic passion about what had become of her beloved American
ideals. She, too, felt that what she was talking about was not proper
therapy talk. Only when I resisted making reductive interpretations
was she able to explore what Andrew Samuels (1993) has called the
political psyche, and this experience taught me that we ought to
add the capacity for civic passion and action to Freud's two criteria
for health, the ability to love well and to work well. Finally, in
"Cultural hierarchies, splitting, and the heterosexist unconscious"
(2002), I discussed an enactment in which a lesbian client's desire
for me led me to "reassure" her, but really me, that we would not

be sexual together. She was complaining that her partner never touches her in the right way, and for several days before that she had been telling me about elaborate sexual fantasies that she was having about me. Only vaguely aware of my anxiety, I said that here she did not have to worry about me touching her in the wrong way, since here we would not become sexual. She felt shamed and she stopped talking about her sexual desire immediately. Over the course of the next months, she began to experiment with "girly" things, clothes, manicures, that she had never tried before. Analysing this sequence later, I thought about the way psychoanalytic developmental theories have made identification and desire either/ ors, and the way this either/or supports compulsory heterosexuality (see O'Connor & Ryan, 1993), as the developmental norm is to identify with the same-sexed parent and desire the opposite-sexed parent. I surmised that my comment, which had clearly stemmed from my own anxiety, had perhaps "heterosexualized" her in just the way heterosexualization might happen developmentally— where, for example, a mother's anxiety about her daughter's desire for her might cause the child to repress desire and replace it with a non-erotic form of identification, if such there is (Layton, 2000). Had I dealt with my own erotic feelings, I might have sustained with her the ambiguities of sexual desire; instead, I sustained a straight–gay split, and, in so doing, upheld the heterosexual norm. In this case that meant shaming the gay patient, precisely what the enforcement of heterosexual norms is designed to do. Fearing arousal of my own homosexual desire, I shut sexuality down.

These examples all reveal one way that culture crashes into the clinic, and the way relational perspectives on enactment, mutuality, and complicity engage socially constructed unconscious processes.

From couch to culture

Earlier, I mentioned Mitchell's insight that "one is always in some sense at the mercy of adults" (1988, pp. 275–276). In her 2004 book, *Precarious Life*, Judith Butler takes this crucial insight from relational thinking in an important political direction. In the book's chapter, "Violence, mourning, politics", first published in the primarily relational analytic journal, *Studies in Gender & Sexuality*, Butler argues that the self is constituted by relations with actual others from the outset, others to whom we are vulnerable and on whom we depend. Vulnerability is thus a key attribute of being human. Personal experiences of loss, grief, and desire all reveal to us the ways that we are in "thrall" to our others; they reveal that relationships can turn our lives upside down, transform us, and make us lose the sense of boundedness that usually governs our self-perceptions. The self constituted in relationships can thus not know in any clear way where I end and the other begins. Moving to the terrain of ethics, Butler argues that it is not the Other itself, but rather the Other's vulnerability and precariousness that call on me to take care of the other. Given these premises, Butler begins to define a new kind of politics: alongside a politics that presumes an autonomous, bounded individual, a necessary presumption, Butler feels, for a politics of sexual, racial, and abortion rights, she argues for a politics grounded in the fact that we are all born vulnerable to and dependent on others.[1]

"Loss," Butler says, "has made a tenuous 'we' of us all" (2004, p. 20). She herself is clearly wrecked by the losses incurred from AIDS, from 9/11, from the Iraq and Afghan wars, from Palestinian suicide bombers and Israeli occupiers. One of her agendas in the book is to reveal the way that public discourses authorize some losses to be grieved while others remain invisible and thus ungrievable. The Iraqi dead, for example, are nowhere represented in the USA.

Benjamin, too, formulates a politics based on the ways we are tied to one another. Rather than privilege loss and grief, however, she privileges the development of mutual recognition, which, as I said above, grows out of the mutual attunements co-created by parent and child. Thus, the pleasures of attunement and what Benjamin (2004) will call "surrender", a "certain letting go of the self" that lets us take in the point of view of the other, have a lawfulness quite different in kind from oedipal law. Where oedipal law prohibits, erects boundaries, instantiates the *nom du père*, the pleasures of attunement and mutual recognition exist in a Winnicottian potential space in which self and other are able to sustain difference while remaining connected.

Both Benjamin and Butler complicate analytic and political work on the concept of recognition by stressing that societies have *norms* of recognition, norms that dictate who will be recognized as human and how they will be recognized. As Butler puts it, "The 'I' who cannot come into being without a 'you' is also fundamentally dependent on a set of norms of recognition that originated neither with the 'I' nor with the 'you' ". "The task," she concludes, "is . . . to think through [humans'] primary impressionability and vulnerability with a theory of power and recognition" (2004, p. 45).

Butler draws our attention, then, to the misuses of the other's vulnerability, citing two of Levinas's assertions that I feel need to be thought together rather than separately: the first is that "ethics is precisely a struggle to keep fear and anxiety from turning into murderous action" (xviii). The second is Levinas's assertion that the fact that the other dies calls on me not to be indifferent to his/ her death. These assertions, it seems to me, resonate with what I earlier spoke of as Benjamin's psychoanalytic ethics: where doer– done to relations were, there mutual recognition between subjects shall be. In "Retaliatory discourse. The politics of attack and withdrawal" (Layton, 2006c), I discussed my experience with patients who repeatedly re-create doer–done to relational configurations because of their shame about their vulnerability, which they construe as "weakness". Repeated relational traumas have made them despise their own vulnerability, dependency, and need for the other. They feel it is their fault that their vulnerability was misused. While they struggle to feel safe with others, in fact they keep staging experiences in which they are either the perpetrator or the victim, in which they either attack the other or angrily withdraw.

Extrapolating—cautiously—to the political realm, I think that what we see in the USA currently is a politics of attack and withdrawal that is based on stoking fear and anxiety and simultaneously making it shameful to be fearful and anxious. We see a politics of attack on the part of an odd coalition of Republican neoconservatives and neo-liberals, whose policies have brought about economic insecurity for just about everyone, in league with Christian and non-Christian social conservatives engaged in a backlash operation against gays, women, blacks, Muslims, immigrants, and many other categories traditionally labelled Other. And we see a politics of withdrawal on the part of the Democratic Party, liberal élites, and even many progressives who feel helpless in the face of global corporate power, media consolidation, and a right-wing government that takes pride in waging pre-emptive war abroad and destroying social services and safety nets at home. (Between the time I wrote this paper and the time of preparing it for publication, there has been some change in US politics. In November 2006, Democrats won a majority in the House and a very slim majority in the Senate. There have been some legislative attempts to question the Bush administration's encroachments on civil liberties and to curb or halt the Iraq War, although Bush has vetoed the Iraq legislation to date. Yet, there is truth to the Democrats' rhetoric that they were elected to end the war, and Bush's incredibly low poll ratings, 28% at this writing, suggest that the public supports neither his foreign nor his domestic policies.) In both the politics of attack and the politics of withdrawal, vulnerability is defended against and ties to the vulnerability of others are denied.

In thinking about this political impasse, I have found helpful Jessica Benjamin's (2004) elaboration of a relational concept of "thirdness", which focuses on the way the analyst inevitably becomes complicit in the repetition of doer–done to dynamics and must continually find a space outside those dynamics so patients can find their way out. Thirdness, she says, is constituted in "early, presymbolic experiences of accommodation, mutuality, and the intention to recognize and be recognized by the other . . ." (p. 19). When patient and analyst are caught in those inevitable impasses in which each feels done to by the other, Benjamin calls for the analyst to act as a moral third, "to sustain the tension of difference between my needs and yours while still being attuned to you" (p. 13). The analyst is called upon to break the deadlock of mutual helplessness by saying "I'll go first", by making a gesture that ends the cycle of shame and blame (p. 33). The analyst surrenders to an awareness of reciprocal influence (p. 11), where surrender "implies freedom from any intent to control or coerce" (p. 8). Such surrender creates what she calls symbolic or interpersonal thirdness.

Who will take this first step on the political stage? Who will say, "I'll go first?"

There has been much talk of political Third Ways, talk that too often issues from centrist governments that pose no real challenge to free market ideologies. A real third way, given the state of affairs in the USA at the moment, would require a media and government that takes Levinas's and Benjamin's psychoanalytic ethical stance seriously, that provides containment for fear and anxiety rather than stoking it either to murderous rage or selfish, save your own skin withdrawal. Butler's relational suggestion that we make vulnerability the ground of a politics that might get us outside of doer–done to retaliatory discourse takes us in the right direction. Were the powerful in the USA able to tolerate their vulnerability and truly recognize our interdependence with others in the world, we might see different economic, environmental, and arms policies, and we might see a re-establishment of the social safety net that made all too brief an appearance on the stage of US history. But money and privilege allow the powerful to protect themselves against feeling vulnerable. The 2006 US Senate and House elections suggest, however, that the disaffected and angry population may be preparing to "go first". Battered as we are by anxieties about being able to hang on to what we have, distracted as we are by "infotainment", we are perhaps beginning the process of questioning the fantasies of glory we have been seduced by, and beginning to deal with our shame about vulnerability. Perhaps we are in the process of connecting our own vulnerability to that of those we have sent to fight our wars and die; perhaps we are ready to emerge from our state of helpless withdrawal and take to the streets.

I hope to have shown some of the possibilities, for both individuals and groups, of a relational understanding of identity, connection, autonomy, and interdependence, as well as of impasse and struggle. To return to my opening vignette, I reiterate that what relational psychoanalytic thinking offers, both for individual treatment and for political process, is a counter-cultural discourse on vulnerability, interdependence, and the need to acknowledge our inevitable complicity in the suffering of others.

Note

1. I find Butler's argument elegant and persuasive. But I wonder if she cedes too much to the bounded self of individualism when she accepts the dualism of two kinds of self and two kinds of politics. It seems to me that a politics of rights can also be grounded in a relational understanding of selfhood, and, if it were, different narratives might serve to express, for example, a woman's right to choose abortion. Indeed,

perhaps some of the politically divisive problems to which rights-based theories give rise are due to their grounding in a bounded self. Nancy Fraser (1997) discusses some of these problems, for example, the way that rights discourses, in demanding recognition of difference, can in fact rigidify difference, minimize similarity, and create greater tension between groups.

References

Altman, N. (1995). *The Analyst in the Inner City*. Hillsdale, NJ: Analytic Press.

Aron, L. (1996). *A Meeting of Minds. Mutuality in Psychoanalysis*. Hillsdale, NJ: The Analytic Press.

Benjamin, J. (1988). *The Bonds of Love: Psychoanalysis, Feminism, and the Problem of Domination*. New York: Pantheon.

Benjamin, J. (1990). An outline of intersubjectivity: the development of recognition. *Psychoanalytic Psychology*, 7(Suppl.): 33–46.

Benjamin, J. (2004). Beyond doer and done-to: an intersubjective view of thirdness. *Psychoanalytic Quarterly*, LXIII(1): 5–46.

Boston Change Process Study Group (2007). The foundational level of psychoanalytic meaning: implicit process in relation to conflict, defense and the dynamic unconscious. *International Journal of Psychoanalysis*, 88: 389–860.

Bourdieu, P. (1984). *Distinction*. R. Nice (Trans.). Cambridge, MA: Harvard University Press.

Bromberg, P. (2003). Something wicked this way comes. Trauma, dissociation, and conflict: the space where psychoanalysis, cognitive-science, and neuroscience overlap. *Psychoanalytic Psychology*, 20(3): 558–574.

Butler, J. (2004). *Precarious Life. The Powers of Mourning and Violence*. London: Verso.

Corbett, K. (2001). Non-traditional family romance. *Psychoanalytic Quarterly*, 70: 599–624.

Dinnerstein, D. (1976). *The Mermaid and the Minotaur*. New York: Harper & Row.

Dimen, M. (2003). *Sexuality, Intimacy, Power*. Hillsdale, NJ: Analytic Press.

Domenici, T., & Lesser, R. C. (1995). *Disorienting Sexuality. Psychoanalytic Reappraisals of Sexual Identities*. New York: Routledge.

Eichenbaum, L., & Orbach, S. (1983). *What Do Women Want? Exploding the Myth of Dependency*. London: Michael Joseph.

Ferro, A. (2002). *In the Analyst's Consulting Room.* P. Slotkin (Trans.). Hove: Brunner-Routledge.

Fraser, N. (1997). *Justice Interruptus.* New York: Routledge.

Gill, M. (1995). Classical and relational psychoanalysis. *Psychoanalytic Psychology, 12*(1): 89–107.

Goldner, V. (1991). Toward a critical relational theory of gender. *Psychoanalytic Dialogues, 1*(3) : 249–272.

Greenberg, J., & Mitchell, S. A. (1983). *Object Relations in Psychoanalytic Theory.* Cambridge, MA: Harvard University Press.

Harris, A. (2005). *Gender as Soft Assembly.* Hillsdale, NJ: Analytic Press.

Hirsch, I. (1998). Further thoughts about interpersonal and relational perspectives. Reply to Jay Frankel. *Contemporary Psychoanalysis, 34*(4): 501–538.

Hoffman, I. Z. (1983). The patient as interpreter of the analyst's experience. *Contemporary Psychoanalysis, 19:* 389–422.

Joseph, B. (1985). Transference. The total situation. *International Journal of Psycho-Analysis, 66:* 447–454.

Layton, L. (1998). *Who's That Girl? Who's That Boy? Clinical Practice Meets Postmodern Gender Theory.* Hillsdale, NJ: Analytic Press, 2004.

Layton, L. (2000). The psychopolitics of bisexuality. *Studies in Gender and Sexuality, 1*(1): 41–60.

Layton, L. (2002). Cultural hierarchies, splitting, and the heterosexist unconscious. In S. Fairfield, L. Layton, & C. Stack (Eds.), *Bringing the Plague. Toward a Postmodern Psychoanalysis* (pp. 195–223). New York: Other Press.

Layton, L. (2004). A fork in the royal road: on "defining" the unconscious and its stakes for social theory. *Psychoanalysis, Culture & Society, 9*(1): 33–51.

Layton, L. (2006a). Racial identities, racial enactments, and normative unconscious processes. *Psychoanalytic Quarterly, LXXV*(1): 237–269.

Layton, L. (2006b). Attacks on linking: the unconscious pull to dissociate individuals from their social context. In: L. Layton, N. C. Hollander, & S. Gutwill (Eds.), *Psychoanalysis, Class and Politics: Encounters in the Clinical Setting* (pp. 107–117). London: Routledge.

Layton, L. (2006c). Retaliatory discourse. The politics of attack and withdrawal. *International Journal of Applied Psychoanalytic Studies, 3*(2): 143–155.

Leary, K. (1997). Race, self-disclosure, and "forbidden talk": race and ethnicity in contemporary clinical practice. *Psychoanalytic Quarterly, LXVI:* 163–189.

Levenson, E. A. (1972). *The Fallacy of Understanding* [reprinted with *The Ambiguity of Change*. Hillsdale, NJ: Analytic Press, 2005].

Levenson, E. (1983). *The Ambiguity of Change* [reprinted with *The Fallacy of Understanding*, Hillsdale, NJ: Analytic Press, 2005].

Mitchell, S. A. (1988). *Relational Concepts in Psychoanalysis*. Cambridge, MA: Harvard University Press.

Mitchell, S.A. (2004). My psychoanalytic journey. *Psychoanalytic Inquiry*, 24(4): 531–541.

O'Connor, N., & Ryan, J. (1993). *Wild Desires & Mistaken Identities*. New York: Columbia University Press.

Pizer, S. (1998). *Building Bridges: Negotiation and Paradox in Psychoanalysis*. Hillsdale, NJ: Analytic Press.

Samuels, A. (1993). *The Political Psyche*. London: Routledge.

Sander, L. (1983). Polarity, paradox, and the organizing process in development. In: J. D. Call, E. Galenson, & R. L. Tyson (Eds.), *Frontiers of Infant Psychiatry*, 1 (pp. 333–346). New York: Basic Books.

Stern, D. B. (1997). *Unformulated Experience*. Hillsdale, NJ: Analytic Press.

Stern, D. B. (2004). The eye sees itself. Dissociation, enactment, and the achievement of conflict. *Contemporary Psychoanalysis*, 40(2):197–237.

Stern, D. N. (1985). *The Interpersonal World of the Infant*. New York: Basic Books.

Sullivan, H. S. (1953). *The Interpersonal Theory of Psychiatry*. New York: Norton.

CHAPTER TWO

Democratizing psychoanalysis

Susie Orbach

Relational routes in (mainly) British psychoanalysis

From the 1930s to the 1970s, there was an extraordinary intellectual flowering within psychoanalysis. The Balints, object relations theory, Winnicott, Fairbairn, Guntrip, Bowlby and attachment theory, the work of R. D. Laing and his colleagues, the anti-psychiatry movement, all attempted to resituate and recast what psychoanalysis had turned into. Then, Independents such as Bollas and Rycroft, contemporary Freudians such as the Sandlers and Fonagy, the clinical and theoretical innovations of The Women's Therapy Centre, Nafsyat and other equally radical therapy initiatives, all these different tendencies focused on the actual experience of patients, their history, and the ways in which intrapsychic development was an outcome of the internalizations of relationships they had experienced from the earliest moment of their entry into the world.

This emphasis on the actual, has swept through nearly all psychoanalytic schools: Jungian, Object Relations, contemporary Freudian, Kohutian. It was always the basis, in the USA, of the work of the Interpersonalists, the Intersubjectivists, and of latterly what has become known as the Relational School. (Of course, similar developments within humanistic psychotherapy were also occurring.) The emphasis on the actual has dovetailed with the work of infant researchers, Mahler, Bergman, and Pine; Stern; Trevarthen; Beebe; and Steele and Steele, who have been demonstrating the very active, relationship-seeking requisites of the baby and the ways in which the character of parental responses structures the infant's relation to self. Beebe's work in particular, which scrutinizes the frame-by-frame of mother–baby interactions, shows the intricate play between mother and infant, the efforts the baby makes to engage the mother, the way the baby responds to the mother's initiatives and the emotional impact of failing attempts to engage with each other.

Routes to relational psychoanalysis from radical movements

Relational psychoanalytic practices reflect much of what Luise Eichenbaum and I were writing in the late 1970s and early 1980s about our work with women at The Women's Therapy Centre. At that time we did not have a term we were happy with for what we were doing. The closest were social object relations theory and feminist object relations. We were repositioning both the mother and the psychotherapist, not solely as the (failing) and fixed object of the analysand, but also as subjects in the process of becoming (Orbach & Eichenbaum, 1982, 1995).

Stephen Mitchell published *Relational Concepts in Psychoanalysis* in 1983, and although he recognized the analytic routes of his reconceptualization, particularly Fairbairn's work, he did not recognize developments that came from social movements such as feminism, the New Left, and what is largely called radical therapy. These were movements that were engaging with psychoanalysis, group and individual psychotherapy, women's consciousness raising groups, self-help groups for mental patients, and so on, that were contextualizing the intrapsychic life of the individual as an outcome of relationship: relationship that was embedded in a set of classed, raced, religious, ethnic, and gendered relations that was reflected in the particular nuances of psychological relations (Eichenbaum & Orbach, 1982, 2003). Following Reich and Fanon,

radical explorations of personality in the 1970s turned on an understanding of how we came to have the particular psychologies we
inhabited. How was femininity fit for a patriarchal society? How
might we describe the intrapsychic features that created women's
experiences? How had racism become internalized by everyone in
the West? What were the functions of "othering"? How did class
and class disavowal construct our various self experience? How did
women become heterosexual? And so on. These agendas became
much excavated, at least in the therapist's head and in radical therapy orientated study groups and seminars, engendering new
theory and new ways of understanding and working clinically
(Eichenbaum & Orbach, 1982; Flax, 1978; Samuels, 1989). Structures
such as the Oedipus complex, penis envy, separation individuation,
and so on were meanwhile challenged and rethought to see what
relevance they might have for radically orientated therapy. The
confluence of these streams became relational psychoanalysis.

Democracy in the consulting room

Relational psychoanalysis has a democratic, co-created view of the
therapeutic relationship. Instead of a sense of the patient as other,
as the object of the therapeutic gaze, relational psychoanalysis
always sees the person in therapy as an influencing and an influ-
ence-able subject. Similarly, the analyst is not a static figure on to
whom the patient projects their transference, but an active member
of the therapeutic dyad who, as Lew Aron (1996) would argue,
brings her or his subjectivity to the therapeutic relationship.

In relational approaches, the therapist's subjectivity is always
present. If the analyst comes to feel uneasy when with a patient or
thinking about a person they are working with, this feeling is scru-
tinized for what it might reveal about what is going on in the therapeutic dyad. The patient's behaviours and affects are not pre-
described or interpretable according to a formula. What an analyst
experienced during the course of a session—the countertransference material (although Aron, 1996, would call this the analyst's
subjectivity rather than the countertransference)—is never simply
evaluated for what the patient "did" or "put into" the analyst. I
mention this because, despite openness to one's analysands being a

principle of all psychoanalysis and psychotherapy, in practice, within mainstream psychoanalysis in the UK, there are rules about what to think about when an individual in therapy does x or y that causes the analyst discomfort. Often the import of these "rules" seems to be about deconstructing the individual's defence structure with the clinical aim of showing her or him the destructive nature of much of their internal world. This is a very different aim from that of relational psychoanalysis, and I want to state quite clearly what I see as some differences between relational psychoanalysis and conventional psychoanalysis with regard to therapeutic stance.

Example 1

> I sit in on a seminar. I notice that the interpretation of an analysand's behaviour is carried on as though it were a sport. If a participant presents a case in which a patient brings flowers to the therapist, this solicits a set of attitudes from the assembled therapists about what the bringing of flowers means, with the tinge that really the patient shouldn't be doing so; she should know better, she is seductive. If the presenting therapist says, these flowers were sent rather than presented, a series of interpretations about the invasiveness of the patient is then offered, as though the patient were endeavouring to get under the therapist's radar screen that the patient would have known would have prevented the therapist from accepting the flowers in the first instance. Thus, the patient is described as both sneaky and intrusive. The meaning of wanting to give is excavated to foster a particular result: that the patient does not know her/himself and must be shown the ways in which their initiative is an expression of the "darker" side of themselves. It reminds one of the old analytic cliché: arrive too early and one risks being labelled over-anxious; arrive late, and one is controlling. The patient, when told these things, experiences shame as though she has transgressed. Interestingly, the therapist's discomfort is not explored, but accepted as a simple consequence of the inappropriateness of the analysand's behaviour.

A hallmark of relational psychoanalysis is that there is no "off the shelf" understanding of what is happening in the consulting room between patient and analyst. There is only a bespoke one— one that fits that particular analytic couple at that moment in that therapy. One could argue that of course this is what happens in any "good" therapy. But experience at seminars where a flowers type incident has emerged conveys a sense that "good" therapy is infrequent, for this example has been offered many times in seminars and has invariably elicited the same type of interpretive response.

By contrast, the entry point to the relational analyst would be to register how the analyst herself feels about the flowers. There may be a complex set of feelings in some cases, or it might be quite straightforward in others. If the feelings were discordant, the analyst would inquire to herself about her own unease—to what extent was the unease personal to her; what kind of unease was it? Was it specific to being with this particular person? Was it a common feeling in this therapy, or an unexpected and unusual one? On the other hand, if the analyst felt comfortable with the receipt of the flowers, she would also reflect on why she felt that way. If there was discomfort, the relational analyst would try to understand what was offered or attempted in the delivery of the flowers: why flowers, why now? Such questions, specific in space and time (why here? why now?), are posed from a neutral stance, a position of curiosity and interest, a something that might be comprehensible between the two parties but emphatically not an act with a given *a priori* meaning.

In the example cited, it was the case that it was Rosh Hoshanna, the Jewish New Year, and the patient wished to send a gift to the analyst to arrive on the right day. The patient was not shamed by exploring why she sent the gift, but was eager to talk about her desire to give and to have her giving received. The theme of being able to give and have that giving acknowledged was an important one in her therapy.

The therapist, for her part, has to allow herself to receive, and in the process she may have to explore her own conflicts or issues about receiving (Eichenbaum & Orbach, 1982, 1987).

Example 2

A colleague working with a child of Ethiopian refugees was very moved by the child's stories of missing animals. She felt a desire to take him to visit the zoo even though she knew this was inadequate to his loss. The child's home circumstances were dire and she felt sad for him. In supervision, *her desire* to take the child to the zoo (which was

something she kept to herself in the session) was interpreted as being
invoked in her by the child's envy for what she had and could so easily
give in her own middle-class parenting. Furthermore, the sadness she
felt when thinking about this boy was, she was told, a response to what
the child had put into her. A relational analyst would more probably
view her desire as a sign of attachment and the child's ability to want
and perhaps to be able to receive after traumatic separation and loss.

The relational approach to the therapist's desire would start
from assumption of the child's desire—and yet the anguish and
difficulty of bringing his two worlds together. What he may have
evoked in the analyst might be understood as a sign of potential
attachment in both therapist and child, that the losses experienced
by the child were being brought to the therapy relationship.

Example 3

In various psychotherapy establishments, therapists walk around the
hallways with their eyes addressed to the floor, lest they see or be seen
by a patient. If one does see or is seen inside or outside the building by
a patient, this is not generally acknowledged. When I have asked about
this I am told that it is for the patient to bring up the encounter. If I
press further, I am told that it would be invasive, an imposition on the
patient for the patient to be acknowledged. These responses strike me
as peculiarly at odds with the often immaculate manners of these same
colleagues in non-therapy settings. In trying to puzzle out why there
should be this extraordinary difference in behaviour, I am led to believe
that the patient is seen as an object rather than a subject, where the aim
is to produce discomfort so that the normal niceties of daily life are
removed and the defence structure is put under pressure. If such an
encounter occurs for a relational analyst, one respects the privacy of the
individual with a discreet nod or hello, and the follow-up to this, if not
taken up by the analysand, would be brought up by the therapist. In
relational work there is little conflict about accidentally encountering
the client as a subject outside the consulting room.

Finally there is also a sense that for an analyst to feel close to his
or her patients is simply not kosher therapy. (Of course we know
that most practitioners do care very much for their analysands, but
the conceptualization around this is very much represented in
forms one can only judge as confusingly bizarre.) The collaborative

stance of relational psychoanalysis permits a relatively open exploration and experience of intimate feelings in the consulting rather
than a frightened withdrawal or an authoritarian or distancing
stance.

How we become human

The understanding of relational analysis starts from the premise
that the individual is born into a set of social and psychological
circumstances. The human infant is *a set of possibilities*, not id based,
not instinctually driven, but, in order to become recognized as
human, will need to attach. For those compelled by the notion of
instinct theory, this was reframed in the 1940s by Fairbairn as a
need for relationship, and by Bowlby as a need for attachment. The
nature of the relationships the child is exposed to, experiences, and,
of course, seeks to shape by her actions, is the template for that individual's self experience and relations to others. Relational psychoanalysis does not seek to understand the structures in a reductionist
way, or by use of sociological tools. Its agenda is to understand how
both the satisfactory and the problematic aspects of those
profoundly influential relationships create the internal structuring
of the individual. The relationship(s) also forms the sense of how
the individual approaches the world: the ways she feels able to act
upon it and in it, the aspects she fears, how she conceptualizes and
experiences her relations to self and other. In addition, relational
theory proposes a conflict-relational model. It does not propose that
becoming is conflict free. It conceptualizes the struggle to be an
individual as an inevitable dialectic conflict between the wish to
connect and to experience one's distinctiveness while understanding that one can only connect with another if one is distinct and
one's distinctiveness has been recognized.

Living as enactment

Being is constituted out of the enactment and living of both
conscious behaviour and behaviour of which we are unaware.
Transference, or to put it another way, the emotional imagos of

early relationship, incline us to see relationships in the present as resonating at a feeling level with structural aspects of those original relationships. Our present stance in relationship involves foisting on to the relationship a template about historic relationship (be it authoritarian, benign, push–pull, withholding, merged, or, more commonly, a combination of different elements). Our present encodes ways of being and experiencing that are less open than we might desire or think. We may see what is not there and miss what is. It is not so much that subjectivity is determined, but that long-ings and desires—those that we can be aware of and those we inter-act with—are necessarily infused by the understandings and the experiences we have imbibed in the course of development. These understandings may be out of conscious knowledge and may oper-ate in a conflictual manner with our longings. *Being and becoming are processes.* There is, from the perspective of relational psychoanaly-sis, no other way to understand and be. And it is a version of those internalized relationship as *felt, understood, and enacted by the indi-vidual* that will precipitate down and form a significant part of the experience of the therapy relationship.

Relational psychoanalysis recognizes that the individual is on the *search for relationship.* An individual's defence structure may embody many impediments to relationship, and those impedi-ments will be brought to and lived out in the analysand's life as well as within the therapy relationship. Inevitably, relational psychoanalysis says, the desire for, fear of, and the complex shape of the wanted forms of relating, will pull the analyst in. The analyst is not outside of the field, observing and interpreting the impact of the patient's various forms of relating, and thus sitting and inter-preting. Of course, she is doing some of that. (I should say that I, myself, am very unhappy with notion of interpreting. Historically, interpretation meant that the analyst interprets unconscious mater-ial. That was her or his function. Today, we do not only "interpret", and my unease stems from the reification of analysts' utterances being claimed as interpretations instead of simple interventions, attempts at understanding, connecting, sense-making, and so on.) The analyst is inevitably drawn into and is an active participant in the relational field. Relational psychoanalysis does not see the analysand as doing things to the analyst, as putting things into the analyst, or see challenging behaviour as acting out or an attempt to

draw the analyst in, as though that were some kind of misde-
meanour. Rather, we anticipate that the analyst *will* be drawn in to
the relational field, *for that is in the nature of relationship. We affect one
another. We cannot not.* We are not doing psychic surgery, dissecting
and then shaking off the countertransference and describing it to
the patient in some theoretically neutral or (accusatory) way. We do
not believe that there is such a thing as therapeutic neutrality. There
is engagement, and this can be understood and related to in many
different ways. But one form of engagement we reject is that which
interprets the longing or desire of the patient as some kind of unacceptable demand on the therapist.

Therapeutic neutrality and the relational analyst

The therapist's stance is one in which we are co-participants in the
therapeutic endeavour. Our job is to make ourselves available to the
analysand, to absorb what is being said, the ways it is being said,
and what is not being said. Our minds make pictures out of the
dilemmas we hear described and we ascribe various understandings to what we hear. But when I say available, I mean also that we
are receptive to being affected and moved. What we hear and see
in the consulting room reverberates on us. And because this is an
analytic setting, what we do with what we experience becomes part
of the analytic field of study. We study ourselves and our
analysands in the process of self reflection.

Our emotional and intellectual availability is, in the first
instance, something we "talk privately with ourselves about"
(Casement, 1985). We create a kind of split in our experience in
which we are both present, observing and analysing the nature of
our presence. This is, of course, a parallel process to that which the
analysand comes to do as well. We endeavour to have the same
kind of curiosity towards our own responses that we hope that our
analysand can have towards their own. When we encounter attitudes or emotions, or are invited to participate in interactions we
find difficult, even repellent, we hope not to send the repellent
feeling back in a retaliatory way or in a way that is personally idiosyncratic. The analytic space and the therapist's theoretical understandings provide the therapist with tools that allow her or him to

act more thoughtfully and judicially than she or he might in ordinary social intercourse.

In making our interventions, we scrutinize what we believe is being conveyed to us *in the feeling that we are experiencing* (the countertransference). We examine how our countertransference might be an aspect of our personal defence structure. We hope to assess what could be useful in helping us to connect with the difficulties being experienced by the individual we are seeing. Let us say a patient starts to masturbate when she is in the room; we hope not to just say "Stop that", we hope to be able to bear the discomfort of it sufficiently to be able to think about it beyond being alarmed. We slow time enough to notice, and then formulate what is important to us in order to be able to interpret the quality of what we feel impelled to say or not say in a manner we hope is digestible and potentially transformative.

In working out the quality of what we feel, relational psychoanalysis goes beyond an understanding of the countertransference as exclusively a diagnostic tool. We take as given that what is expressed is a communication and that, because of how we understand ourselves when we are with this particular individual, we have a personal response that is an expression of our own subjectivity.

Harvey

For the past few weeks, Harvey, a fifty-year-old man well employed in the arts, has been coming in talking like a cross between the National Front and the Daily Mail. Furious, he rails about what has happened to his country, his England. The child of a quite cruel middle-class and prosperous father and a working-class turned middle-class inconsistent mother, he grew up in the suburbs around Edinburgh and was sent to a boarding school. When he got his A levels, he came to London and became part of the generation that embraced alternate ideas. He welcomed the end of privilege, sexual liberation, and made his way through the cultural spaces that were opening up in London.

Harvey is both defiant about and somewhat alarmed by the words that currently come out of his mouth. There is a comfort in his defiance having something to do with positioning himself with what he imagines is a growing majority position. He is now no longer a beleaguered but morally righteous left-wing individual, fighting a minority battle against everyone. He is joined with his fellow countrymen who find themselves suddenly aware of being dispossessed from their England, an England that ceased to exist many years ago and, indeed, an England that he fought to disassemble himself, but, nevertheless, an England that he now fails to recognize.

While he loves the loosening of restrictions in everyday life, the greater sexual freedom, the liveliness of the restaurants, clothing, and the ethnic scenes, what he cannot come to terms with are the degraded work practices in his profession, where product has replaced risk, demographics has replaced originality, and where cost-cutting and the destruction of the unions have broken the working practices of the unit he is in. People now work very long hours, feel they have less stake in the product, and have little respect for the executives, who are only concerned with churning out product.

Harvey does not recognize an England rife with poverty and with drugs, with a great divide between rich and poor. He does not recognize an England in which the dominant voice is not white and middle-class; he does not recognize an England that has become a playground for the rich from other countries, and he does not recognize an England that has become a place in which the tortured or disenfranchised from elsewhere seek to settle.

His sentiments, which in more benevolent times would be expressed as a wish to change things towards what might be broadly thought of as an equality agenda, are turned now towards a populist sloganeering of the *Daily Mail* variety.

We are highly trained to reflect, to think, to listen, and to understand inside the responses of my patient Harvey that yes, for a postwar baby, that stultifying Britain that they tore down with such a sense of personal and collective agency in the 1960s and 1970s has been transformed into a new culture greatly at odds with its postwar sensibilities and with the progressive sensibilities through a combination of Thatcherism, globalism, the demise of politics, and the omnipresent offerings of consumerism and celebrity.

By neither responding with a counter polemic nor simply concurring with our patients, we allow different sorts of thoughts to form. Harvey can explore his ideas but, in hearing himself doing so without external censure or concurrence, he enters into a study of his own subjectivity. He brings a third ear to himself and to his own polemical rant. He begins to be curious about his conclusions: why the explanations that he is now offering himself have salience. He is not shamed by his responses. They cause him discomfort, and in the therapy he can engage that discomfort. He does not have to either become defensive or hide his new attitudes.

We talk about loss. The loss of something known, an England he recognized, an England he felt entitled to bash up and transform, an England in which he saw himself having a stake. By acknowledging loss, a space is open for Harvey's displacement and his anger to find less targeted responses. He reflects on loss and the ways in which, in times of change, new circumstances can become sites of fear for him. The conversation between us moves on. We do not resolve his feelings in one session. We do not, as it were, reform him and the venality of his responses. Therapy is not a place for the exchange of one political coat for another. It is a place for deconstructing. It is a place for mixing up the easy, the commonplace, for adding texture, for being confused without fright, for exploring what we are feeling and what it means to think with complexity, with compassion, towards self and with an understanding of defence structures that limit our capacity actually to address new situations rather than impose old emotional and psychic tableaux on them.

But, of course, Harvey's story affects me deeply. I, too have lived these times. I, too, experience confusion, delight, dismay about the changes the UK has gone through. As he talks, I am forced, if I wish to stay open to what he is struggling with, to explore my own prejudices, my own values, not just as a progressive, but the ways in which a kind of nationalistic, Murdochized, heavy media have structured my responses to the social, economic, and political, to the extraordinary social changes that have occurred since 1984. I have to find a way to engage with Harvey that denies neither my subjectivity nor his. I employ a version of analytic neutrality that is *not* about being a blank screen, but is marked by attentiveness and interest towards *my responses* to Harvey's utterances and feelings.

As it happens, this story has a happy ending. In time, Harvey was able to see how he squeezed his upset about not understanding Britain into a piece of rhetoric that gave him a temporary sense of belonging; a sense of belonging that had eluded him through his childhood, had briefly emerged in his twenties and thirties when he was part of the counter-cultural movement, but that had disappeared again in the past period, where the values he held seemed once again at odds with the culture. Therapy helped him to understand the ways in which the longing to be "part of" joined with the devilish psychological dynamic of adherence to historical emotional tableaux of identifying with the very set of emotional resonances that cause pain. Our past relationships, and the ways in which we have internalized them and the positions that we have held in them, form our individual relationship to the world.

Psychotherapy tells us unequivocally that we cannot relinquish the power and dominance of past relationships in our psychic functioning until we accept them as they were. We increase our powerlessness to the extent that we are always railing against those who so affected us and unable to come to terms with our relative powerlessness about what was. In the recognition of that powerlessness and the inner psychic battles we fought to deny it, we endeavour to move towards acceptance and the ways in which we can have the past be in the past, so that our present expresses our *actual* and *potential* power rather than the victimized or angry stance of thwarted power.

The therapist's subjectivity

So, what is Harvey's impact on the therapist's subjectivity and our impact on Harvey? Of course, it is individual and particular to each therapeutic couple. We will all have different responses. We will have heard different parts of the story. We will not even have heard the same story, for we will either have stalled it, helped him enlarge it, or taken it in different directions. Our own responses to Harvey will encode our subjectivity, our interests, and our views about what is psychologically and, explicitly in this instance, politically salient. The very endeavour of therapy will necessarily encode a politic. What the politics are, where they lead the patient and the therapist, depends upon the political sensibilities of both parties, but especially that of the therapist, who can and does both wittingly and unwittingly direct the attention of the therapy in particular directions. We can imagine another therapist, with different politics, and a different psychological theory, not looking at loss and conflicts over belonging, but focusing in another direction altogether: on what has been taken away, issues of rage about deprivation and a fear of spoiling the new.

In whatever ways we are drawn, we will be responding to Harvey's longings for contact and understanding from our own response to both the transferential field and how Harvey's distress affects us. His isolation and agonies will necessarily stimulate our own. We might even anticipate that, in the therapy relationship, we might enact, without wishing to, the prohibiting, critical parental imago that Harvey has internalized and that he unconsciously anticipates we will take up, despite his wish to find a different, more embracing understanding. We can predict, too, that at one point or another, the therapist will enact some aspect of Harvey's world of inner relationships to confirm for him that he *cannot* be understood, he cannot belong. The therapist will, in effect, become disappointing. This, for the relational analyst, will not be judged as a failure of our personality or therapeutic fitness, but *as what is almost bound to occur at some point in the therapy relationship as a way of literalizing and enacting, between the two of us, what in Harvey's psychic structure holds him in positions that he finds disabling.*

The literalizing of the struggle between us does not emerge out of conscious intent. It happens because the therapy relationship is co-created between analyst and analysand. Our desires mutually, if asymmetrically, influence one another, and the recognition of the bi-directionality of the therapeutic relationship is a crucial aspect of relational analysis. Working on what has been literalized is another therapeutic moment.

Therapeutic neutrality

This takes me back to the problem of neutrality. Therapeutic neutrality has been idealized and fetishized. The idealization is a function of the distance the therapist wishes to take from the patient. It is an expression of the desire not to be influenced or be affected, because it was thought that the analyst was a kind of psychic detective or surgeon. But I think we can accept today that *relationship is influence and affect, or it is not relationship*. If we remain unaffected, we are quasi "autistic", or constrained by our own splitting capacities. To be influenced and affected is not to give up our own agency or our own skills as analysts. It is a push to the centre stage of contemporary understandings of the analytic endeavour: that what the patient is struggling with is "being" and that the process of being involves the engagement of an other, a thinking, feeling other with whom to explore the difficulties of being. This endeavour will create space, impingements, psychic rearrangements. In democratizing the relationship, the analytic capacity to observe ourselves while *being* is deemed to belong to both of us. We can both become partially adequate and skilled at doing this and recognize the limitations we are bound to feel. To go back to the masturbating example, neutrality here means developing curiosity, a kind of 360° curiosity towards our own responses and that of the person who is causing us alarm or discomfort by his or her behaviour.

Self disclosure

This brings me briefly to self disclosure, one of the shibboleths by which relationality is criticized. If the analyst is a co-participant and co-creator of the therapeutic relationship, she or he is also disclosing who they are. The relational analyst does not walk into the room and don a psychological uniform. She goes in with her skills and theory, her emotional and intellectual availability, ready to engage. The forms of engagement that transpire will disclose much about who she is with *this particular person. The way she is, is disclosure*. She is not concealing, nor is she revealing intentionally. Her way of being is an expression of self and inevitably self-disclosing. This is not the self disclosure of telling an analysand what I did in *x* situation. My experience of having been in *x* situation will be embodied in my engagement with her or him. I have a history and human agency that is as transformative (and struggles with repetitions) as that which I hope the analytic process can give her or him. Self disclosure is not about saying or not saying. It is about an authenticity of being.

Dependency and recognition

I want now to discuss what is, for me, one of the most critical issues of relational psychoanalysis. Dependency and recognition, of course, have enormous implications for our institutional, class, and gender arrangements. Relational psychoanalysis recognizes that, within the therapy relationship, issues of dependency and recognition will be central. Dependency is the term that Luise Eichenbaum and I have used; recognition is that of Jessica Benjamin's. Fairbairn's was mature dependency. In essence, we are all talking about the developmental need for attachment, to be seen and to be accepted, and the defences that develop when dependency needs are not met and their not being met goes unacknowledged. The individual internalizes a sense that their desires, their longings, their dependency, their need for nurture and care and to be seen, in short, that which arises from inside of them, their very self, is wrong. They may express this "wrongness" in many different ways, from shame to insistence, but behind the various defences will be a sense of unentitlement.

Within the therapy, this sense of unentitlement, of not daring to want or wanting so much (which is itself a variant of not being comfortable with wanting because there is no expectation that wanting leads to receiving), comes directly into the therapy relationship. It will form the explicit and the latent content of the therapy and it will shape the therapeutic relationship. Then, too, the therapist's own stance towards, and defences against, their personal dependency issues will challenge them in many ways. Within psychoanalysis, dependency has been a kind of dirty word, with women especially being described as overly dependent, clingy, and needing to separate. Gender conscious therapy brought to the fore the ways in which therapists' and patients' unconsciously shared fears of dependency needs meant that dependency needs within the therapy were collusively warded off by both parties. We suggested that looking at dependency, and not defending against it, is crucial. By looking, we meant being able to invite and commit ourselves to grappling with dependency issues between the patient and therapist, including, of course, all the defences, which range from being free of need for the therapist to feeling desperately and unreachably needy. These included defences that we ourselves embodied. Just as in the analysand, these defences could be stirred up in us by the analysand (Eichenbaum & Orbach, 1982).

Autonomy can *only* emerge out of connection, what Luise Eichenbaum and I have termed "separated attachments". A sense of personal agency is intersubjectively located and arises out of dependency needs being addressed. Connection occurs through the capacity to see the other as an other as well as related to self, and to experience oneself as both attached and separate simultaneously (Eichenbaum & Orbach, 1983; 1987). The political implications of separated attachments and dependency are important in light of the ideological arguments on what constitutes a social, political, and economic world in the past twenty, post-Thatcherite years. We could see Thatcherism (and I include Blairism as a variant of Thatcherism) as the preparation for Britain's relation to globalism, with its emphasis on pseudo-connection, the marauding of the other, and the exploitation of complex economic dependencies. When we think about the forms of institutional arrangements and institution-to-institution arrangements, rethinking dependency issues, not to avoid them, but to recognize and rebalance them, is crucial.

The democratization of fee structures

Money has always been problematic in the history of psychoanalysis. When distorted by the influence of private medicine in the USA, a theory was put in place stating that unless the patient paid the therapy was not worth anything. From a European perspective, where indirect payment is as common as direct payment (as indeed it was in the USA for a period of time, when psychoanalysis was taken to a larger population base through free clinics, the Veterans Administration, and outpatient psychotherapy services), such a view appears anachronistic.

It has been disturbing to encounter an ideological position about the importance of direct payment, weighted down with interpretation about a patient's behaviour in regard to money, when actually the majority of UK patients are seen without fee. The insistence —you must pay as an expression of valuing yourself and the therapy—of some clinics and clinicians becomes both tokenistic and totemic. The existence of the fee is then hailed as the site for the working out of issues about need, entitlement, contempt, and so on.

While such a rationale might have had general relevance in a model where the analyst was perceived to be a blank screen and the only directly analyst-personal material related was to do with money and holidays, this is simply not the case in relational psychoanalysis, where the analyst offers her or himself for engagement within the session and where their subjectivity is in view and being struggled with (internally and interpersonally) rather than all challenges by the patient being referred back to the analysand's individual pathology.

So, for those in relational psychoanalysis who have absorbed the culture of mainstream psychoanalysis, it is necessary to excavate one's theories about fees and to think them through afresh. A tenet of practice at The Women's Therapy Centre in its first five years (1976–1981) was firmly committed to as little direct payment as possible. (Unfortunately, because of funding difficulties, this could only be offered to people who were on social security and very low personal incomes.) We found absolutely no difference in terms of an individual's commitment to therapy whether they were paying directly or not. Indeed, certain clinical issues did become particularly focused precisely because the fee was absent, and could not be sloughed away inside the fee. These issues were often around the theme of emotional receiving, of struggling with issues of dependency and attachment. Without a direct fee payment as carapace, the therapeutic couple had to confront and live through what was transpiring, being given, being risked, and being received. Interestingly, with several of my own fee-paying people, there have been attempts to "use" the fee almost to reverse the dependency issues in such a way that I come to be dependent on the people paying me.

Of course, indeed, therapists are dependent on fees financially. We need to be paid and we need to find humane and democratic ways to structure our financial arrangements with the people we see. We need to provide fee structures that work for us, but I believe that a rigid fee structure is too inflexible for many people. The fees that rest on that idea of the analysand taking exactly the same holiday dates as the therapist and being financially responsible for sessions that are unattended because of half-term, or a need to travel, seems, in today's climate, therapeutically indefensible. I, for instance, have a practice that is a combination of individuals who come week-in, week-out for once, twice, or more sessions in which their times vary only very occasionally. But I also see people who travel, or who work in the theatre, and cannot commit to a weekly or twice-weekly time despite their interest in coming. How then to structure fees?

Colleagues and I have always assessed our fees on a nominal forty weeks a year basis (in our own minds). This may mean that one is charging marginally more per session, but it allows for people taking their half-terms or going on a trek which might be wonderful for them without it threatening the therapist's income, who then interprets such activities as "an attack on the therapy".

Of course, each individual therapist has to have clear what she or he will work with. The therapist needs to think through for her or himself what she actually thinks about individuals who want to take their holidays when it suits them rather than suits the schedule of the therapist. A therapist also has to think through whether cancellation for illness is billable. And, if so, what kind of advance notice do they require? None of this is to say that there will not be a particular individual in one's practice who is unable to take the therapy seriously without paying. This will sometimes be the case, but what relational psychoanalysis has to take on is that an idea of convenience for the therapist (regular income) does not become a false god of therapy or simply doing what one's own analyst did.

As therapists, we are emotionally inconvenienced by the things we come to feel in our sessions. We are also dependent on the people we see. We do not necessarily hold them better by insisting on payment for when they go on holiday. Indeed, I think we may lose them. When we insist, I fear we are subverting the therapy for our own agenda; an agenda that may have made some sense at some point but is not justifiable today.

Conclusion

This account of relational psychoanalysis is not meant to exclude several main features of therapy: the finding of words to tell of experience previously unformulated or unheard, making narratives that can create new understandings of one's past and one's present, and linking up affect that has become separated off from the emotional circumstances that produced it so that, in relinking, one may digest the difficult feelings and increase one's emotional vocabulary. This is the ordinary activity of therapy. How it is done will be theory-laden and, in the case of relational psychoanalysis, it will reflect a sense that psychoanalysis does not seek *a* truth but many truths—truths that contradict one another, that change in time, and are always perspectival and partial. Among its great strength for today's purposes is that we study people in the process of change and reflect on those changes as they happen to us and to our patients in the therapeutic couple.

References

Aron, L. (1996). *A Meeting of Minds. Mutuality in Psychoanalysis.* Hillsdale, NJ: The Analytic Press.

Casement, P. (1985). *On Learning from the Patient.* London: Routledge.

Eichenbaum, L., & Orbach, S. (1982). *Outside In, Inside Out.* Revised (1984) as *Understanding Women.* Harmondsworth: Penguin.

Eichenbaum, L., & Orbach, S. (1983). *What Do Women Want? Exploding the Myth of Dependency.* London: Michael Joseph.

Eichenbaum, L., & Orbach, S. (1987). *Between Women.* Harmondsworth: Penguin.

Eichenbaum, L., & Orbach, S. (2003). Relational psychoanalysis and feminism: a crossing of historical paths. *Psychotherapy and Politics International*, 1:17–26.

Flax, J. (1978). The conflict between nurturance and autonomy in the mother–daughter relationship and within feminism. *Feminist Studies*, 4: 171–179.

Mitchell, S. A. (1988). *Relational Concepts in Psychoanalysis: An Integration.* Cambridge, MA: Harvard University Press.

Orbach, S., & Eichenbaum, L. (1995). From objects to subjects. *British Journal of Psychotherapy*, 12: 89–93.

Samuels, A. (1989). *The Plural Psyche: Personality, Morality and the Father.* London: Routledge.

CHAPTER THREE

Staying close to the subject

Paul Zeal

I n this chapter, in order to place relationality, I investigate the nature of psychoanalytic discourse and consider at what levels psychoanalytic relating takes place given that both participants are subjects. (I am registered as a psychoanalytic psychotherapist. Distinctions between that title and psychoanalyst are, in the context of this chapter, porous to say the least.) I consider connections and disconnections between presenting self and subject. Paradoxically, to do so I discuss the subject of addiction, which, it is generally agreed, presents obstacles to psychoanalytic discourse and relating. I also touch on the appetites of consumerism in a psychoanalytic perspective.

In *Relationality: From Attachment to Intersubjectivity*, Stephen Mitchell (2003) situates relational psychoanalysis in psychoanalytic tradition and begins his Preface, "Psychoanalysis has always been centrally concerned with human relatedness" (p. ix). He writes that the domain of the psychoneuroses that Freud wrested from the neurology of his day was a domain of mental events having largely to do with relations with other people. Freud then abandoned his seduction theory (child as innocent, corrupted from outside) in favour of instinct drive theory, in which significant others were largely fantasized. Mitchell writes, "But Freudian drive theory always remained, necessarily, a *kind* of object relations theory, in which fantasies about others rather than the actions of others were crucial" (*ibid.*). He continues that the clinical process of psychoanalysis has always been fundamentally relational, but there have been long stretches in the history of psychoanalytic ideas when the nature of human relatedness has not been studied directly (*ibid*). Instead, the patient's mind was understood to derive from body-based, constitutionally wired primal fantasies, and psychoanalysis became definitively intrapsychic, in which actual others were considered "accidental" factors.

Freud's modernist project, his grand narrative, was to pursue universality in the processes of oedipalization and symbolic castration. In our postmodern era, relativity in all things is the new universal, thus the renascent interest in psychoanalytic relating, the analyst as co-creator of what happens between. However, it does not follow from the fact that both participants are possessed of unconscious minds made of internalized accidents and consequent baggage that they are identically placed in relation to each other. There are important symbolic order differences. The analyst is in the position of the one who is supposed to know ("le sujet supposé savoir"—a Lacanian ascription for the role of the analyst). It does not follow that he does, or that he knows better—but that he knows differently or at least something, and his job is to hold that place despite transference assaults. But uneasy oscillations between universal (analyst is always analyst, patient always patient) and particular (each at times is caught in issues of lack and jouissance) are unavoidable, given what we are made of, despite our birth into speech and language and the symbolic markers of difference they give us in principle. (Jouissance seeks enjoyment in excess. It is desire overflowing need, a signifier for being fully human. However, its shadow side is its denial of lack. Lack is part of the human condition that is subject to symbolic castration or oedipalization, by accepting which we take up a place in the human community. Lack is hard to bear, and tends to be unbearable when nurture and recognition are lacking. Jouissance, then, is dangerous, because when it denies lack it becomes subject to a repetition of lack in the form of the death drive expressed in destructiveness. Jouissance transgresses the homeostatic law of the pleasure principle, whereby through discharge the psyche seeks relief from tension, and is thus beyond the pleasure principle. [These notes are adapted from Alan Sheridan's "Translator's note" in Lacan, 1977, p. xi].)

Relational psychoanalysis has come to be linked with attachment theory (witness Mitchell's title), understandably, because John Bowlby's work had everything to do with the crucial relational impact of the accidental in the child's development. Ignored for decades by the psychoanalytic establishment, his discoveries are posthumously out of the cold (Holmes, 2004). However, Mitchell devotes much of his book to the work and vision of Hans Loewald, and, by doing so, gives lineage to a dialectical tradition in psychoanalysis. He says Loewald spent three years studying philosophy with Heidegger in Freiburg, and attributes his preoccupation with problems of being and time to that experience. But "[I]f the problems that gripped Loewald were Heideggerian, the conceptual world that he lived in and loved was Freudian" (Mitchell, 2003, p. 31).

> In many respects, Loewald's life's work might be regarded as a kind of Heideggerian reworking of Freud's basic concepts. Nowhere is Heidegger's influence more palpably felt than in the centrality Loewald placed on language. "Language", Heidegger suggested, "is the house of Being. Man dwells in this house." [*ibid.*, pp. 11–12].

Mitchell continues,

> The centrality of language in the psychoanalytic experience makes possible a reanimation of psychic life through the excavation and revitalisation of words in their original dense, sensory context in the early years of the patient's life. [*ibid.*, p. 12]

—a depth movement from desultory empty speech, into embodied full speech (Lacan, 2002, p. 206).

Poetic reverie, theorized by Loewald in his calling for evocative psychoanalytic speech and listening, was implicit in Freud's invitation (for example, 1910a, p. 29) to let things freely associate or occur, while he, too, was in a state of evenly suspended attention. In *What Is Called Thinking?* (1968), Heidegger elucidates and illuminates thinking as calling, giving thanks, and taking to heart. Embodied speech is what it is all about. Heidegger also profoundly influenced Lacan and R. D. Laing. And Lacan, Laing, Heidegger, and Freud were all profoundly influenced by Nietzsche and Socratic Greek dialectical philosophy. There is a cluster of European traditions here, deeper than all of us, and in which we participate even without knowing it.

We know that the analyst is not an observing outsider but an actively invested participant. But is he inevitably "drawn into" the patient's material with implied loss of meta-analytic neutrality? Such analytic enactments, which happen under transference pressure on the analyst's role-responsiveness, were, for the Sandlers (1998, pp. 47–56), a means to investigate blind spots in counter-transference. It is still of value to hold to the specific place in the symbolic order that Freud opened up for us. It helps the work to remain grounded in a deepening experience of the bi-directional, multi-layered and multi-generational unconscious.

My first analyst was chatty and "relational", no doubt thinking that that was the way through to me, whereas I felt offended, unconsciously waiting to defend my narcissistic identifications. Yet, it loosened me sufficiently for an analysis in more classical style. During that initial meeting I said eventually, "Yes, I think I'd like to see you." She retorted, "You don't come here to see me, it's not a relationship." I received that with some sense of relief. I was living in a very congested network of relationships around Laing and our therapeutic communities, and I remember thinking "one place in the world where I can be with someone and not have to have a relationship". I also knew, with doubtful irony, that some kind of relationship would be bound to develop if the analysis took. In that context, interpersonal relationship was not important to me.

For psychoanalytic relating to take place, it has to be with a view to the unconscious, the unknown, repressed, dissociated, or foreclosed, and this usually requires the analyst's personal restraint from ordinary interpersonal relating if it is not to lapse into person-centredness. Freud took up the Socratic theme of the self as decentred. "Freud tells us," says Lacan, that "intelligence has nothing to do with the subject, the subject is not on the same axis, it is ex-centric. The subject as such . . . is something other than an organism which adapts itself. . . . [T]he subject is decentred in relation to the individual. That is what *I is an other* means" (1988, p. 9), where the centre of gravity is in the unconscious unknown rather than where the speaker says I. "I" *represents* the subjects of the unconscious. There often needs to be an odd sense of not relating at the normal surfaces and interfaces, in order to hear what is underneath, hidden, split off, elsewhere. Thus, there might be rather little inter-personal connection, while establishing relatedness in the uncon-scious felt through the body in projective, introjective, adhesive identifications, or articulated through dreams and other symbolic formations. However, with more psychotically disordered patients, the therapist might have to reach and stretch out more to make "normal" contact. Or, if the therapy involves only a weekly session, the more temptation/necessity there might be to engage in ordi-nary relating in order to "mind the gap".

It is a fine line between being an active participant and being "drawn in" and losing one's symbolic function. However, when I have had experiences of becoming drawn in and losing the place of passionate neutrality, I have felt very uncomfortable. In so far as one becomes an inner world figure in patients' transference, signi-fiers of one's own independent existence disturb them. They also prefer to avoid contact outside sessions, at least while intensively engaged. There may be chance meetings in corridors, at the school gate, in the supermarket, and sometimes patients can become excited in perverse fascination with bringing those about. But mostly the therapist's circumspection is appreciated. If one has become too muddlingly close, one has less room for interpretations made on the basis of specialized knowledge and which are thus not necessarily an abuse of power. It depends how they are "couched". Interpretations of envy can be power abusive, but they can be expe-rienced with a sense of relief. If they foster paranoid–schizoid relat-ing there is no good in them, but if they make for depressive–reparative, self and other acceptance, they are surely to the good.

Trauma and doing things to the body

Psychoanalysis attempts to create a safe setting, confidentially bound, for the telling and working of intimacies. I have chosen to discuss addictions, especially to alcohol, foodstuffs (sugars, fats, and fermentations), and nicotine, because they challenge the limits and capacity of psychoanalytic endeavour in that addictions substitute for, or take the place of, speech, and the subject of the unconscious is obscured in them; thus, one may be drawn out of analytic position. Many foods and alcohol that culturally we take for granted over-acidify the body addictively and stressfully, disturbing the PH balance and making for illness. (See Robert and Shelley Young: *Sick and Tired* [2001].) Not everyone who has a drink, eats a cake, or smokes a cigarette becomes addicted, however close to the wind they might sail. But where there are childhood patterns of neglect, abuse, or transgenerational trauma that go against innate expectations for nurture and love, resulting in what Masud Khan (1963) calls cumulative trauma, there is vulnerability to addiction. The child's innate expectations that render him or her vulnerable to deficits of love and abuses of trust make for loyalty at whatever cost, and addictive substances fill lack and repeat excess. Responding to, and agreeing with, Professor Nutt's research that ranks alcohol and tobacco as more dangerous than cannabis, LSD, and ecstasy (Randerson, 2007), I concluded a letter in the Guardian (Zeal, 2007) with the observation that all substance addictions attempt to make up for and to reconfigure primary lack—often compounding, I would add, transgenerational entanglements.

The subject of addiction has tended to be left out of psychoanalytic enquiry ever since Freud turned away from cocaine and kept smoking ("sometimes a cigar is only a cigar"). Rik Loose (2002), in an excellent Lacanian enquiry, gives reasons why addiction has been omitted. The word "addiction" has in it "diction"—announcing or saying—yet addiction will not say what it means, it is "a-diction", anti-diction, refusing to speak (*ibid.*, p. xviii). There is a fundamental antagonism between speech or diction and addiction/a-diction. The habit "speaks volumes", but its habitué, under its spell, is silent where speaking is necessary for change. McDougall (1991) tells stories of analyses with drinkers and smokers who have become ruled by extravagant excess. She says "the work of analysis is always a story recreated by two people" (p. 171), but she struggles against the limitations imposed by addiction. When people are in the grip of cumulatively traumatic patterns of excess or deficit they are driven in all kinds of ways to compensate, substitute, displace, and repeat them. Freud's (1918b) concept of *Nachträglichkeit*, afterwardsness or deferred action, gathers in it the way that early traumas that could not be assimilated at the time, get taken up and elaborated as life develops and becomes more complex. The psychoanalyst's concern is how to wrest the affects of loss, deficit, and excess from what is held locked in a-diction, unspoken and unspeakable, immutably mute. Meanings might be readily available cerebrally, at the level of thought, but to be felt dynamically in ways that render them mutable to change is another matter.

Words are containers—but where within and between whom are the words to be contained? Yvette and Will each gave me permission to write about some of the issues of addiction we encounter in their respective therapies, Will on condition that he could read the book. As I fictionalize moments of their therapies, in my mind's ear they are signatories to my text because I hear what I write through my anticipation of their reading—"It is the ear of the other that signs" (Derrida, 1988, p. 51). As I co-create their analyses with me, they in my mind co-create my writing. Every therapist is an invisible but audible presence in the patient's relational field—audible through the therapist's skeins of verbal signifiers that become part of the patient's speech. (Will phones to apologize for forgetting to show up yesterday, the last session before a break. "Went clean from my mind. Funny thing is, me and my wife were talking about you at the time I should have left. Didn't remember until 9.30 last night.") Thus, the patient signs the therapist's language, assigns it a place in their world outside the therapy. From the beginning, patients' analyses have been woven into the development of the psychoanalytic field, weft to the warp (some kind of *double-entendre*?) of theory. André Green (1997, pp. 4–5) explains that he eschews "case material" because no clinical observation has the validity to settle a theoretical debate, and because a "theoretical" paper is also clinical in that it stimulates associations in an analyst reader. Freud was savvy to the postmodern realizations as to the indivisibility of theory and practice, both being narratives in pursuit of meaning.

Neuro-scientific research into addiction has found evidence that childhood stress results in fewer dopamine receptors in the brain, and that this lack renders the subject less able to resist addictive substances. The capacity of the individual to resist is one question, but beyond it—or within it—is another: the question of the

individual's jouissance, their enjoyment in excess, beyond the pleasure principle where lurks the death drive waiting. Jouissance, the
enjoyment of rights and property, with slang sexual reference, "to
come", is a good. But when it is linked via a denial of lack to the
death drive, it is bound to destruct.

Yvette is a beautiful young woman who "wants to be able to
wear her size tens", and to enjoy looking and feeling good. Dodgy
ground? She talking to her male therapist about her shape? It is
important to her to tell me what shape she is in. When she unconsciously feels subject to her lack of a love life and her loneliness
kicks in with evocations of infancy, then the part of herself that says
"No" to compulsive eating loses will and voice. Her psychotherapy
is helping her to find strength and continuity in the part that goes
missing, so that her ordeal of excess is shorter-lived. In so far as the
question of her jouissance is untouched, she is in psychotherapy
rather than analysis.

> *February 2006.* She was with friends on Saturday evening. They were
> going to have dessert, she was not going to. They decided not to, but
> by then she was going to, but didn't—so felt deserted. She became
> impatient to get home to go late-night shopping. The pattern is that she
> refuses when with friends, but is then unsafe when alone, having to
> binge. And once it has started it just has to run its course, resulting in
> her being unable to face work or other people and crying off sick. Once
> she is in its grip, the craving becomes a ravening beast that has to be
> fed. Separated from her mother at birth and not breast-fed, Yvette
> refused substitutes, so for two days was fed by nasal tube. Her craving
> for fats and sugars may have its precipitation there, in the substances
> administered, and in the gap in primal bonding.

> *December 2006.* The part of her that wants to be "thin" falls silent when
> the greedy compulsive self grabs the world. I was interested in her
> word "thin". She resisted, but began to hear how the word seems to
> refuse life. She is trying to establish things to do over the Christ-
> mas break so she doesn't go to her parents all the time. She has a
> tendency to hurry and scurry, eating chocolate bars surreptitiously
> so she doesn't savour the one she's eating now and wants more.
> She endured a frenzy of such eating on the drive here—until, in order
> to leave a clear space in herself for the session, she threw the rest of
> it in the hedge. I commented that as she got nearer to me she felt
> safer.

January 2007. After the Christmas ordeal she achieved remission from the lure of fats and sugars, so there was room to enquire as to her real sense of self, underneath all that frantic activity. I pointed out that it is there she has voice and agency. She is determined not to go back on anti-depressants. I pointed out that sooner or later she may say "No" to those foodstuffs, to become ready for life despite unhappiness, rather than be at the mercy of manufacturers and retailers who, like drug-dealers, but with insidious GNP approval, put lures and temptations everywhere. Her father, it seems, is not able to hold her in mind, and it is not safe to approach him. Not liking the feminine as weak, dependent, and at the mercy of masculine strength, she has identified with the aggressor (Anna Freud, 1936). With a boyfriend who was laid back and easy going, "It was boring—I don't know why I said that." "It was your unconscious speaking." To stay alive in the field of desire she needs a fight but fears it. She wants to stay away from dad and close to mum. A sister has confided in Yvette and their mum, excluding their dad, that she is dating a man outside her marriage. Thus is the family's symbolic order disordered, the women caught in excluding men. She saw that, therefore, she has no internal bar to regression.

Will (*January 2006*) said he wants more from me. He thinks I collude with his avoidance. The part of him that is terrified of death is smoking him into an early grave, and there is nothing he can do about it; it is like his thoughts of driving into a wall and ending it all. I said that I feel I am up against two, he and the smoking—indeed, up against three, including the drinking. The smoking and drinking, in which parts of himself are entangled, gang up on me—they are his minders. They take good care of him, so he doesn't feel too much pain—emotional pain, that is. Those minders take their toll on the body, and he, we, are powerless to resist. He said the front of his head is heavy, and from the back of his head he is out of touch.

He began (*February*), "Smoking takes care of the pain—of stopping smoking." I heard that gap—he heard that gap. It was his response to what I had been saying. That smoking began as something to cling on to. Desperately insecure, Joney, his soft toy, no longer allowed in the dorm, and he all of aged nine, there was nothing to hang on to but bravado. From being cheery, happy (go lucky), and top in middle school, it all went wrong. He got bullied, suspended, and started smoking. Smoking was a friend, part of an image he struck that got the girls. But internally he was weepy, forlorn, hands down, " didn't mean it", etc. So smoking became a bully. Smoking as a means of achieving continuity of care could only go bad. His identification with smoking substitutes for the nurturing he craves and feels he is not getting from anywhere or anyone—I acknowledge that he is saying that to me. So there is defiance in smoking. But on this side of the gap, where conscious discourse takes place, "smoking takes care of the pain".

"I *must* stop smoking" (*October*). I was interested. But he disclosed a surreal disconnect from the words he had apparently spoken, as if *he* hadn't said them. It was said to please me—identifying with his new aggressor in so far as I want him to stop, to end my being passive witness to his pain. Does anyone care enough to bear with his doing something difficult? Do I? Am I supposed to? What is the analytic contract?

A limitation in psychoanalysis is that there are only two participants; all others are either talked about in the third person, or their impact is felt obscurely in the psychodynamics of the transference matrix and given coherence in the narratives of hermeneutic interpretation. I am discovering that it can be revealing to invite patients to set up what is called a family constellation in the room with me in order to open out the field of relationships in which they are enmeshed. (Family constellation therapy is a systemic approach developed by Hellinger [1998] out of systemic family therapy, psychoanalysis, phenomenology, and other influences. Usually practised in groups, it is adaptable to one to one therapy. I completed a foundation training with HIB [Hellinger in Britain], now called CSISS [Centre for the Study of Intimate and Social Systems].)

Will expressed himself as beleaguered and hounded by one of his older brothers, and distressed by his own affinity with Regan, a younger brother and heroin addict, so I invited him to set them up in the room as if they were there.

The older brother stood astride the room looking at Will and me with angry contempt. Regan lay down on the couch! I pointed out that Regan was blocking Will's access to it and what it symbolizes, and he immediately became very choked and emotional. In the next session he said he wanted to let go some of his responsibilities, and gestured towards the couch. I reflected his gesture—he said he hadn't forgotten.

"I love my excesses," (*November*) he said, with a defiant gleam in his eye. But it turns out he does not love smoking. I interpreted his love for his excesses as masochistic because he is bound to them and they persecute him. But I accept that he gets genuine enjoyment from alcohol. Smoking is his shadow, his fatalism attached to it. "I'll give you £10,000 if you stop me smoking," he said with a flourish as he left. I replied that he pays me a fair fee, and if *we* can stop him smoking, then he could give to a charity if he wished to. But the project depends on his participation. (It felt like a hollow appeal, because it is nothing to do with his "I" speaking, and everything to do with his availability to the subject in him.)

Psychoanalytic therapy is threatening because it makes for regression in psychic functioning from egoic secondary process distinctions to the realm of the subject, where there is turbulence as to distinctions between self and other, past and present, here and there, male and female, etc., due to the dynamic presence of pre-differentiated non-egoic primary processes. Psychotic patients who are into part-object functioning may follow your hand gestures rather than your face, obvious symbol for the illusion of whole person relating. McDougall (1991) discusses patients who seem to be in fierce opposition to analysing or discovering anything felt about their inner world, insisting on external reality as the only dimension of interest. But despair and experience of inner death lie behind their angry protestations. They resist psychic change fearing it can only be for the worse. "Immobility is felt to be the only protection against a return to an unbearable and inexpressible traumatic state" (*ibid.*, p. 93).

As Will's young brother was still lying on the couch, so to speak, it felt necessary to do more in constellation genre. So I asked where would his subliminal self place his mother? On the couch with Regan. Given Will's mergy, omnipotent relation to his mother, in which he is as much mother to her, and she too interested in how he is doing and he tempted to tell too much, I suggested he might ask her to leave. Reluctantly she did, which left Regan giggling maniacally, making it impossible for us to proceed. I wondered whether Will could ask him to leave, too. At Will's first attempts, Regan turned away on the couch and went to sleep, so he then energetically, and not disrespectfully with regard to his brother's place in his inner world, demanded that, at least for the time being, he leave.

In January he said his therapy sessions interrupt his Internet play sessions. I asked what is the first interruption he remembers in his life.

"What comes immediately to mind is school." I pointed out the metonymy, that the interruption was between *home* and school, which "school" stands in for, and that therapy has become school interrupting his play. There is a darker side: he envies his children and gives them a hard time, and then punishes his body by filling the gap in himself with excess. His body, wracked by the consequences, is itself in metonymical relation to his emotional self, his lungs and other internal organs feeling the pain of interruption that he cannot bear.

In February he came looking for his exit strategy. I was left fumbling as to how to rescue our work, and felt a cut across my midriff. I asked him how he felt at that decision.

"Disappointed," he said.

"I've no idea whether you do or don't," I replied.

"That's rude. I've thought about it a lot." He harangued me. It seemed I should not have asked him what he felt because he could "only be compliant".

Later in the month he was still looking for his exit strategy. "You talk the good talk," I said.

"I know I do. I don't want to break down." I said if he felt his real feelings it might be breakthrough—and that for the time being they need to be held in therapy. It transpired that, although smoking will destroy him in the end, it will keep him all right while his children grow up.

"So smoking is not only self-destructive, it is also self-sacrificial," I said. He found that poignant recognition difficult to bear.

"I'll take your word for it, but I can't hear it. I often don't hear what people say." Smoking is a cost he is prepared to pay to enable him to stay in his children's young lives. Without it he would erupt and explode. The sacrifice is worthwhile.

In the next session he declared, "I'm a hedonist." His internal attack on linking had destroyed any felt connection between smoking and drinking and self-sacrifice. I pointed this out, and sought to remind him that his addiction to excess enables him to stay in place as dad, husband, provider, and that it is hard for him to be interested in lack. The hedonistic headlong pursuit is to cover over lack, depression, boredom, and fear of lack and boredom. He is addicted to excess in substitution for lack. Once I had reminded him of the sacrificial motivation, and after he had acknowledged and agreed that he is depressed, he began to be interested a little in lack and possible experiences of it. He might write

RELATE
HEXHAM

03/06/2016 FRI   09:53

DEPT4   £2.00
DEPT4   £2.50
TOTAL   £4.50
CASH   £5.00
CHANGE   £0.50
CLERK 1   035700   000000

again. "Let it out that way—but no one in my family must know about it or read it." It is hard for him to share his real feelings even with his partner. Winnicott (1976) writes that, "At the centre of each person is an incommunicado element, and this is sacred and most worthy of preservation" (p. 187). Will knows he has to develop a sense of privacy and here, maybe, are the beginnings of a capacity to do so. He does not have to be so defiant about self-destructiveness, now that I have recognized for him the aspect of it that is sacrificial love.

March: "I was flying a plane, black, and had to get it to land. I was circling around, and got it safely on to the field—no runway. Then a lion—*a lioness*—grabbed me by the arm, the right arm, and was dragging me away to eat under a tree. There would be nothing left but bones. I tried waving, but there was no one there." A vivid presentation of his distress in which, lacking sufficient sense of maternal nurturing, the nurture lacked turns against him, and he fears that if he stays alive as an act of love, especially without drinking and smoking, he will be consumed by the gnawing effects of that lack.

Back after the Easter break, he said he had said to his wife, "I'm bored with going to Paul, therapy therapy and more therapy. *I* haven't had a break."

"So, you envy me mine," I replied. "Yes," he said. He spoke again about being driven by excess. I reminded him, "It's your way of coping with lack and loss."

"It's about the tummy button—don't know where *that* came from," he blushed.

"Your unconscious speaking."

"It's got me going."

"It's the place of the first cut of loss," I replied, and remembered my feeling that cut across my midriff when he had been speaking about an exit strategy. He said he wanted to learn about meditation, so I said, "How's your tummy button feeling?"

"Full of fluff. That's not fair. It's a gimmick, hypnosis, like Paul McKenna might do. Makes me angry. How's yours?"

"I located mine before asking."

"Did you? Then I apologize."

The rest of the session was devoted to mooring him in a sense of the value of lack.

In May he began with a joke I enjoyed, but he said he was afraid he was entertaining me.

I said, "Like if you don't throw me chunks of meat I'll bite your head off?"

"Yes, a bit like that."

"Like in your dream: the plane's landed, there's just you and me here and I'm about to . . ."

". . . drag me away and devour me," he added.

"So there would be just bones," I said.

"But it's a haven too," he replied. "I've been thinking about lack, but I can only get so far and no further. I come to a blank with excess. I feel my excesses are attempts to fill lack, they make me feel normal, normally connected."

Gregory Bateson (1972, p. 309) explores exactly that point: "surrender to alcoholic intoxication provides a partial and subjective short cut to a more correct state of mind".

"Last night in a kind of dream," Will continued, "I was squeezing myself into a narrower and narrower place, weird."

"Like being born," I said. We discussed memory, the difference between seeing himself in a playground aged four as in a photo, and seeing through his eyes aged four. The latter he could glimpse.

"Is that my lack," he asked, "lacking connection with the child I was?"

Orientations

Lacan, like Loewald, retains Freudian traditional terminology and reinvents it, in his case with an ear for linguistic and structuralist developments. "One can trace over the years a growing aversion regarding the functions of speech and the field of language" (Lacan, 2006, p. 201). He writes of

the temptation that presents itself to the analyst to abandon the foundation of speech, and this precisely in areas where its use, verging on the ineffable, would seem to require examination more than ever: namely the child's education by its mother, Samaritan-type aid, and dialectical mastery. [ibid., p. 202]

He opposes American psychoanalytic developments in ego psychology that inflect toward the adaptation of the individual to the social environment, and distinguishes ego from subject (*ibid.*, p. 204).

> The ego is something that the subject can present itself with to others, but the subject and the ego cannot be collapsed into each other. The status of the subject is one of being represented. [Loose, 2002, p. 108]

The ego facilitates the subject's arrival in analysis, but it "is a 'false connection' with the internal and external world of the subject" (*ibid.*), so it gets in the way of the subject (in and of the unconscious unknown) being heard.

In our terminological Tower of Babel, this seems to link and not link to Mitchell's (2003) concept of intersubjectivity. Mitchell presents four modes of relating: nonreflective behaviour, affective permeability, self–other configurations, and intersubjectivity (pp. 59–66). He says the first three modes might all be considered in terms of Kohut's concept of self-objects, because in these three modes "others are not organized and experienced as independent subjects in their own right . . . . Only in Mode 4 [intersubjectivity] are others organized as distinct subjects" (Mitchell, 2003, p. 63). Bacal and Newman (1990, p. 229) offer this definition of self-objects, "An object is a selfobject when it is experienced intrapsychically as providing functions in a relationship that evoke, maintain, or positively affect the sense of self"—i.e. when the self does not yet recognize the object as fully independent of its own perception of it.

However, whereas person is a simple term meaning mask, and that through which sound appears, i.e., is the presenting self, subject is not so easy. It may not be distinct as in an identity. The word "subject" has an etymological derivation from the past participle of *iacere* (Latin), to *throw*, plus *sub*, under—thus it means something or someone thrown under. In other words, analytically, a subject is not simply a person or self, but a dynamic concern in the unconscious unknown thrown under consciousness.

Mitchell comments that in the broad sea change now understood and envisioned, "the analytic relationship, the personal relationship between the two participants, is now granted a fundamental, transformative role" (*ibid.*, p. 64). This "pervasive paradigm shift" has come from several major traditions: (i) British middle group object relations (and, I would add, contemporary Freudians); (ii) American self psychologists who have replaced paternal and patriarchal classical psychoanalytic metaphors with the analyst's role as maternal presence; and (iii) interpersonal psychoanalysis from which has emerged an iconography of psychoanalysis as a much more personal, truly intersubjective, "authentic" encounter. Relational psychoanalysis is a blending of the diverse currents of these traditions. Mitchell argues,

> From the object relations traditions there came a textured develop-
> mental perspective and rationale for a constructive restraint, but
> the lack of a place for the more active forms of the analyst's
> personal engagement. [*ibid.*, p. 65]

From the interpersonal tradition of Harry Stack Sullivan, who regarded neurotic beliefs and behaviours as nonsensical "security operations", and Erich Fromm, who felt that people deceive them-selves as to how they really feel and so emphasized frankness and honesty, came a directness that made room for active analytic engagement.

In London, during the same decades, from the 1950s onwards, there was a very similar creative dynamic of rivalrous resemblance between object relations theory and existential analysis. Laing, himself a middle group analyst, was very influenced by Sullivan, and by Sartre, with his concept of bad faith. But Laing became wild and turbulent, fuelled by alcohol, and it was difficult for those around him to theorize "wild" initiatives in analytic intersubjective relating in a coherent manner. In the current climate of regulation and elitism people are cautious in saying what they really do. In practice, they might take short-cuts with technique, but would not put such initiatives into their publications. Thus, a layer of super-egoic pretence as to what really goes on is built up, with tyrannical effect. While it is necessary in a psychoanalytic training to learn the ropes of basic transference and countertransference awareness and interpretation, and to develop an acuity of perception as to the differences between what the patient generates in us and our own stuff, and throughout a career to be alert to the same dynamics, analysts develop individuated styles of subjective intervention and participation as they become seasoned in good practice. Relational psychoanalysis gives the opportunity to lift the veil of secrecy around practices divergent from presumptive norms. It is not so much what one does as whether one can justify it that counts. But it does not follow that there is yet clarity around the concept of "the subject". Interestingly, Mitchell (2003) has several indexed references to intersubjectivity, but none to subject.

He describes his work with Connie (*ibid.*, pp. 96–101). A productive patient from the start, but incredulous that she might have feelings about Mitchell, she suddenly one day became distressed that his greetings were impersonal, not even using her name. He said it was his customary practice simply to say "Hello" to patients and invite them in. But he agreed to begin to use her name if he could find a way that was genuine for him. He did so, and this has influenced him to engage similarly with others sometimes. I was recently challenged in the same way, but I said I did not use the patient's name because I did not assume I knew who was arriving. He might not feel he was himself that day and I did not want to collude, or maybe some other internalized relationship was presenting itself that day, and anyway, there was a whole time of life from conception to naming when he was unnamed. He understood that my practice was something I had thought about, could justify, and that it involved recognition of the complexity of our relationship, and he felt cared for. I suppose I want for myself a certain restraint in order to find my jouissance in the gap between interpersonal and intersubjective. Sometimes, it seems to me, interpersonal relating can get in the way of the subject being heard.

There are massive and pervasive social pressures and problems to do with the lurch into addictive behaviours. There is a rampant cultural, consumerist, superego demanding tyrannically, "You will enjoy". Why? An accountant who had suffered breakdown and lost his career, as he began to regather a sense of self, said mournfully, "I'm not even a good consumer." It seems we all have our part to play in the shadow side of Adam Smith's *Wealth of Nations*: consume or die. After "9/11", President Bush said to the American people that Americans "must not be afraid—to go shopping". "Shop till you drop" puts shopping and shoppers in the service of the death drive, an excess of negative jouissance over life, calm, and peace. Psychotherapy has a part to play in helping to elucidate underlying causes and vulnerabilities, thereby increasing both participants' capacity to tolerate pain and distress. And maybe we can do more, outside the consulting room, to oppose market forces and their addiction to the death drive, in favour of acceptance of lack and consequent freedom.

There is a tendency for analysts to seem to feel superior to their patients' parents, colluding with their complaints about them, and then wanting to supply what patients lack. Hellinger (2007) suggests that therapists are at the bottom of the patient's system—this, I find, is a good, safe place to be. Psychoanalysis, with its ready immersion in the psychodynamics of the transference matrix at whatever cost, can look like a last throw of romantic agony (Mario Praz, 1962). But, if it is remembered that Freud's original discovery of the transference was as a symptom of resistance to be interpreted so that analysis could continue (1912b, p. 104), and if that original discovery is employed as a paradoxical injunction against the romantic agony of full immersion, then the stance of psychoanalyst and phenomenologically-guided systemic constellator are similar, though their behaviours are different. Both discover their truth in close subjective observation of the relational field in which they exist. Both receive transferences, but distribute them differently, the psychoanalyst taking them into his own person, and the constellator allowing them to appear in the multi-generational relational field. Both are empathically involved, and both stay close to what Lacan calls the subject—a word that does not predicate a self but refers to matters of the unconscious. And for both, the presenting self of the practitioner is a means not an end.

Interpersonal relationship, transference–countertransference matrix, and intersubjective relationship intricately over- and underlap each other in the work, closely woven. Each involves three presences—self, other, and the relationship or matrix as itself a speaking presence. The interpersonal is the most superficial, for it is the domain of competing egos or presenting selves, the most person-centred and the least decentred. The transference matrix is the least personal, as by definition it excludes everything that is interpersonal. The intersubjective is the most inclusive, because the decentred self or subject manifests in both transference matrix and interpersonal field. It is also the most unnerving for the analyst, because his or her subject(s) (matters of the unconscious unknown), may be too present being present too, triggered by patients' material.

Mitchell (2003, p. 90) explains Loewald's notion that we organize our experience on different levels simultaneously. All levels of mind, from primitive drives held in "primal density" to whatever levels of developmental relationality have been achieved, are simultaneously and synchronously present. Loewald depicts a "primary process" organized around a primal density of experience in which dichotomies like self–other, past–present, inner–outer, male–female do not exist, and a "secondary process" in which the customary categories of conventional, adaptive living apply. I would say the subject for analysis is made of their interplay. Loewald (1988, cited in Mitchell) stresses his difference from Winnicott's concerns: early subjective experiences are not necessarily suffused with omnipotence and illusion, but, especially those of non-differentiation, constitute alternative and equally valid forms of organization. As Mitchell says, the task of psychoanalysis is to open up "the severed, potentially enriching links *between* fantasy and actuality" (2003, p. 90). Thus, therapeutic regression undoes the presenting self's self-gatherings. As to which depths of mind become analytically present depends on present evocations in the embodiments of speaking and listening. In a world where surfeit and excess dominate lack, which nevertheless waits to devour us, it could be felt to be a matter of urgency to listen otherwise than normally in order to evoke otherwise than normal speech as a basis for action.

References

Bacal, H., & Newman, K. (1990). *Theories of Object Relations: Bridges to Self Psychology*. New York: Columbia University Press.

Bateson, G. (1972). The cybernetics of "self". In: *Steps to an Ecology of Mind* (pp. 309–327). San Francisco, CA: Chandler.

Derrida, J. (1988). *The Ear of the Other: Otobiography, Transference, Translation*. Lincoln, NB: University of Nebraska Press.

Freud, A. (1936). *The Ego and the Mechanisms of Defence*. London: Hogarth, 1966.

Freud, S. (1910a). *Five Lectures on Psychoanalysis. Third Lecture. S.E., 11*: 29–39. London: Hogarth.

Freud, S. (1912b). The dynamics of transference. *S.E.*, 7: 97–108. London: Hogarth.

Green, A. (1997). *On Private Madness*. London: Karnac.

Heidegger, M. (1968). *What Is Called Thinking?* New York: Harper & Row.

Hellinger, B. (1998). *Love's Hidden Symmetry*. Phoenix, AZ: Zeig, Tucker.

Hellinger, B. (2007). Seminar in Oslo, April.

Holmes, J. (2004). *The Search for the Secure Base*. Hove: Brunner-Routledge.

Khan, M. (1963). The concept of cumulative trauma. In: *The Privacy of the Self*. London: Hogarth, 1981.

Lacan, J. (1977). *Écrits*. A. Sheridan (Trans.). London: Tavistock.

Lacan, J. (1988). *The Seminar of Jaques Lacan: Book Two—The Ego in Freud's Theory and in the Technique of Psychoanalysis*. Cambridge: Cambridge University Press.

Lacan, J. (2006). *Écrits*. B. Fink (Trans.). New York: Norton.

Loewald, H. (1988). *Sublimation*. New Haven, CT: Yale University Press.

Loose, R. (2002). *The Subject of Addiction*. London: Karnac.

McDougall, J. (1991). *Theatres of the Body*. London: Free Association.

Mitchell, S. (2003). *Relationality: From Attachment to Intersubjectivity*. Hillsdale, NJ: The Analytic Press.

Praz, M. (1962). *The Romantic Agony*. New York: Collins Fontana Books.

Randerson, J. (2007). Alcohol worse than ecstasy: the shock new drugs list. *Guardian* 23 March, p. 1.

Sandler, J., & Sandler, A.-M. (1998). *Internal Objects Revisited*. London: Karnac.

Winnicott, D. W. (1976). *The Maturational Processes and the Facilitating Environment*. London: Hogarth.

Young, R., & Young, S. (2001). *Sick and Tired? Reclaim Your Inner Terrain*. Pleasant Grove, UT: Woodland.

Zeal, P. (2007). letters@guardian.co.uk, 26 March, p. 35.

CHAPTER FOUR

Relational thinking and welfare practice

Paul Hoggett

Introduction

In a recent article Anna Yeatman (2007) has compared what she calls liberal and post-liberal forms of individualism in terms of their conceptions of the human subject and the implications of these conceptions for welfare practice. In this chapter, I draw upon current developments linked to the relational turn in psychoanalysis to try and put some more flesh upon what Yeatman calls a "post-liberal" or "post patrimonial model" of professional practice.

Classical liberalism

Traditional liberal models of the human subject emphasize rationality and autonomy. Rationality is construed in patriarachal terms, something to be counterposed to emotion, passion, and the language of the body. Autonomy refers to the individual sovereign subject, a self-interested subject capable of co-operation with other self-interested subjects, a unitary self, not one torn by internal conflicts or constituted by its relation to others.

The liberal welfare subject is construed in terms of a deficit or pathology model, constituted in a child-like way as someone lacking the capacity to make reasonable judgements about themselves and the others they have responsibility for. Professional practice arises in conditions of advancing modernity that privilege credentialed expertise. The professional is seen unproblematically as the "one who knows", but this knowing is situated in the context of an ethical relationship to the other, the one who is known. Professional ethics stress the duty of care to the other. The discretion of the professional expert is therefore bounded by a set of ethical responsibilities. Yeatman (2007) sees this as part of a wider "ethics of patrimonialism" in which "the liberal individual is ethically obligated to protect and provide for those who come under his private jurisdiction whether this is domestic or professional in nature". The ethical stance of classical professionalism should not be lightly dismissed. Many of the current struggles of teachers, nurses, social workers, and others against the managerialist thrust of successive neo-liberal governments alert us to the continued value of practices that give room for forms of care and discretion, albeit care and discretion cast in a paternalistic fashion.

Social democracy

Some aspects of classical liberalism were challenged by post-war social democratic and socialist thinkers. In the UK, the work of Richard Titmuss offered a crucial challenge to individualistic notions of the autonomous citizen. For Titmuss, the post-war citizen was bound to fellow citizens through relations of shared vulnerability. His concept of the "gift relationship" (Titmuss, 1971), following the work of the anthropologist Marcel Mauss, stressed the centrality of relations of reciprocity and mutuality. This was a solidaristic vision of welfarism, one that gave emphasis to what Titmuss called the "texture of social relationships" (Titmuss, 1974).

But the social democratic vision was also limited in two crucial ways. First, as Fiona Williams (1989) noted, it embodied in an unquestioned way a solidarity of (at that time) largely male breadwinners. This was a patriarchal solidarity, and the community that it valued was an exclusionary community, one indifferent, even hostile, to differences of gender, sexuality, and culture. Second, like the professionalism that it criticized, it was unreflexively modernist. It privileged expert knowledge and the technocratic institutions of government. The state was everything. Critics of Titmuss, such as David Reisman, noted,

> Titmuss's model is remarkable for its lack of active community involvement . . . and notable for its autocratic etatisme: the user is not consulted about his needs but is informed of them by politicians and bureaucrats acting, of course, on the basis of sound professional advice. [Reisman, 1977, p. 37]

New social movements and the critique of professionalism

In the 1960s and 1970s, socialist, feminist, and other social movements subjected classical models of professionalism and social democracy to sustained critique for the way in which they reproduced a disempowered subject of welfare. The state was viewed as an essentially contradictory formation, embodying solidarity and universal rights but in a way that simultaneously excluded whole classes of citizens. Fiona Williams (1989) described this as a "false universalism" because of the way it was still predicated upon rational liberal notions of a (male) subject.

The new movements pioneered critical models of community development, internal critiques of professionalism (anti-psychiatry, case-con, etc.), and the self-organization of service users. Above all, the new movements were alert to the play of power and the reproduction of power relations in both the private and public spheres. The radical edge of the new movements sought to develop alternatives to state models of welfare. Alternative models of service provision sprang up in the community and voluntary sector; the concept of "user control" gained increasing currency. The existing state apparatus and the professions nested within it constituted a formidable problem. Some sought to critique professional practice by adopting anti-racist and anti-sexist models. Others sought a radical decentralization and democratization of the state apparatus itself.

However, outside feminism, the general thrust of these new movements was at first a structuralist critique of the state and its practices. There tended to be less interest in agency; indeed, for some, a focus on the individual subject was seen as a form of bourgeoise individualism, something therefore deeply suspect.

More gradually but, in the long term, more powerfully, a thorough-going challenge to the prevailing liberal model of the human subject was developed through the notion of a feminist ethic of care. This emerging discourse questioned concepts of rationality that devalued the affective and embodied nature of humanity. It challenged the valuation of individual autonomy and the privileging of independence over interdependence. It argued that vulnerability and dependence were an aspect of the human condition, not simply something that occurred to unfortunates. For Sevenhuijsen (1997, p. 147) this meant that the ethics of care was also a solidaristic ethics in which the carer and the cared for were united by their shared existential fate. It also challenged abstract and impartialist ethics, arguing that universal principles could only ever provide a partial guide to the dilemmas of moral life. Such dilemmas were always bound up in particular relationships, involving unique subjects in ambiguous situations where there was no obvious right thing to do. As Sevenhuijsen put it, the ethics of care posits the image of a "relational self", "a moral agent who is embedded in concrete relationships with other people" (ibid., p. 55).

As Yeatman (2007) notes, the cumulative impact of these new movements and their critiques was to recast human subjects in a new way, no longer objects of benign intervention but as participatory, experiencing agents. As she puts it

> Each human being is to count in the relationships in which he or she finds him or herself, because each human being is to be accorded the status of an individual understood as a distinct and unique centre of subjective experience. [p. 46]

Continuing difficulties

I suggest that existing critiques of welfare practice nevertheless still contain weaknesses and limitations. There are two that I wish to focus upon.

The new movements and discourses have not been able to transcend an idealized model of the welfare subject. Their critique of the pathology and deficit models of the welfare subject manifested by classical professionalism has led to a phobic avoidance of criticism of the welfare subject. This, combined with their quite legitimate stress upon the continued role of power relations, oppressive practices, poverty, and exclusion has led to the development of a simplistic "person good/environment bad" way of thinking. This acts as a kind of antithesis, or mirror image, to the pathologizing aspects of Labour's social policy, but it fails to transcend it. As a consequence, radical social policy has only been able to conceive of human agency in terms of its positive and optimistic dimensions. The agency a man uses when silencing his partner through his violent talk or acts, the agency a parent uses when trampling all over the vulnerability of their child, the agency a teenage boy uses when intimidating a peer who is suspected of softness, all these and many other forms of agency that are destructive towards others and ultimately towards self cannot find a comfortable place in radical social policy. Indeed, even the concept of care suffers from this inability to face the negative. When Sevenhuijsen speaks about vulnerability, her analysis is normative. Absent from the vocabulary and experience of the one dependent on another's care is ungratefulness or envy, and absent from the one who cares is irritability or hatred towards the dependent other. As a consequence, care ends up constructed once more in a gendered way, as if it were simply about love and compassion and not also about firmness, the capacity to challenge or criticize, cruelty (as in, sometimes you have to be cruel to be kind), and other constructive uses of aggression.

Second, and linked to the above, radical social policy shares with radical social theory a shallow notion of human experience and identity. It is grasped, but what is grasped often has little depth. Here, I take as my starting point Stuart Hall's (1996) reflections on what he calls the "impasse in identity theory". Recent theorizations of identity in the human sciences have borrowed extensively from post-structuralism and the legacy of Lacan and Foucault. But, as Hall notes, while this approach has been strong on the conceptualization of power, of how power relations enter into the interstices of the subject, they have been weaker in providing a place from which to understand human resistance, creativity, and transformation.

Contemporary identity theory still lacks a proper understanding of the subject as someone who is not just the bearer of discourse, as someone who is not just positioned by race, class, and gender. What is missing is a concept of a loving and hating subject with an internal world that comprises real and imagined relations. In other words, there is no proper sense of internalization, of the inner world of the welfare subject.

This is exemplified by current social theory in the USA, which uses Freud's "Mourning and melancholia" (1917e) in order to grasp the way in which the subject is constituted by loss. Judith Butler (1997), for example, uses Freud to develop a model of gender identity in terms of a melancholic subject, forever doomed to repeat unresolved oedipal identifications. And, while this is an important step towards integrating the social and the psychoanalytic, what slips through her fingers is an understanding of mourning: that is, a non-melancholic resolution to loss in which what has to be given up can nevertheless be worked through. In other words, Butler and others are unable to grasp the difference between identification and internalization. To illustrate my point, let me cite Hans Loewald, the influential American analyst, at some length.

> Identification as such leads to an identity of subject and object or of parts or aspects of them. Insofar as, in identification, they become identical, one and the same, there is a merging or confusion of subject and object. *Identification tends to erase difference:* subject becomes object and object becomes subject. While identification is a way-station to internalization, in internalization, if carried to completion, a redifferentiation has taken place by which both subject and object have become reconstituted, each on a new level of organization. When we speak of the internalization of object relations, such as in the resolution of the Oedipus complex and in the work of mourning, it is not, if the processes are brought to completion, a matter of maintaining identification with the objects that are to be relinquished; the latter is the case in melancholia where the object and the identifications with the object cannot be given up ... Internalization as a completed process implies emancipation from the object. [Loewald, 1973, p. 15, my emphasis]

If an environment exists in which the suffering deriving from losses and injuries can be safely felt and thought about, then they can be worked through and digested. It is the digestion of experience that corresponds to internalization, and it is through internalization that an internal world with internal resources is built. Depth is strength, shallowness is weakness. It is as if contemporary social theory and social policy has not yet managed to fully glimpse welfare subjects with strength, resourcefulness, and character.

It is at this point that I want to turn to the emergence of a more relational model of psychoanalysis. The question I want to ask is this: to what extent does this development correspond to the emergence of a post-liberal model of professional (in this case psychoanalytic) practice?

The relational turn in psychoanalysis

Fairbairn, Klein, and Winnicott had a profound impact upon the theory and practice of psychoanalysis, shifting its ground from Freud's energy/instinct model towards a conception of the psyche as something fundamentally relational. Winnicott exemplifies this shift with his well-known dictum that there is no such thing as the infant: rather, what we always have is an infant–mother relation. But, in a puzzling way, this relationality was always viewed one-sidedly. Either the presence of the mother (and, by implication, of the environment) was considered primarily in terms of its absence (a good enough mother was one, first and foremost, who was reliably present in both a physical and emotional way) or, for the Kleinians, the environment was considered in terms of its power either to confirm or disconfirm the infant's phantasies. What is missing is any grasp of the environment as something that intrudes or acts upon the infant.

Freud also struggled to grasp a fuller sense of the environment's impact. As is well known, his original theory of hysteria assumed that some kind of actual seduction had occurred to his patients during their childhood. Later, Freud was to abandon his theory of an actual event that intruded upon a life. For the later Freud, the seduction is imagined, a product of sexually-charged phantasy. It becomes a matter of either/or—an interpsychic theory is replaced by an intrapsychic theory. But Freud never fully gives up his curiosity about an intrusive or invasive environment; it returns in his theory of trauma (written up in *Beyond the Pleasure Principle* (1920g) soon after the trauma of the First World War).

The point is that if the interpsychical dimension is absent, then power relations are also absent. Psychoanalysis has tended to conceive of the social environment primarily in terms the idea of failure (absence of good enough nurturance), it has not been able to grasp the impact of the social in its active form—as force, violence, invasiveness, intrusiveness. At times, one can see how later writers, influenced by Klein and Winnicott, have continued to wrestle with this. Masud Khan (1974), for example, conceptualizes cumulative trauma not in terms of "gross intrusions" but in terms of "maladaption to the infant's anaclitic needs" (Khan, 1974, p. 47). But later, in the same paper, he speaks of the intrusive mother (*ibid.*, p. 51) and of the need of the child for protection from internal *and* external stimuli (*ibid.*, p. 52).

The criticism of Klein and others is therefore not so much that they have focused obsessively upon hatred and the negative emotions, but that they have not focused enough or, rather, they have only focused one-sidedly. They have not followed through. If we really are so much in thrall to violent and sadistic impulses, then it follows that we must emerge from the shadow of these impulses as they fall upon us in the family home and public life. If we really do regularly resort to violent forms of projective identification, then it follows that each one of us was subject to the projective identifications of our parents as we grew up. In other words, the Kleinians have failed to consider violence interpsychically by construing it largely in intrapsychic terms. As Gianna Williams (1997, p. 928) put it,

> we tend to understand persecutory anxiety as the consequence of a fear of retaliation from sadistically attacked objects, also as a consequence of excessive projective identification, but the extreme and pervasive dread of being invaded and intruded upon . . . may also be related to early persecutory experiences of being at the receiving end of projections perceived as inimical.

Returning to the condition of melancholia, if we can grasp this intrapsychically *and* interpsychically, then we can see how depression can be a result of both one's own ambivalent love *and* the hatred that the other felt for you. And internalizations are not just the precipitate of abandoned object cathexes, that is, the history of loss, but also the result of forced introjections arising from the experience of being an object to other's projective identifications; as Christopher Bollas put it, "people bare memories of being the mother's and father's object . . ." (Bollas, 1987, p. 41).

From this perspective, the object relations which constitute our character are partly the product of unconscious imaginings, the outcome of our internal psycho-logic (denial, reaction formation, splitting, etc.), and partly the outcome of the internalization of real self–other relations in which, at times, the subject takes the position of object and at times the position of agent (for example, at times the persecuted and at times the persecutor). A fully relational psychoanalysis is therefore one that can grasp the continued interplay between the real and the imagined, "the actual mother and the mother constituted out of unconscious phantasy . . . the historical and the fantastical, the actual and the imaginary, are engaged in an endless and inevitable dialectic" (*ibid.*, p. 6).

Projective identification, then, becomes the process of re-evoking these real/imagined past relations in the present, either directly or inversely (the abused child becomes the abusing parent). According to Maria Ponsi, such an internal relation is "a readily recognisable and self-perpetuating relational configuration—that is, an object relationship" (1997, p. 256). Bollas (1987, pp. 59–60) construes this in terms of the "ego grammar" of the person's "character". From this perspective identity is therefore built up from these internal(ized) relations. At any moment we can therefore ask of the subject, "Who is speaking? What part of the self is speaking and what part of the self is being addressed?" (Bollas, 1987, pp. 1–2, 44).

This is where the master–slave dynamic comes in. For Hegel, according to Benjamin, this is the foundation of human relations, which are also always power relations. Benjamin (1998, 2004) uses Hegel's dialectic of the master–slave relation to describe a process of breakdown and repair in human relations (including group relations, as in South Africa—see her 1998 book *The Shadow of the Object*). Where relations break down, self and other (us and them) engage in an agonistic struggle where each enacts violence on the other yet each believes themselves to be victim (this sounds very similar to a paranoid–schizoid mode of relating). The interesting point is (and this is where Benjamin's relational perspective comes in very strongly—she sees that this happens just as easily in the analytic encounter) that the analyst, psychotherapist, or group consultant does not stand aloof; they enact the violence as much as the patient or group member (and Benjamin appears to argue here and elsewhere that one of the main ways they do this is by assuming the position of "the one who knows"). Again following Hegel, Benjamin counterposes breakdown to what seems to be the desired state of "mutual recognition", in which each self is able to recognize the existence of different minds who are real subjects rather than extensions of self. This requires the reclaiming of what self has disowned and projected into other (and this sounds very similar to the depressive position). As Benjamin puts it, "to recognize that the object of our feelings, needs, actions and thoughts is actually another subject, an equivalent centre of being, is the real difficulty" (Benjamin, 2004, p. 6).

The implications for analytical practice are considerable. First, there is a recognition that the analyst's expertise, if handled unreflexively, leads to either compliance by the patient (and the interpretation works through the power of suggestion) or to breakdown and struggle. Second, there is a validation of the knowing of the patient and the corresponding need for a dialogic engagement with this knowing, thinking, and inquiring part of the subject. Third, it follows that to facilitate such dialogue, the analyst must be prepared to be more transparent. To quote Winnicott,

> Interpretation outside the ripeness of the material is indoctrination and produces compliance. A corollary is that resistance arises out of interpretation given outside the overlap of the patient's and analysts' playing together. [Winnicott, 1971, p. 51]

For Bollas, Winnicott's thoughts were meant to be played with, not regarded as "official versions of the truth". Bollas adds, "I try to put my thoughts to the patient in such a way that he does not feel himself to be cornered" (Bollas, 1987, p. 206) and "I believe that it can be valuable for the clinician to report selected subjective states to his patient for mutual observation and analysis" (*ibid.*, p. 228), but he adds, so long as the analyst does so in the overall interest of the analysis and s/he tunes into and offers further thoughts about the patient's response to such "disclosure". This is *not* about transgressing professional boundaries, it *is* about being prepared to share the grounds of one's own thinking with the person (or group) you are thinking about.

Dialogue

I am groping towards something. Let us call it dialogue. Bion refers to it in terms of container–contained, that first labour of love through which a mutually enriching interchange between two human beings occurs. He has in mind an asymmetrical relationship, in which one has a capacity to think what the other can only feel. But thinking about this in terms of symmetrical relations, relations between equals such as friends, colleagues, or lovers, we would need to think about a mutually containing relationship, one in which each has the capacity to think beyond the other (interdependency).

Habermas's concept of "communicative action" is another way of conceptualizing this, but only if we include a psychoanalytical appreciation of the subjects concerned. To Habermas, the feminists added difference "without engagement, confrontation, dialogue and even a 'struggle for recognition' in the Hegelian sense, we tend to constitute the otherness of the other by projection and fantasy or ignore it in indifference (Benhabib, 1992, p. 168); assumptions and prejudices need to be defused, "confronted, discussed, worked out and worked through in an open dialogue with concrete others" (*ibid.*, p. 167).

Bion and Winnicott add further dimensions. For Bion, within each subject there is a propensity not-to-think, indeed, to hate thinking, to hate relationship, to hate connection, to attack linking, to hate creativity, to hate intercourse. In his paper "Attacks on linking" (Bion, 1959) one can clearly discern the embryo of the concept of destructive narcissism and the "gang in the mind". For Winnicott, dialogue is not primarily about doing or being done to, it is about being and being with. This is the free association of collective improvization. Playing occurs in the intermediate area between being (the life of the dream) and doing (external reality). Winnicott says (1971, p. 51), "in playing, the child manipulates external phenomena in the service of the dream". The paradox is this. One must be able to do in order to be, the musician must be able to "do" his instrument, the surfer to "do" his board. There must be some element of competence or mastery. But to do one must first have the capacity to be, and to be one must have acquired some capacity to do. To communicate one must be able to "do words". We can speak in order to "do" to the other (struggle, strategic action) or in order to be with the other (dialogue, mutual enrichment, touch/contact). In dialogue, we are subjects seeking understanding and to be understood rather than objects seeking to act upon or to be acted upon.

Following Benjamin (2004, p. 14), the question is, shall we eat together or eat each other?

Dialogic welfare practice

I am suggesting that the relational turn in psychoanalysis is leading psychoanalysis towards a more dialogical model of professional practice. A dialogical model that nevertheless is not based upon some naïve view of what James Gufstafson (1979) once termed "pseudomutuality" (one which assumes that for relationships to be equal they must be symmetrical) but one in which the asymmetry of the relationship is recognized, as is the sense of authority that the professional derives from their craft. I think of it as a model of democratic authority in which the expert acknowledges and validates the knowing of the client/user/patient (as well as the limits of this knowing) and uses their own authority (and the limits of their knowing) in a reflexive and transparent way.

In a recent debate, Jessica Benjamin and Ron Britton (a leading contemporary Kleinian) have offered their different views about where "insight" comes from. Benjamin (2004) emphasizes the insightfulness of the dialogical couple, Britton (2004) emphasizes the importance of the analyst's independent thinking. My sense is that Benjamin is reluctant to acknowledge that at times the analyst does have to be tough, confronting, and able to preserve her/his own way of thinking in the face of resistance or attack from the one s/he seeks to help. What remains a constant, however, and has always been a characteristic of the psychoanalytic stance, is that the patient's subjective experience, including that part of her/his experience that cannot be put into words but is embodied, projected, or enacted, remains at the heart of the work.

So, where does all this take us with regard to our starting point, the classical liberal model of professionalism and the critiques of it? The classical model hinges upon an ethics of service that casts the recipient of this service as an "unfortunate" who is deficient in autonomy and subject to the responsible but sovereign discretion of the "one who knows" (the professional). The radical (what Yeatman calls "post-liberal") critiques of the classical model expose the power relations embedded in the paternalistic ethics of service, problematize the unreflexive nature of professional power, and restore value to dependence and interdependence. However, their stress upon the destructive nature of societal relations leads them to underemphasize the agency of welfare subjects, and their critique of deficit/pathology models of the "welfare unfortunate" leads them to an idealized construction of this subject as noble victim. Furthermore, their critique of professionalism leads to an undertheorization of an alternative vision of professional practice.

Building on work that has led to the development of the feminist ethic of care, how could the relational turn in psychoanalysis lead us beyond the present impasse? First, I suggest that it provides us with a model of democratic authority that relegitimates expertise understood as a form of reflexive and transparent practice. In the public realm of welfare practice, as opposed to the more private domain of psychoanalysis, this transparency also implies accountability, and accountability not just to one's own profession (and its self-regulatory frameworks) but more directly to the users and potential users of the service being provided. Both user and professional are recognized as knowing and inquiring subjects *and* as defended subjects; each is knowing but also unknowing, and it is the unknowing that forms the basis of a fundamental interdependency between professional and client/user from which a dialectic of recognition can emerge (Froggett, 2002). There is no such thing as "the client"; rather, following Winnicott, there is only ever the client–professional relationship. Effective professional practice hinges upon the quality of this encounter.

This brings us on to dialogue. According to Yeatman, the professional has to rethink how she practises her expertise so that it is done "in a dialogical relationship of respect for and listening to the subjective experience of the client". There is considerable congruency between the demands of the new social movements and the practice of psychoanalysis here; recognition of the individual as a unique centre of subjective experience is a central value to both. People with learning difficulties and mental health problems, the old and frail, children, and many other groups are still not given this respect. As Brenda Lovegrove states, in her reflections on working as a psychotherapist with a Down's syndrome teenage girl,

> psychoanalytic psychotherapy is an unusual choice for parents of a child with Down syndrome because these children and adults, due to their cognitive limitation, are treated behaviourally without much attention to their inner experience. [Lovegrove, 2005]

Lovegrove's reflections connect to a bigger and more fundamental issue. In conditions of late modernity, new disciplinary technologies, many drawing upon contemporary psychology with its anti-hermeneutic and positivist stance, are encroaching into many areas of welfare practice (mental health, probation, and so on). These technologies recast the subject of welfare as an object of intervention rather than a centre of experience, as someone who needs reskilling and reprogramming rather than as someone who needs to be given time, respect, voice, and understanding. A friend of mine, who has been HIV positive for many years, recounts how her local branch of the Terence Higgins Trust has now abandoned user involvement, buddying, a drop-in service, and so on, and replaced them with an apparently more "professional" model of screening and assessment which then places new users on a treatment programme consisting of an eight-week bloc on self-management followed by a six-week bloc on another programme, and so on. As she put it to me, what is completely missed is any space in which the grief of the user can be worked through and, because experience is no longer attended to, many of those being placed on programmes are completely unable to grasp the opportunities for "agency" that are apparently on offer. Agency cannot be "willed" upon the welfare subject, but rationalist models of the individual, now resurgent in the exponentially expanding profession of psychology, offer "quick fix" concepts of change such as CBT (cognitive–behavioural therapy) that ease themselves smoothly into the empty performativity of the "New Labour" vision.

Social suffering: the object of welfare practice

The democratic model of professional authority and dialogic model of professional practice I have outlined constitute the cart that follows the horse, the means to address the ends. But the ends should take precedence, so what are the ends, what is the object of welfare practice? As we have seen, both the new social movements and psychoanalysis offer a fundamental critique of the human subject of classical liberalism. At the centre of their critique is an alternative vision of the subject as a unique centre of experience. Both are concerned with forms of human suffering, either as a consequence of the exigencies of human relationships or of oppression and disempowerment.

I suggest we make a distinction between two forms of suffering: the first I will call "existential suffering" and the second, following Bourdieu (1999), I will call "social suffering". There is no hard and fast boundary between the two; they are overlapping areas of human experience. Existential suffering arises primarily because of loss and our frailty before loss; the losses bound up with ageing, illness, injury, accident, the vagaries of love, the alterity and unknowability of the other, and so on. Of course, our experience of such things is culturally bound, and, of course, it is also mediated by class, poverty, race, and other factors. And this is the area of overlap with "social suffering", that is, suffering that is a direct consequence of the way in which a society is organized. As Richard Titmuss (1976) once put it, poverty and disadvantage is the price some people pay for other people's progress.

What I like about Bourdieu's concept, however, is the way in which it draws our attention to what is felt and experienced by the poor, the marginalized, and the discriminated against. One is reminded here of Sennett & Cobb's (1993) "hidden injuries" of class, to which we might add the hidden injuries of race, and so on. In other words we are drawn to the psychical consequences of power relations, the way in which poverty and discrimination affects the soul. It is interesting that there is now a vast body of research literature on what is called "stress and coping", which looks at the incidence of mental stress in relation to indicators such as social class, ethnicity, and so on. But virtually all of this literature is based upon quantitative methodologies; hardly any of it provides insights into the actual subjective experiences and lived lives of those concerned.

The following example comes from a youth worker with over twenty years' experience who ran a remarkably successful youth club on a housing estate that has long had a notorious reputation. He is referring to a recent incident in which some youths trashed his club and then three of them—two brothers and their friend's cousin—turned on each other. The younger brother is known to be dangerous and has used knives in the past.

> The younger brother and the other protagonist were just yelling abuse at each other. And they just sounded so hysterical, fragile and upset, I mean that was quite upsetting, because they were both saying really hurtful things to each other. I mean when I find this, all of them have actually got quite a lot of pain in their backgrounds and they scratch at each other's pain, they don't let it, they don't show solidarity for other people. On these situations they actually pull at the scabs you know, yelling awful things about their parents, the majority of which were true, you know.

The example gives us a glimpse of something else that is not often talked about by governments or the media: the rage, the pain, and the despair with which welfare professionals work on a daily basis. I propose to call this "social suffering", and I will argue that the quality of government in Western-style democracies can partly be measured in terms of the nature of its relationship to this suffering. While not the primary focus of this chapter, it is worth pausing to think about the nature of this suffering and the forms that it takes. Much of the "stress and coping" literature focuses upon stressful life events, but the part of the literature that I find most illuminating is that which argues that, for the multiply disadvantaged, "stressors" are chronic and continuing features of everyday life rather than discrete "life events" (Titterton, 1992). I think the concept of "no exit" situations also gives us glimpses of the unrelenting nature of this everyday reality. Writers about social class, such as Diane Reay (2005), who draw attention to the centrality of shame and disrespect, and those such as Farhad Dalal (2002), who use concepts such as projective identification to explore how racism becomes internalized, also illuminate aspects of social suffering. There is also quite a long history now of attempts to use concepts of loss, grief, and melancholia to understand the experiences of those whose communities are destroyed by processes of urban modernization (Marris, 1974) or, more generally, who are the powerless objects of economic and social restructuring (Sennett, 1998). Moglen (2005) has suggested the possible value of Masud Khan's concept of "cumulative trauma" (but see my earlier reservations) to describe the effects of such chronic and continuing impingements upon people's lives, and Moglen's work is part of a substantial body of North American literature that, as I noted earlier, deploys Freud's analysis of melancholia to explore forms of suffering that cannot be worked through psychically as there are no available means for articulating and symbolizing them (Eng & Kazanjian, 2003).

The idea that social suffering has a melancholic dimension is also helpful because, by drawing attention to that which cannot be worked through, we are reminded of the ways in which suffering must then be somatized and embodied (an important factor accounting for the social inequalities of health), enacted ("acting out" under the old social pathology paradigm) or projected (on to partners, children, neighbours, strangers, etc.). Whereas somatization draws attention to the ways in which social inequalities of health may be compounded by the conversion of aspects of social suffering into a physical symptomatology, projection can help illuminate the lack of solidarity, the "scratching at the other's pain", which is also an aspect of this suffering. We need to remember that coping strategies are also mechanisms of defence—suffering can be dealt with by splitting, projection, idealization, and denigration just as it is by alcohol, drugs, or other addictions. As well as agents and victims, the more we suffer the more we may also adopt the subject position of "own worst enemy" or "other's worst enemy" (Hoggett, 2001). As a consequence, the subjects of social suffering are not those who draw easily upon our compassion, since they often do not comport themselves as innocent victims but as aggressive, resentful, or suspicious beings whose hurt is directed at others rather than at themselves (Hoggett, 2006).

In Western-type democracies, the welfare state and welfarism arose as a consequence of the existence of such suffering, particularly social suffering. Much of the business of this aspect of the state concerns relationships with disadvantaged communities (including racialized minorities) and excluded groups such as people with disabilities or mental health problems. I suggest that one of what Claus Offe once termed the "contradictions of the welfare state" is that modern democracies are concerned as much with the management and control of social suffering as they are with its alleviation. This is not just an issue of resources and the management of demand; more fundamentally, it gives expression to both a cultural and a political problem. Politically, the existence of social suffering reminds us of the continued existence of social inequality, and, in the case of Britain, these inequalities are proving surprisingly resistant to government intervention even while, under Labour, the incomes of the most affluent have continued to rise quickly (Instititute of Fiscal Studies, 2007). Culturally, there are grounds to believe that suffering is itself the Other to modernity (Ferguson, 2003, p. 121). As I have argued elsewhere (Hoggett, 2000), suffering gives expression to the passive rather than active voice, to our needs as dependent rather than independent beings, to what is often chronic and enduring rather than what is open to social engineering and quick fixes. So, for both political and cultural reasons, Western-style democracies are partly in flight from suffering and those who are the subjects of suffering become the "Othered" of an achievement-orientated, change-embracing modernity.

I believe that by adding psychoanalytic insights to Bourdieu's concept of social suffering, a new way of thinking about the proper object of welfare practice can come into view. This would be a perspective that could at last do justice to people's lived experience of powerlessness and material scarcity, but in a non-idealized way. The tragedy is that none of us automatically responds to hardship, humiliation, or the abusive exercise of power through noble resistance; we are just as likely to turn our sense of grievance upon ourselves or innocent others. This is suffering turned upon itself, and it is this double suffering that is the real object of professional practice in welfare work.

Conclusion

I have tried to reframe a critical social policy in terms of a post-liberal theory of the human subject, one that places human experience at the centre of the lens. I think we do have the beginnings of a way in which an interpsychic account of social violence can be integrated with an intrapsychic model of human frailty, but this has had to wait until relational models of psychoanalysis could become fully relational. Only by integrating the interpsychic and the intrapsychic can we glimpse a human subject with internal resources and strengths as well as hatreds and vulnerabilities, that is, as someone with both transformational and destructive possibilities. And, of course, this model of human subjectivity applies equally to the professional practitioner as to the user of welfare services. Only with this understanding in mind can reflexive practice become possible and authority be exercised in a truly democratic manner. Formal models of participation are a necessary but not sufficient condition for fully democratic forms of social relations. Radical social policy needs to advance beyond its formal understandings towards something that is more fully lived, suffered, enjoyed, and experienced.

References

Benhabib, S. (1992). *Situating the Self.* Cambridge: Polity Press.

Benjamin, J. (1998). *Shadow of the Other: Intersubjectivity and Gender in Psychoanalysis.* New York: Routledge.

Benjamin, J. (2004). Beyond doer and done-to: an intersubjective view of thirdness. *Psychoanalytic Quarterly, LXIII*(1): 5–46.

Bion, W. (1959). Attacks on linking. *International Journal of Psychoanalysis, 40*: 308–315.

Bollas, C. (1987). *The Shadow of the Object.* London: Free Association.

Bourdieu, P. (1999). *The Weight of the World: Social Suffering in Contemporary Society.* Cambridge: Polity.

Britton, R. (2004). Subjectivity, objectivity and triangular space. *Psychoanalytic Quarterly, LXXIII*: 5–46.

Butler, J. (1997). *The Psychic Life of Power.* Stanford, CA: Stanford University Press.

Dalal, F. (2002). *Race, Colour and the Processes of Racialization: New Perspectives from Group Analysis,Psychoanalysis and Sociology.* New York: Brunner-Routledge.

Eng, D., & Kazanjian, D. (2003). *Loss: The Politics of Mourning.* Berkeley, CA: University of California Press.

Ferguson, H. (2003). *Protecting Children in Time.* Basingstoke: Palgrave Macmillan.

Freud, S. (1917e). Mourning and melancholia. *S.E., 14*: 237–258. London: Hogarth.

Freud, S. (1920g). *Beyond the Pleasure Principle. S.E., 18*: 1–64. London: Hogarth.

Froggett, L. (2002). *Love, Hate and Welfare: Psychosocial Approaches to Policy and Practice.* Bristol: Policy.

Gufstafson, J. (1979). The pseudomutual small group or institution. In: G. Lawrence (Ed.), *Exploring Individual and Organizational Boundaries* (pp. 69–76). Chichester: John Wiley.

Hall, S. (1996). Who needs identity? In: S. Hall & P. DuGay (Eds.), *Questions of Cultural Identity* (pp. 1–17). London: Sage.

Hoggett, P. (2000). *Emotional Life and the Politics of Welfare,* Basingstoke: Macmillan.

Hoggett, P. (2001). Agency, rationality and social policy, *Journal of Social Policy, 30*(1): 37–56.

Hoggett, P. (2006). Pity, compassion, solidarity. In: S. Clarke, P. Hoggett, & S. Thompson (Eds.), *Emotion, Politics and Society* (pp. 145–161). Basingstoke: Palgrave Macmillan.

Institute of Fiscal Studies (2007). Poverty and inequality in the UK: 2007. *IFS Briefing Note, BN 73.* London: Institute for Fiscal Studies.

Khan, M. (1974). The concept of cumulative trauma. In: *The Privacy of the Self.* London: Hogarth.

Loewald, H. (1973). On internalisation. *International Journal of Psychoanalysis, 54*: 1: 9–17.

Lovegrove, B. (2005). Developing a sense of self in an average world: the treatment of a woman with Down Syndrome. Paper given to the Annual Conference of the Association for Psychoanalysis, Culture & Society, Rutgers University, 4–6 November.

Marris, P. (1974). *Loss and Change.* London: Routledge & Kegan Paul.

Moglen, S. (2005). On mourning social injury. *Psychoanalysis, Culture & Society, 10*(2) : 151–167.

Reisman, D. (1977). *Richard Titmuss: Welfare & Society.* London: Heinemann.

Ponsi, M. (1997). Interaction and transference. *International Journal of Psychoanalysis, 78*, 243–263.

Reay, D. (2005). Beyond consciousness? The psychic landscape of social class. *Sociology, 39*(5): 911–928.

Sennett, R. (1998). *The Corrosion of Character.* New York: Norton & Norton.

Sennett, R., & Cobb, J. (1993). *The Hidden Injuries of Class.* London: Faber and Faber.

Sevenhuijsen, S. (1998). *Citizenship and The Ethics of Care: Feminist Considerations on Justice, Morality and Politics.* London: Routledge.

Titmuss, R. (1971). *The Gift Relationship.* London: Pantheon.

Titmuss, R. (1974). *Social Policy: an Introduction.* London: George Allen & Unwin.

Titmuss, R. (1976). *Commitment to Welfare* (2nd edn). London: Allen & Unwin.

Titterton, M. (1992). Managing threats to welfare: the search for a new paradigm of welfare. *Journal of Social Policy, 21*(1): 1–23.

Williams, F. (1989). *Social Policy: A Critical Introduction.* Cambridge: Polity Press.

Williams, G. (1997). Reflections on some dynamics of eating disorders: "no entry" defences and foreign bodies, *International Journal of Psycho-Analysis, 78*: 927–941.

Winnicott, D. W. (1971). *Playing and Reality,* London: Tavistock.

Yeatman, A. (2007). Varieties of individualism. In: C. Howard (Ed.), *Contested Individualization* (pp. 45–59). Basingstoke: Palgrave Macmillan.

CHAPTER FIVE

Artistic output as intersubjective third

Lynn Froggett

Seeing the other in community-based practice

In Chapter Four, "Relational thinking and welfare practice", Paul Hoggett argues that both classical liberal professionalism and its opponents who wish to see a less oppressive and more responsive welfare practice share a somewhat "thin" and idealized view of the supposedly rational and unitary welfare subject. The paternalistic stance of classical welfare, with its tendency to efface the particularity of the client, has been assailed by new social movements, user and advocacy groups that, in the name of diversity, have exposed the demeaning consequences of "top-down" welfare models and expert-led care. Under the banner of anti-oppressive practice, these critics of liberal welfare have struggled to create new spaces in which the people who use services can be seen and heard. A huge literature, which is partly underpinned by post-structuralist social science, has addressed the power relations that perpetuate inequality and oppression within welfare systems. However, Hoggett draws attention to the fact that something important eludes a welfare practice based on the micro-politics of power, and that derives from a shallow conception of the welfare subject who, positioned in the endless play of power relations, is seen as fundamentally inert, incapable of a desiring, resisting, creative, and destructive agency. How, then, might it be possible to "fill out the hollow welfare subject" so that they become a partner with depth, substance, and agency produced in a complex interplay of actual and phantasized social relations.

> Contemporary identity theory still lacks a proper understanding of the subject as someone who is not just the bearer of discourse, as someone who is not just positioned by race, class, and gender. What is missing is a concept of a loving and hating subject with an internal world that comprises real and imagined relations. In other words, there is no proper sense of internalization . . . [Hoggett, 2008, p. 70]

Much of the current practice guidance of the health and welfare professions has been concerned to redress the balance of power relations in interactions between users and professionals, to the extent that empowerment seems to have become "the new care". Empowerment commitments have become central to mission statements, institutional procedures, organizational and managerial structures, and regulatory frameworks. Discursively speaking, the battle for anti-oppressive practice appears to have been won. However, it is far from clear that the modernization of public services has emancipated the people who use them—perhaps consumerist models of empowerment have become as thin and insubstantial as the ideal consumer-subject of rational choice theory. The conflicted and destructive young people who populate the youth justice system are a long way from becoming self-responsible, empowered consumers, but they are not generally amenable to liberal professional paternalism. Not only are they antagonistic to the disciplinary procedures of the law and its representatives, they are quite likely to attack the very welfare orientation that underpins the legal treatment of juveniles.

Restorative justice as reparation

Restorative practices, which, at the time of writing, are high on the government agenda in the UK, have become increasingly popular in the youth justice system and among those professionals working with children and young people who have committed criminal acts or are at risk of offending. Restorative justice aims to combine welfare with discipline in the hope of restoring the fractured relationships between young offenders, victims, and communities. This chapter argues that its success depends on a richer and more relational model of restoration and community-based professional practice than is presently available—one that implies seeing the other as an equivalent centre of subjective experience (Benjamin, 1988; Hoggett, 2008). This is the basis for relationships of reciprocal recognition.

The young people who come into contact with the Youth Justice System have largely fallen out of mainstream schooling. Many are in Pupil Referral Units or other special provision, if they can be persuaded to engage in formal education at all. A large number have suffered family breakdown and have supposedly been "looked after" by Local Authorities. Some are skinny and hungry, most are sad and at times fearsomely vindictive and angry. Their horizons are restricted to the estates where they live, the shopping centre, police station, and courts. The next town is beyond the limits of the known world. They are fatalistic about following their fathers, uncles, brothers, and peers into prison or their mothers, aunts, sisters, and friends into early pregnancy and life on benefits. Many are candidates for mental health care, though whether they will get it is highly uncertain.

The discourse of restorative justice focuses explicitly on fractured social relationships and seeks to restore a sense of connection between victim and offender in which both parties acknowledge themselves to belong to the same moral community and share a sense of mutual responsibility (Blather, 1999; Zehr & Toews, 2004). Restorative practices emphasize recognition processes in which the nature of the offence and the harm done is explored in the real or symbolic presence of the person or persons wronged. The harm caused by delinquency is thus regarded as a failure to see the other as having the same capacity for feeling and suffering as the self. In so far as this is understood to be failure on the part of both community and offender, it depends on a public understanding of the effects of systematic exclusion and deprivation and a willingness to respond to the offender as a moral subject. Restorative practices are those in which a dynamic of mutual recognition between parties can be established. The encounter between victim and offender—imagined or real—is thought to produce a transformative moral crisis in the offender and moral learning within the community. Providing depressive anxieties can be contained and worked through; this is expected to stimulate reparation, forgiveness, and reintegration (Froggett, Farrier, & Poursanidou, 2007).

In principle, therefore, the community represents a symbolic third space (Banton, Clifford, Frosh, Lousada, & Rosenthall, 1985; Cooper & Lousada, 2005; Foster & Zagier Roberts, 1998), an arena in which wrong-doer and wronged might seek a basis for mutual recognition, juridical rights, and social solidarity (Honneth, 1995). However, the community as a place where the needs and wishes of others define the limits and opportunities of the self is not the same as the idealized space of communality where differences of interest and desire are submerged in a transcendent unity. In much day to day talk of restorative justice, the notion of community, in so far as it invokes a local, spatially-defined population bound together by shared interests and civic values, is a romanticized flight from reality. The actual communities from which the young people who took part in our research (Farrier, Froggett, & Poursanidou, 20009, forthcoming; Froggett, 2007; Froggett, Farrier, & Poursanidou, 2007) are drawn are degraded environments and reservoirs of social suffering that induce division: poverty, ill-health, low educational and occupational mobility, inter-ethnic tension. Social capital is low, crime high, and bonds between neighbours fragile. Persecutory anxiety escalates and with good reason: the streets that pass for public space are dangerous places to be.

Public policy is Janus-faced and unhelpful here, swinging to and fro on whether to reform or punish young criminals: the rehabilitative ideal is well embedded in community-based youth justice while, at the same time, Britain contrives to lock up more of its young people, and at an earlier age, than most other European countries. Despite intellectual understanding of the link between social disadvantage and anti-social behaviour, there seems to be difficulty on the part of the public in comprehending how the actual child of a disrupted family, with limited opportunities, may feel impelled to visit his sense of victimization on others. Nor are retaliatory impulses the exclusive preserve of the offender. In the town that is host to the Youth Offending Team considered here, a well-meaning attempt to distribute surplus supermarket fruit to mal-nourished teenagers incited howls of rage in the local press. Real communities can be severely challenged by the threats posed by young offenders and are prone to familiar forms of splitting. On the one hand, wrong-doers are regarded as feral social pests who (within their limited means) appear to do pretty much as they like; on the other they are deprived innocents—the abandoned children who might be reclaimed when maternal and paternal care are reunited in "tough love". Nevertheless, the illusion of "the good community" has an important symbolic function, providing a yard-stick by which real communities may be assessed, and the possibil-ity of a public space where the anxiety that induces polarizations can be held, processed, and modified.

Matters might be helped if the professionals and advocates who accent the creative potential of the young people they work with were also able to acknowledge their destructiveness (Hoggett, 2007). The over-social view of the subject that conceives restorative justice solely in terms of the reconstitution of social relations between victim, offender, and community needs to be qualified by a depth psychology that understands restoration as reparation in the inner world of the offender: that is, in the object relational sense. Relational psychoanalysis may have something to offer here, in so far as it interprets the intra and intersubjective interplay of creativ-ity and destructiveness as integrally related within and between selves. This produces the internal struggle that animates the moral faculty and seems to be one of the conditions of intersubjective recognition in criminal justice settings: the sense between victim, offender, and community that the others are "like subjects" to be "felt with" (Benjamin, 1995, 2004)—but that empathy and identifi-cation constantly break down, especially in "suffering" communi-ties where access to goods and cultural resources are so unevenly distributed that each party can seem both victim and aggressor to the other.

Neither welfare paternalism nor welfare consumerism can facili-tate recognition of interdependency between offenders, victims, and communities. In Benjamin's terms (2004), the problem with welfare paternalism would be that its hierarchical social relations produce a coercive dependency based on the complementarity of doer and done to. Welfare consumerism, on the other hand, assumes an essentially monadic subject who has little to gain from relational practice. Similar themes have resonated through psychoanalytically informed thinking on welfare reform for years (for example, Cooper & Lousada, 2005; Froggett, 2002; Hoggett, 2000), some of it inspired by feminist writing on care, recognition, and democracy (Fraser, 1995; Gilligan, 1982; Sevenhuijsen, 1998; Tronto, 1994), along with Axel Honneth's (1995) work, *The Struggle for Recognition*. Yet, this body of work has had limited influence on welfare practice, even though practitioners may wish to resist the reductionist views of human agency presumed by managerialized welfare institutions. Practices of recognition are easily overwhelmed by procedural imperatives of eligibility, forensic defensibility, and measurable effectiveness. Within restorative justice, a behavioural model of human motivation undermines the reparative ideal by endorsing a culture of blaming (Gadd & Jefferson, 2007), dignified by the theory of "re-integrative shaming" (Braithwaite, 1989). Once again, the underlying model is that of the self-responsible subject, fully in command of his or her choices and immune in decision-making to the disruptions of emotions and bodily states. What appears to be lacking in much current practice is an understanding of the generative intersubjective space in which the relationships between practitioners and the people they work with are the prime medium of intervention. In what kind of intersubjective field do recognition relations between such subjects become possible?

Within community-based provision in third sector and mixed partnerships, there are people positioned in a very interesting field of tensions. They have activist orientations to grass-roots mobilization and social pedagogy, and have been mainly concerned with material and social disadvantage and strategies of empowerment and inclusion. These professionals, community-based workers, and volunteers share a practice that is now penetrated by intrusive forms of regulation and is bedevilled by short-term funding, yet they still operate at arm's length from the prescriptive centralism of formal services. Moreover, they are often in flight from excessive managerialism and the "institutionalisation of shallowness" (Hoggett, 1992) that characterizes the mainstream, and they try to remain connected to the communities among whom they work. These practitioners, who are at the precarious innovative edge of formal services, are likely to remain exercised by the problem of how to see the other as a centre of subjective experience, partly because local forms of communicative democracy (Young, 1996) and responsiveness to people who are excluded or disenfranchised are their overriding rationale. Many, such as the community artist and YOT (Youth Offending Team) who are the subject of this chapter, are also in partnerships with mainstream services.

These workers are involved with individuals and communities where subjection to practices of "othering" is a mark of social suffering (Bourdieu, 1999; Hoggett, 2008). They are, therefore, in a position to apprehend that the other in question is neither rational nor unitary, but conflicted, defended, ambivalent, and embodied. Coping with the routine insults of being "othered" and "done to", if it is not to lead to enraged self-destructiveness or criminality, means finding a third position from which to think, thus avoiding the impulse to split and retaliate. Restorative practices that aim at overcoming polarities and repairing division must, therefore, create the conditions for third-position thinking among professionals and among the people they work with. If, as has been suggested, the community is to function as a third space, individuals must find the capacity to occupy the third position within the self. This is the condition of sustaining recognition processes that involve the ability to apprehend the separate positions of self and other, while acknowledging the interdependence between both parties. In Britton's formulation, it requires the capacity to observe the self while being oneself, and from this position of self-awareness and one's own point of view, to hold the perspective of self and other simultaneously in mind. The triangular space that allows one to do this—in this instance the space between the good community (real or imagined), victim and offender—is a condition of creativity and mental freedom (Britton, 1989, 1998). A question that concerns this chapter is how such a space can be found or facilitated within restorative justice contexts. The material that follows is taken from a research project with a Youth Offending team which has been experimenting with creative, arts-based approaches to relational practice (Farrier, Froggett, & Poursanidou, 2009, forthcoming; Froggett, 2007, Froggett, Farrier, & Poursanidou, 2007). A more extended discussion of inter- and intra-subjective thirdness will follow the case example.

The YOT as a setting for relational practice

The youth justice and community workers within the YOT that was the subject of this research are feeling their way towards practices that derive from and reproduce a relational view of the subject. Professional practitioners have been collaborating with community artists and education, care, and leisure agencies. Central government takes a keen interest in youth crime, and the challenge of developing relational thinking in this highly regulated environment is considerable. Work with individuals is under constant scrutiny from the courts and local press, who are keen to see that any form of intervention has a direct and measurable impact on reoffending rates. The YOT staff are convinced that a precondition of restoring social bonds between victim, offender, and community lies not only in directly addressing offending behaviour, but at the same time nurturing everyday forms of creative living. They try to foster a latent creativity among young people at risk of offending and on court orders, and, to this end, they make intensive use of the arts. The arts effectively sensitize both staff and young people to the aesthetic dimensions of communication and an attunement to the "erotics of experience" (Bollas, 1992). This is the condition for expression and perception of what Bollas calls "personal idiom" (equivalent to Winnicott's [1971] "true self", but with the accent on the self's implicit "theory of form"). The perception of one's personal idiom by the other is a condition of recognition in that it accounts for the sensing of what is *irreducibly unique* about the self as centre of subjective experience. In this case, the medium for idiomatic self-expression is arts-based interaction and the moral reflection it stimulates, through the production of an intersubjective third. In the case material and discussion that follow, the oedipal third arises from the biographical and object relational dimensions of the young man's experience while Benjamin's discussion of the energetic, moral, and symbolic thirds (Benjamin, 2004) helps to illuminate the intersubjective field established in the creative writing process.

Just "being me"

The young people who took part in this study were hard to reach and even harder to interview. Case studies were built up from a variety of sources: assessment information held on file, conversations with key workers, biographical narrative interviews with the young people concerned and observation of videotaped records of interactive art-based activities. The latter provided by far the richest data. The extract below was taken from footage collected in the course of a session with Bob the poet, and Tom, a slight, pale seventeen-year-old who looks younger than his years and less dangerous than his reputation.

> Tom has received numerous community sentences for offences committed after drinking or drugs-taking. He is curfewed, electronically tagged, and has done time in a lock-up. During the project he begins working on a part-time, short-term basis at a local garage. He is ejected from home after an argument with his mother and later allowed back.

> Tom seems uncomfortable talking about his childhood. His relationship with his mother has been stormy and he has been "chucked out" whenever she hasn't been able to stand the arguments and bad behaviour. He reports this in a matter of fact, deadpan way with no evident resentment. When allowed home, he lives there with his younger brother, who is a partner in crime. Tom's father died some time in his second year and he remembers nothing. He is exaggeratedly casual about this—"not fussed" (though he admits he used to be) and he is vague about the death: possibly heart attack—he hasn't asked. He struggles to name a father figure but looks up to an older brother who works as a dustman and has a little girl. Tom is fiercely protective of her.

> He links drinking with offending: criminal damage and common assault. He downs two litres of cider on a good night. He claims he is going easier now, but will turn eighteen soon and wonders how to get drunk with an electronic tag. Tom's off-hand story has very little tragicomic drinker heroism in it. There are no tales of improbable quantities, hilarious exploits, drowning sorrows or drunken fellowship. Being drunk is a prosaic, matter-of-fact ordinary sort of event—more about avoiding definition, keeping things out of focus—being fuzzed rather than fussed.

> Much of what Tom says is delivered with a shrug, hands in pockets, face blank. His posture emphasizes his small stature and he slouches on the hard, upright chairs. But "stuff matters" and when it does he loses even more definition—speech mumbles, jumbles, and trails off, or he buries his head in his hands and ruffles his hair, or he shuffles his feet. At these points he looks even younger, even less poised.

Bob, the poet, is forty-something, big and burly, affable, loud, comical, whacky, wears pink stripy sweat shirts and talks in thick local vernacular. In the past he has played in a band, dug graves, worked as a teacher and stand-up comedian. He occupies the liminal position of artist, somewhere in-between the justice system and the streets. He has a battery of cues, prompts, and provocations and varies his delivery, seeking responses from Tom on whatever he wants to talk about. Bob never pushes a topic—just fishes around, casting lines, waiting to see which Tom will catch and swim with. The cues are designed to find out who or what is Tom. They play around with youth identities: gangsta, chav, hooligan. Does Tom aspire to the black rap glamour of 50 Cent or the close-to-home laddishness of white working-class Wayne Rooney? "I'm just me," he announces, and this theme heralds a search for an image of himself that he can credibly inhabit. It resonates through every session. To start with Tom is bored, slouchy, slightly contemptuous, but Bob is engaging and confrontational by turns. Pretty soon we see Tom leaning forward, making eye contact, tapping out the rap rhythms, reflecting them back. There is rapid repartee and bodily mirroring between them. Bob is on the look-out for anything that can be crafted into verse. Tom provides the words, Bob picks them up and works on them. Tom takes them back and inflects them with something of his own. This is how they co-create a poem. Tom is finally "hooked" when he triumphantly completes a jingle. He will return week after week, using the sessions to discuss friends, family, prison, work, children, girls, his hopes and disappointments, mistakes, values, and his touchingly conventional view of the good life: "a job, home, car and a fit wife".

The rhythmicity that is evident on the film cannot be inferred from the transcript, but here is a short extract (a transcript of a video clip) that gives something of the flavour of the dialogue:

B: Let's talk about music for a bit then. Who's your favourite singer . . . rapper . . . MC?

T: 50 Cent.

B: Why's he good?

T: Yeah, he's ace

B: Why though?

T: 'Cos his music's ace

B: Is it? How's it make you feel?

T: I dunno [laughs] "gangsta".

B: What's a "gangsta" then? Is it spelt g-a-n-g . . .

T: Some of my mates . . . really like him [inaudible] say "50 pence"

B: [Laughs] Are you a "gangsta"?

T: No, am I 'eck.

B: So what are you?

T: Nothing, I'm just me.

B: Ah! Are you a "chav"?

T: Yeah.

B: I thought you said you were nothing?

T: [bored and irritable] Well . . . I don't know [inaudible] when I'm older I'm not gonna wear . . . I'm gonna wear jeans and stuff.

B: Are you a chav now?

T: I wear chav clothes, but not really bad. Some of 'em wear their socks tucked in . . . look like rejects some of 'em

B: You're not a gangsta . . .

T: No. I wish I was.

B: What are you . . .

T: Like 50 Cent or summat.

[Interruption by Tom's brother. Tom waves him out and firmly shuts door.]

B: Are you a yob?

T: [contemptuous] No. Definitely not. Yob is the wrong word.

B: Yeah. Are you a hooligan?

T: [brightens up] No, but I would be a football hooligan with Leeds United.

B: Would ya? [Laughs] Would you like to be?

T: [Smiles] Yeah. It'd be mint. Against the Manchester scum . . . Manchester United. You know that *Football Factory*?

B: Have you read that book?

T: No, but I seen the film.

B: What d'you think?

T: The film's ace. So's *Green Street*.

B: We'll talk about that in a bit, *Football Factory* . . . er [reads]

I wear chav clothes
but I'm just me
I'm not a gangsta
I'm just me
I'm not a yob
I'm just me
I'm not a hooligan
But I would be
Leeds United
It'd be mint

T: [Smiles, shakes head, looks dubious]

B: Getting there . . . Tell us about *Football Factory* . . .

T: [Interrupts, leans forward, and grabs notepad] You know you're going "me me me"?

B: [Loudly] Me! Me! Me!

T: [with animation] Listen!

. . . but I would be
Leeds United
That's my cup of tea

B: Yes! We have ourselves a . . . you gonna read it out?

Watching the footage, the research team tries to take in the inter-action as a whole then shifts focus from one party to the other. Much of the spoken language is hard to catch, so we concentrate on physical presence and tone of voice as this is the first and most compelling evidence of an affective field developing between Tom and Bob. We are seeing a process of spontaneous bodily attunement and a resonance between the speech rhythms. The two of them are sitting in a poky little office, but their interaction has something of a dance about it as each mirrors the other's movements. The patterns they create align and break down (around line 15, where

Tom's speech becomes inaudible, his tone irritable, and his body slack). They begin to repair with mention of Leeds United. It often happens that Bob uses rap to get the exchange going, but the interaction acquires a momentum of its own, giving way to bits of significant conversation—about what Tom thinks and wants from life. Then the tension disperses and the pair momentarily disengage. Tom slumps, scratches, fiddles. His eyes wander vacantly around the room and he shrugs and grunts, then he re-engages once more. In this way, the tension constantly dissipates and re-forms giving rise to conversational highs and lows, moments of collaboration followed by irritable dissonance. This keeps going over the weeks as a process of moral reflection takes shape. The content is about Tom rather than Bob, and it has all the asymmetry of the professional relationship. However, the resonance between them is only possible on the basis of mutuality, and this becomes very clear when Bob becomes didactic or tries too hard to push the youth justice agenda. Tom seems to experience this as intrusive and emotionally withdraws from the exchange.

In this particular episode, which takes place in session three, there is a critical turning point when Tom finally grabs the notepad and takes over responsibility for the poem they have been working on. From this point on, and in subsequent sessions, he readily engages and is more conversationally forthcoming. Filling the existential intuition of "being me" with content that can do justice to his conflicted and contradictory states of mind, finding out who that is becomes the overriding task. Bob alternately challenges and encourages him in this search for authenticity. Tom is increasingly willing to discuss his future hopes and consider what has happened to friends who have escaped from criminal trajectories—perhaps under the influence of a girlfriend—and those who have ended up in prison. The tone is increasingly one of a young man beginning to see the futility of the life he had been leading, and able to understand the damage he has done to self and others. A persistent refrain is his liking for children and eventually an admission that he would like to work with them. He responds to Bob's encouragement and takes responsibility for keeping the younger boys in line at the garage. At one point he realizes that his criminal record may have ruined his chances and he "crumples", burying his head in his hands.

After the creative writing sessions are over, Tom gives this assessment of the process:

> [Bob] asks you five things about your family and you don't realize but . . . he gets them out of you and puts them into a poem and you see how it's making you feel and stuff like that.

Bodies, words, and thirds

The video clip described above is an excellent example of two people "doing" recognition. In the process they create an intersubjective field—a space of the third between them. In the extract above their collaboration also results in the production of a poem—a third object—that is the outcome of gestures, notions, and words that they have passed to and fro in an expressive exchange. There are different versions of thirdness or triangularity within psychoanalytic theory, and this material may help to draw some distinctions since there are clearly different thirds at play in the interaction.

Benjamin distinguishes between the energetic, symbolic and moral thirds that are produced within the space of the third. *The energetic third*, which arises in the non-verbal intersubjective exchange, can be seen in the bodily mirroring between Tom and Bob. It is based not on language but on a co-ordinated rhythmicity, such as that which allows the development of proto-conversations between mothers and infants (Trevarthen, 2003). Such exchanges have, in the case of babies and mothers, been analysed spectrographically (Malloch, 1999) and found to display a musical structure with intrinsic respect for metre, and even a narrative flow: introduction—development—climax—resolution. In this context, where the two are attempting to write verse, the spontaneous rhythmicity is quickly apparent to the observer and fuels the creative process.

Tom's use of the relational space appears at first to depend on a mutual attunement that is possible because the conditions of creative writing involve an ongoing co-production within a potential space of thirdness (Winnicott, 1971). Bob is quite anxious at first that the poems are not all Tom's "own" work in the sense that his words have been partially selected and recast by Bob. But Tom appears to take genuine pleasure in the co-creation. To an outsider, the verse may be little more than doggerel, but the real art is in the way both parties give themselves over to the process of creating energetic thirdness and the particular quality of mutual attention that allows them to work in this way. Benjamin calls it "letting go into being with"—a process of surrender by which they overcome the complementarity of twoness and enter a potential space. This space is never a point of rest, but an in-between that involves the continual reconfiguration of inner and outer, me and not me. It is in this space that the self's idiom (akin to Winnicott's "true self" [Winnicott, 1971]) is evoked by the other. The sense of "being with" may seem momentarily like fusion as Bob and Tom move and think together. However, the illusion of unity is productive precisely because it is unstable. It quickly breaks down into complementarity as they trip over each other, get bored, interrupt, irritate, produce lines that don't gel.

When the energetic third falters, Bob and Tom visibly struggle to reconstitute dialogue in words, producing *a symbolic third* of which the outward manifestation is the good conversation, and sometimes verse. The use of language enables each to maintain his own position while holding the other in mind. Language, for young people like Tom, can often be a marker of their exclusion from work and formal education, whereas street vernacular provides access to deviant identities. In this case we see a growing facility and confidence in the use of language as Tom finds a potential for authorship and hence the irreducible particularity of being "just me".

As attunement is reconstituted in the interaction between Tom and Bob—partly through bodily mirroring and partly through words, *a moral third* emerges where the tension is held between the needs of self and other, and it may be this that stimulates Tom to think about his offending. As it happens, this aligns the creative process—the play in which they are pleasurably indulging—with the formal demands of restorative justice: that Tom engage in moral self reflection. This happens, for example, when he compares himself to peers who have escaped or fallen further into crime, or where he wonders whether he might ever be seen in the eyes of others as sufficiently responsible to care for children. The outcome of this process is not merely submission to the law, in that Tom seems to be developing a wish to move away from a criminal career, but also recognition of the needs of others and guilt and concern for harm he has done. As the sessions proceed, Tom continues to raise the issue of morality and personal responsibility as if under some inner impulsion.

When a poem is completed, it is read out to the research camera with the gravity of a poet laureate on a state occasion, and Tom is visibly proud. The camera, too, creates triangularity—not so much the judgementalism of *Big Brother* as a reference to the principle of moral self-evaluation that underlies restorative justice.

Benjamin's account of the intersubjective thirds focuses on the interpersonal dynamics of encounters between two people, which, in the case of the energetic third, is already present within the mother–infant dyad. This, in her view, also generates the intrasubjective capacity for thirdness, or triangular thinking, which is then elaborated with language use and the experience of relationships with others. The information we have on Tom's family relationships is collected in the creative writing sessions and in a subsequent interview when he talks about—or rather exaggeratedly shrugs off—the death of his father, or his on/off relationship with his mother. We also know of the years of drinking and drug-taking, and the violent offences committed while under their influence. It is worth considering these aspects of his life and relationships from a developmental perspective.

Heuves (2003) outlines the distinctions between *diadic* and *triadic positions* in the development of adolescents, where the dyadic position appears to correspond to Benjamin's impasse of complementarity. The triadic position, on the other hand, involves the capacity to surrender to a dialogic process (a space of thirdness) and to engage in the production of an intersubjective third. This is the condition of learning from experience, achieving mutuality in relationships and of co-operation with others in education and work. In the dyadic position, the achievement of autonomy seems to involve a continued struggle in phantasy with primal objects and in actuality with parental figures, dependence on whom is increasingly resented. To the adolescent in this situation, the only possible outcome is the assertion of self over other who must be forced to submit to the self's own narcissistic needs and adapt to the precarious identity he has managed to construct. This struggle is paranoid–schizoid in the sense that it feels like a zero sum game: victory and annihilation of the parental object seems like a condition of psychic survival; negotiation is experienced as submission. When the creative writing project takes place, Tom and his mother seem to have been enacting such a conflict for some time. Their relationship with each other has been more off than on. Tom gets kicked out after rows in which the two reach an impasse. He has nothing to say about these episodes—they are not available for thought, but are just part of the banal everyday here-and-gone rhythm of things, like getting drunk and getting into trouble. Just as with the death of his father, Tom tries not to appear "fussed". These events are reported but not processed. Where the interpreting subject should be, the "fuzziness" takes over.

By contrast, in the triadic position there is a willingness to adapt to reality and consider the self and other as having independent minds with which to think about the other. Within the sessions between Tom and Bob, we begin to discern an interpersonal responsiveness that can only operate to the extent that they are mindful of each other. The dialogue that ensues veers between rhythmic bodily enactments that precede imaginative play and moments of mature reflective conversation when Tom is thinking about the mess he has got himself into. Although he cannot as yet talk of his own childhood, he returns uninhibitedly to his liking for children. He bosses and cares for the younger boys at the garage where the sessions are taking place. When he realizes he might have blown his chances of ever working with children, his distress is palpable and he asks for help from Bob. In the triadic position there is a willingness and an effort to verbalize feelings, a developing capacity for insight, and when words fail it is the result of inner conflict rather than the destruction of meaning. Tom's anxieties take on a depressive character as he gauges the extent of the harm he has done and moves towards concern and moral responsibility.

Heuves stresses that, rather than the classical Oedipal progression from the dyadic to the triadic relationship, adolescence is a time of especially dramatic shifts between the regressive and progressive positions—hence the volatility and moodiness characteristic of this phase of development and the particularly acute need for parental figures who are not drawn into dyadic configurations but maintain the capacity for independent third position thinking. The task of achieving a triadic, or third, position faces Tom in the same way as any other adolescent. Biographically speaking, it is easy to see why he should have found the resolution of the oedipal situation a challenge. The loss of his father was never plausibly explained, much less grieved for within the family. He speaks of the heart attack as if he knows it is not the whole story. Rather than bearing the symbolic third of language, Tom's father exited the family, leaving behind the unspeakability of his absence. From then on Tom, lacking any other reliable figures of masculine identification, has been trapped in a recurring struggle with his mother in which they swing between mutual acceptance and rejection. Distinction and discrimination are increasingly abandoned in the pseudo-sensuality of alcohol and street drugs, giving rise to episodic bursts of abusive and violent criminality, which just happen, as if from nowhere.

Watching the videos, we see Bob as parent to both the infant and the adolescent. The one-year-old child in Tom, who lost his father just as he was trying to find a first language, at last finds himself mirrored by an adult male who helps him achieve self-definition in words. The "fuzziness" is dispelled and there are moments of triumphal clarity as Tom gains authorship and authenticity through language ("I'm just me") in a cultural field that offers him achievable but denigrated adolescent identities on the one hand, or the unattainable celebrity status of mega-stars on the other.

Mature third position thinking, in Britton's view, depends on the constitution of an *oedipal third*, which depends on tolerance of the oedipal situation, the link between the parents that excludes the child and inaugurates a third position from which object relationships can be observed. However, connecting his own work with that of Lacan (1979), Britton points out that the successful negotiation of oedipal conflicts involves not only the acquisition of language, but the reuniting on a higher level of organization, of the flesh of the mother (*l'imaginaire*) with the father's word (*le symbolique*). The precondition of this accomplishment—and of all meaning—lies in the adequate maternal containment of early infancy. As we have seen, Benjamin (2004) argues that this implies that the potential for the third already exists in the relational dynamics of the mother–infant dyad, and that it shows itself in preverbal patterns of sensuous attunement. It may be that dialogical creative processes, such as the one between Bob and Tom, are effective because they involve an exchange that is both self-reflective and embodied. They therefore reunite the sensuous and the discursive at the level of subjective experience. In this respect, they are unlike the other interventions to which young offenders are subject, such as the judicial or social work based interview.

The aesthetic of self and arts-based practice

Arts-based practice in health and welfare is currently becoming an irrepressible force within hospitals, schools, community settings, and the justice system. It is remarkably under-theorized, given its popularity, and although there is some evaluation research, it is still bedevilled by the injunction to measure outcomes and has failed ask the interesting questions: why the arts? Why now? And *how* do they do what they claim to do? Given that the arts explosion has occurred just as technical rationalism has penetrated most areas of human services, there are reasons to see it as an inchoate but increasingly determined attempt to preserve a responsiveness to the embodied subjectivity of the other and resist the evacuation of relationship from practice. The YOT attended by Tom sees arts-based projects as media for expression of the interiority, depth, and complexity of the young people they work with. It does so on the basis of an intuition that expression of a personal creativity offsets the effects of "othering" to which young offenders are particularly vulnerable. Hence, the markers of young people's identities are registered through a constellation of social signifiers—class, gender, ethnicity, generation, and so on, but the uniqueness of each is apprehended through personal idiom (Bollas, 1992). It is through the expression of idiom that they can negotiate identities acceptable to their communities and at the same time "feel real". Professionals who work intensively with arts-based approaches tacitly adopt a view of the self that Bollas has described as "an aesthetic intelligence" that imprints its unconscious sense of form on the world with which it interacts. According to Bollas, when we attune ourselves to the specific quality of the other's experience, we register their idiom as a distinctive, psychic texture within ourselves.

Art-based activities may be a privileged (though by no means the only) route to expressing this idiom in the sense that all art involves the creation of something that passes through the medium of the self, acquires its imprint, and is animated by it.

Once seen, or rather felt (this requires a radically embodied form of perception), the experience of the other's experiencing gives rise to an area of disturbance or psychic intensity that will then scatter into other trains of personal association or object relating stimulated by the specifics of the encounter. In so far as attunement to the other's idiom occurs by means of imaginative identifications that express themselves in bodily states, it involves a somatic countertransference aroused by the quality of their presence. This has something in common with what happens when we are affected by the unconscious creative intelligence of an artist whose existential signature expresses itself through a painting or piece of music.

In everyday life, this idiom also impresses its self as an aesthetic sensibility or a garden-variety creativity. Although almost impossible to describe in words, it articulates itself in the way someone moves through the world of people and inanimate objects, or how they choose to assemble and combine them. It is present in how they dress, arrange their furniture, move their bodies, listen to music, tidy their desk, eat their food, select their friends, and how they arrange the patterns of their day. When they engage in artistic activities in interaction with others, or with their materials, they are once again driven to express this personal aesthetic or "theory of form". In this sense, art is only a special instance of creative living but it is one that invites a particular kind of imaginative freedom as the artwork passes through the self and emerges as an embodiment of idiom in a third that the other can share. This bears on the subject's sensed and expressed authenticity, and is shaped through the earliest experiences of being transformed in the presence of another through the mother's personal idiom of care (Bollas, 1987): the distinctive way in which she tends, strokes, cleans, and caresses her infant's body. Clearly, the aesthetic of the self's idiom has nothing to do with the postmodern aestheticization of personal identity—its voluntaristic self-assembly through consumer choice (Bauman, 1998). It is rather an emergent property of subjectivity, biographically embedded in our earliest intersubjective exchanges, unconsciously elaborated through our inner object world and its external counterparts, and the source of our ability to "feel real".

Implications

There is a wealth of clinical wisdom on how to create the conditions for the patient to find his or her way to a true self or unhindered manifestation of idiom. In the tradition of Bion (1970), much of it has to do with negative capability or the "evenly hovering attention" that allows the analyst to attune to the patient and thus use him or herself as an instrument of knowing. The non-intrusiveness of the analytic stance is paramount. It is much more difficult to create these conditions in other welfare settings, and the routinization and regulation of practice ensures that the situation will get no easier. Social workers who trained in the 1970s were taught the therapeutic value of the one-to-one encounter and the necessity to provide a space apart where the relationship became the prime medium of intervention and could be psychodynamically understood. It is not just the psychodynamic model, but the intersubjective space itself that has collapsed under current practice conditions.

The kind of arts-based practice I have described here attempts to generate and work creatively within the intersubjective space, but it may be argued that such projects are, at best, on the edge of mainstream welfare and represent a special case that has limited replicability. I would make a bolder claim: while art-making requires and reproduces conditions peculiarly suitable to the process of creating thirdness, the kind of communicative relationship I have described can be generated in a range of creative activities. Moreover, the capacity and enthusiasm for this kind of work is widespread and can draw on experiences from elsewhere. In Europe, it occurs within a well-established tradition of social pedagogy, while in Latin America it is present in the Frierian heritage of political "conscientization" (Friere, 1996). Experimental cultural forms, such as Boal's theatres of internalized and external oppression (Boal, 1995, 1998), have explored democratic dialogue and nourished political resistance. Since beginning this line of research, I have found arts-based and other forms of creative activity in very diverse welfare settings in the UK, and these are inflected with a micro-politics of experience that aims to produce a view of oppression from within. Instances range from multi-million pound agencies with significant budgets and the ability think about creativity in strategic terms, to small, experimental local projects that build on the inspiration of this story-teller, or that geek with digital know-how, or the boy next door with a camera and a pot of paint. There are professionals willing to co-opt such people and learn from their communicative flair and from the state of mind and relationship required to work with the other to produce a third. The inventiveness of these initiatives often goes unrecognized and remains undignified by serious theoretical consideration. It might be easier to defend and generalize such work if its nature and conditions were better understood.

Relational practice is orientated to the use of all the dimensions of thirdness within the intersubjective field, and bodily interaction may be the primary means by which some subjects express themselves and change each other. Elsewhere, I have considered clay modelling in a group of profoundly disabled adults in a community care setting who do not communicate in words (Froggett, 2005, 2006), and the use of artwork to transform the subject's relationship to chronic and debilitating ill-health (Froggett, Chamberlayne, Buckner, & Wengraf, 2005). Such observations suggest that producing thirdness involves, in the first instance, surrender to a sensual exchange unmediated by conceptual thought. Language is not necessarily everyone's prime medium of self-expression, particularly among the disadvantaged client groups of many community-based services. Workers within this field need to attend to the dimensions of action and interaction without the clinical context that allows minute decoding of the pragmatics and semantics of language. For most of the young offenders in the project illustrated here, the language of the street had become a mark of their exclusion from education, and a defiant badge of a socially denigrated identity. For Tom, reconstituting language as a symbolic third depended on finding a link with Bob via an idiomatic, energetic exchange. This stimulated a dialogical process of reflection on his existential and biographical identity. Along the way he managed to imagine in words a restored relationship (as future husband, worker, and parent) to a moral community—an imagined third space of shared values in which it would be possible handle conflicts, stay out of jail, and build a life. It so happens that, a year after the creative writing course, Tom has not been convicted of any further offences and is holding down a full-time job.

Acknowledgement

With thanks to Alan Farrier and Konstantina Poursanidou of the Psychosocial Research Unit at the University of Central Lancashire for their part in this data collection and for their contribution to the preliminary analysis.

References

Banton, R., Clifford, P., Frosh, S., Lousada, J., & Rosenthall, J. (1985). *The Politics of Mental Health*. Basingstoke, Macmillan.

Bauman, Z. (1998). *Globalisation*. Cambridge: Polity Press

Benjamin, J. (1988). *The Bonds of Love*. New York: Pantheon.

Benjamin, J. (1995). *Like Subjects, Love Objects, Essays on Recognition and Sexual Difference*. New Haven, CT: Yale University Press.

Benjamin, J. (2004). Beyond doer and done-to: an intersubjective view of thirdness. *Psychoanalytic Quarterly*, LXIII(1): 5–46.

Bion, W. R. (1970). *Attention and Interpretation*. London: Tavistock.

Blather, C. (1999). Towards a constructive response to young offenders: reparation at the levels of justice and individual psychology. *Journal of Social Work Practice*, 13(2): 211–220.

Boal, A. (1995). *The Rainbow of Desire*. London: Routledge.

Boal, A. (1998). *Legislative Theatre*. London: Routledge.

Bollas, C. (1987). *The Shadow of the Object*. London: Free Association.

Bollas, C. (1992). *Being a Character: Psychoanalysis and Self Experience*. London: Routledge.

Bourdieu, P. (1999). *The Weight of the World: Social Suffering in Contemporary Society*. Cambridge: Polity.

Braithwaite, J. B. (1989). *Crime, Shame and Reintegration*. Cambridge: Cambridge University Press.

Britton, R. (1989). The missing link: parental sexuality in the oedipus complex. In: R. Britton, M. Feldman, & E. O. Shaugnessy (Eds.), *The Oedipus Complex Today* (pp. 83–101). London: Karnac.

Britton, R. (1998). Subjectivity, objectivity and triangular space. In: *Belief and Imagination.*(pp. 41–58). London: Routledge.

Cooper, A., & Lousada, J. (2005). *Borderline Welfare: Feeling and Fear of Feeling in Modern Welfare.* London: Karnac.

Farrier, A., Froggett, L., & Poursanidou, K. (2009 forthcoming). Offender-based restorative justice and poetry: reparation or wishful thinking? *Youth Justice.*

Foster, A., & Zagier Roberts, V. (1998). *Managing Mental Health in the Community: Chaos and Containment.* London: Routledge.

Fraser, N. (1995). From redistribution to recognition: dilemmas of justice in a post-socialist age. *New Left Review, 212:* 68–92.

Friere, P. (1921). *Pedagogy of the Oppressed.* R. Shaull (Trans.). Harmondsworth: Penguin, 1996.

Froggett, L. (2002). *Love, Hate and Welfare: Psychosocial Approaches to Policy and Practice.* Bristol: Policy Press.

Froggett, L. (2005). Social work, art and the politics of recognition. *Social Work and Social Science Review, 11*(3): 29–51.

Froggett, L. (2006). Thinking with the body: artistic perception and critical reflection. In: S. White, J. Fook, & S. Gardner (Eds.), *Critical Reflection in Health and Social Care* (pp. 89–106). Maidenhead: McGraw-Hill Education, Open University Press.

Froggett, L. (2007). Arts based learning in restorative youth justice: embodied, moral and aesthetic. *Journal of Social Work Practice, 21*(2): 347–359.

Froggett, L., Chamberlayne, P., Buckner, S., & Wengraf, T. (2005). *The Bromley by Bow Research and Evaluation Project: Integrated Practice, Focus on Older People.* Research Report, Preston: University of Central Lancashire.

Froggett, L., Farrier, A., & Poursanidou, K. (2007). Making sense of Tom: seeing the reparative in restorative justice. *Journal of Social Work Practice, 21*(1): 103–117.

Gadd, D., & Jefferson, T. (2007). *Psychological Criminology.* London: Sage.

Gilligan, C. (1982). *In a Different Voice.* Cambridge, MA: Harvard University Press.

Heuves, W. (2003). Young adolescents: development and treatment. In: V. Green (Ed.), *Emotional Development in Psychoanalysis, Attachment Theory and Neuroscience: Creating Connections* (pp. 183–202). Hove: Brunner-Routledge.

Hoggett, P. (1992). *Partisans in an Uncertain World: The Psychoanalysis of Engagement.* London: Free Association.

Hoggett, P. (2000). *Emotional Life and the Politics of Welfare*. Basingstoke: Macmillan.

Hoggett, P. (2008). Relational thinking and welfare practice. In: this volume (pp. 65–86). London: Karnac.

Honneth, A. (1995). *The Struggle for Recognition:The Moral Grammar of Social Conflicts*. Cambridge: Polity Press.

Lacan, J. (1979). *The Four Fundamental Concepts of Psychoanalysis*. J. A. Miller (Ed.), A. Sheridan (Trans.). London: Penguin.

Malloch, S. (1999). Mother and infants and communicaive musicality, in "Rhythms, musical narrative, and the origins of human communication", *Musicae Scientiae, special issue*: 13–28.

Sevenhuijsen, S. (1998). *Citizenship and The Ethics of Care: Feminist Considerations on Justice, Morality and Politics*. London: Routledge.

Trevarthen, C. (2003). Neuroscience and intrinsic psychodynamics: current knowledge and potential for therapy. In: J. Corrigall & H. Wilkinson (Eds.), *Revolutionary Connections: Psychotherapy and Neuroscience*. London: Karnac.

Tronto, J. (1994). *Moral Boundaries: A Political Argument for an Ethic of Care*. London: Routledge.

Winnicott, D. W. (1971). *Playing and Reality*. London: Routledge.

Young, I. M. (1996). Communication and the other: beyond deliberative democracy. In: S. Benhabib (Ed.), *Democracy and Difference* (pp. 00–00). Princeton, NJ: Princeton University Press.

Zehr, H., & Toews, B. (2004). Critical Issues in Restorative Justice, Criminal Justice Press, New York and Devon: Willan Publishing Regulation, Mentalization, and the Development of the Self, Karnac Books Ltd. Teaching and Learning as Inquiry. International Work Based Learning Conference, Northampton, March 2006.

CHAPTER SIX

Psycho-social research: relating self, identity, and otherness

Simon Clarke

I n this chapter, I explore the nature of psycho-social research, its origins, development, and its importance in contemporary social science research, in particular when applied to areas such as cultural identities and Otherness. There is something quite distinct about a psycho-social approach to social research; it is more an attitude, a position towards the subject of study rather than one methodology (see Clarke, 2006). Psycho-social research can be seen to be part of a group of methodologies that point towards a distinct position. These may entail the analysis of group dynamics, observation, or a detailed reading of the co-construction of the research environment between participants (we are all participants) and researchers. For me, and this is very much my own personal journey, the most important element of psycho-social research is that it does not reduce to either social or psychic; there is no duality, the two are so related they are inseparable, or at least we cannot talk about one without the other.

I start by looking at the origins of psycho-social research with particular reference to the construction of cultural identity; this, I feel, is exemplified in the work of the Frankfurt School and Frantz Fanon in what is known as critical theory. Critical theory, that early blend of sociology and Freudian psychoanalysis, for me forms the bedrock of what we now call psycho-social studies. I then go on to outline a psycho-social method that is based on Wendy Hollway and Tony Jefferson's pioneering work in the book *Doing Qualitative Research Differently* (2000) and that I have used and adapted in my own social research. Finally, to give an example of current psycho-social research, I discuss a research vignette applying method in practice.

Theoretical psycho-social research

The origins of my own interpretation of psycho-social research lie in the critical theory of the Frankfurt School, in which they attempt to marry sociology and Freudian psychoanalysis into a critical theory or social philosophy of society, societal phenomena, and identity construction. Horkheimer and Adorno's seminal book *Dialectic of Enlightenment* (1947) is a critique of positivism, of science, of Enlightenment ideals, and an exploration of the massive change in our relationship to nature. Horkheimer and Adorno interweave Freudian drive theory with Marxism and the Weberian notion of rationalization to explain the pathological nature of anti-Semitism. After Freud's thesis on civilization (1930a), Horkheimer and Adorno argue that civilization, the modern world, has slowly and methodically prohibited instinctual behaviour.

Anti-Semitism is based in what Horkheimer and Adorno describe as false projection, which is related to a repressed form of mimesis. In mimesis proper, we see an imitation of the natural environment—a mechanism of defence that enables camouflage and protection; we make ourselves like nature in order that we may become one with nature. False projection, conversely, tries to make the environment like us: we try to control and rationalize nature, projecting our own experiences and categories on to natural things and making that which is not natural, natural, through a reification of scientific categories and constructions. Inner and outer worlds are confused and perceived as hostile. Central to this argument is the Freudian notion of projection. The product of false projection is the stereotype, the transference of socially unpalatable thoughts from subject to object. Horkheimer and Adorno argue that the paranoiac cannot help or accept his or her own instincts. In doing so, he or she attacks others, experiencing his or her own aggression as that of the "other", a classic case of projection. The implications of this are twofold. First, the Jew or "other" reminds us of the peace and happiness that we cannot have. The persecuted minorities of Europe form a receptacle for those betrayed by modern society. We cannot have it, so we will eliminate or destroy it in an envious attack. Second, the "other" stands as a direct reminder, sometimes real but often imaginary, of our repressed longings to return to a pre-social state of nature, to return to our mimetic existence. To satisfy these socially banished instinctual needs, we accuse outgroups of behaving like animals, because we long to behave like animals. This should not be taken too literally: what Horkheimer and Adorno mean by this is that we yearn to act on impulse, on our instincts, without the constraints of rationalized modern society. It is, though, Horkheimer and Adorno argue, in this way that the Jew became the persecuted "other". The product of false projection, the stereotype is a product of evil, a product of the ego that has sunk into its own depths, lacking any form of self reflection. Self reflection is central to a psycho-social method and practice.

Horkheimer and Adorno's work on anti-Semitism contains a critique of capitalism, positivism, and scientific rationality on the one hand; on the other, it gives us a basis for the explanation of how we form our idea of self in relation to others, and our changing relationship to nature. It provides one of the first psycho-social accounts of racism by addressing both social structure and affect and, notably, if you take *Dialectic of Enlightenment* and *The Authoritarian Personality* (1950) together, then they provide both a theoretical and philosophical account of social conflict in tandem with empirical social research. (See Clarke, 2003, 2005 for a detailed reading of the work of the Frankfurt School.) This is one of the major threads we see developing in contemporary critical theory, although the emphasis for many theorists has moved away from psychoanalysis to more eclectic psychological ideas—for example, Bauman's (1989) "stranger". Other members of the school are also well known for their psychoanalytic contributions to sociology: Eric Fromm's *Escape from Freedom* (1941) and Herbert Marcuse's *Eros and Civilization* (1956) are among the classic texts of critical theory. It was perhaps Jurgen Habermas, more than any other social thinker, who revitalized the idea of using psychoanalysis as a form of social philosophy.

Habermas's book *Knowledge and Human Interests* (1968) is an attempt to analyse the connections between knowledge itself and the fundamental interests of the human species. It is also a critique of science as the dominant and only form of knowledge. It is Habermas's contention that systematic self reflection is the path to self knowledge; self knowledge helps us to free ourselves from ideological domination. Self reflection, therefore, leads to emancipation. The key to this is to think about a hermeneutic method in terms of reflection, which is why Habermas turns to psychoanalysis. Habermas's notions of the cognitive interests are discussed in depth elsewhere (see Held, 1980, How, 2003; Outhwaite, 1994). To try to explain them simply, all knowledge, for Habermas, is founded in cognitive interests. These interests are the basic interests of the human species and are the underlying modes through which reality is disclosed and acted upon. They delineate a general orientation that yields a viewpoint from which reality is constructed. Cognitive strategies are determined by the conditions and problems governing the reproduction of the human species. So, we have the technical interest with the according social sphere: the world of work. A practical interest embedded in the social domain of interaction and communication, and finally the emancipatory interest, which is connected to the world of power relations. The corresponding types of knowledge are empirico analytic, historico hermeneutic, and critical theory.

For Habermas, it is very much the idea of psychoanalysis as a hermeneutic interpretative science based in self reflection that lends itself as model for the mapping of the cognitive interests. Freud provided a model that reflected on its presuppositions and, after all, that is what critical theory is all about: critical sustained self reflection on our methods and practices. Habermas argues that, initially, psychoanalysis appears only as a special form of interpretation, but on closer inspection we can see that it involves a much deeper form of hermeneutics: in other words, a depth hermeneutics that addresses both conscious forces (as Dilthey's hermeneutics did) and unconscious or unknown memories that make up historical life. Habermas points to the method and role that psychoanalysis can play in uncovering distortions and meanings in everyday language, in linguistic expressions, and text. For Freud, as we know, the royal road to the unconscious was through dream analysis and, as Habermas notes, for Freud the dream was the "normal" model of pathological conditions. The dreamer awakes, but does not understand his or her own creation—the dream. Psychoanalysis goes beyond the hermeneutic because not only does it try to grasp the meaning of distorted text, but also the meaning of the text distortion itself. Transposing this to society, we can start to see a method for uncovering distorted communication and ideology. The emancipatory cognitive interest aims at the pursuit of reflection: "in the power of self-reflection, knowledge and interest are one" (Habermas, 1968, p. 314).

Therefore, for Habermas, freedom equals knowledge of the real processes underlying human consciousness and motivation. What makes us "unfree" is that we are driven by both internal and external forces that we are not aware of. Internal forces are covered by repression; external forces are masked by ideology. Self reflection can free us from both these internal and external constraints. In doing this, Habermas is trying to introduce us to a way in which a substantive rationality unclouded by ideology can be introduced back into the project of modernity. So, it is in these classic studies that we first see a marriage between sociological and psychoanalytic ideas, couched as either critical theory or critical sociological theory. I think we also see the development of a psycho-social perspective that takes into account both the internal and external forces that shape social life. In his later work, Habermas (1981) develops a theory of communicative action in which we see some notion of relationality in his notion of the ideal speech situation.

What we now term a psycho-social perspective can be seen in the ideas of the Frankfurt School, and, for me, in terms of identity construction in the work of a very different writer—Frantz Fanon. Fanon (1968), in his now widely read book *Black Skin, White Masks*, saw the construction of colonial black identity and oppression as the product of both a political economy of hatred and a psychodynamic of racism. Fanon was influenced by both Freudian and Sartrean existential ideas, in what he terms "psychoexistentialism". The main feature of Fanon's understanding of the psychology of oppression is that inferiority is the outcome a double process, both socio-historic and psychological: "If there is an inferiority complex, it is the outcome of a double process: primarily economic; subsequently, the internalisation, or better, the epidermalization of this inferiority" (*ibid.*, p. 13). There is, therefore, a link between the sociogenesis and psychogenesis of racism, and these processes are violent and exclusionary. When Sartre talks of anti-Semitism as a passion, it is not the Jewish person who produces the experience; rather, it is the (projected) identification of the Jew that produces the experience. Fanon illustrates this internalization of projection: "My body was given back to me sprawled out, distorted, recoloured, clad in mourning in that white winterday. The negro is an animal, the negro is bad, the negro is ugly" (*ibid.*, p. 113). If we apply a Kleinian lens to Fanon's thinking, and understand the reference to the breaking up bodies, to being sprawled out and distorted in terms of more than a mere metaphor, then these processes, which have consequences on the sociogenic level, are the outcome of processes of projective identification. The white person makes the black person in the image of their projections, literally forcing identity into another, as Fanon notes: ". . . the white man has woven me out of a thousand details . . . I was battered down with tom-toms, cannibalism, intellectual deficiency, fetishism, racial defects, slave ships . . ." (*ibid.*, p. 112).

The black person lives these projections, trapped in an imaginary that white people have constructed; trapped by both economic processes and by powerful projective mechanisms that both create and control the Other. This, of course, highlights the paradoxical nature of projective identification. White people's phantasies about black sexuality, about bodies and biology in general, are fears that centre on otherness, otherness that they themselves have created and brought into being. This is what Fanon means when he says that he was "battered down", "woven out of a thousand details": cultural identity is a stereotype of the black person constructed in the mind of the white person, and then forced back into the black person as the black historical subject (see Dalal, 2002; Macey, 2000). This indeed is a false consciousness. Fanon shows us, like Foucault (1967, 1977), how power is an important element in the constitution of our identities and how this is often an oppressive force.

Thus, these authors form the theoretical backdrop to my own psycho-social position, albeit one that is influenced by Kleinian thinking rather than the Freudian ideas of these earlier thinkers. For me, though, the most important thing about psycho-social studies is the emphasis on empirical research in which the emotional life of both researcher and respondent are explored. This enables, after Habermas, a critical and sustained self reflection on our methods and practice. So, for example, how are we to understand identity if we do not look at both the socio-structural determinants of a person's life and the way in which they impinge on the inner world of emotion and vice versa? After all, we live in a world where one person's fiction is another's fact; one person's rationality is another's irrationality. So, how do we "do" psycho-social research? There is a growing interest in mainstream research in the social sciences in work that has a psycho-social dimension; indeed, this is evident in the latest ESRC Identities and Social Action Programme, where a number of projects use psycho-social methods. The next section of this chapter introduces the reader to some of the basic methodological practices of psycho-social research and some of the challenges it issues to mainstream social science thinking.

Psycho-social method and practice

I think perhaps the idea of relationality is best seen and developed within psycho-social research methods, where the form of sustained self reflection advocated by the Frankfurt School leads to a critical examination of the relationship between researcher and researched. Although wide ranging inroads have been made into social science disciplines by psycho-social perspectives, this is a relatively new area of research. These inroads challenge masculinist notions of rationality structured not only in positivism, but in the social sciences in general, and can be seen as a relativist challenge to the duality of the researcher as the purveyor of all known knowledge. Thus, the emphasis is on the co-construction of data and the research environment. This can be seen by example in Hollway and Jefferson's (2000) work, which I discuss later in this section, in Frosh, Phoenix, and Pattman's (2002, 2003) work on young masculinities, and Walkerdine, Lucey, and Melody's *Growing up Girl* (2001). (See also Lucey, Melody, & Walkerdine, 2003.) More recently, Hoggett, Beedell, Jimenez, Mayo, and Miller (2006) use a psycho-social method to understand the nature of personal identifications, for example, class and gender, that underpin the commitment of welfare workers to their jobs, and in this volume Wendy Hollway looks at the process of becoming a mother in Tower Hamlets (with Anne Phoenix). Those involved in psycho-social research come from varying academic disciplines that include psychology, critical psychology, sociology, social policy, and political studies. In this next section, I want to outline a basic psycho-social research method before going on to talk about its application through a vignette or research story.

In a recent paper in *Qualitative Research* (Clarke, 2002) I suggested what a psycho-social research method for the social sciences would look like, using a small qualitative study of black students in higher education as an example. The method was largely built on Wendy Hollway and Tony Jefferson's psycho-social model in *Doing Qualitative Research Differently* (2000). Hollway and Jefferson argue that using a psycho-social perspective in research practice necessarily involves conceptualizing both researcher and respondent as co-producers of meanings. There is an emphasis in their work on the unconscious dynamics between researcher and researched and the use of free association through narrative interviews. Hollway and Jefferson (2000) use the "Free association narrative interview", which "can be summarised in terms of four principles, each designed to facilitate the production of the interviewee's meaning frame" (*ibid.*, p. 34). The first is to use *open-ended questions*. So, for example, in a recent research project on notions of home, identity, and the construction of "whiteness" in contemporary Britain (see Clarke & Garner, 2005), I would simply ask the respondent what the notion of "home" meant to them, rather than attempting to use a fairly closed and leading question, which may have evoked either a yes or no answer, or made the respondent feel that they had to think of a particular incident. This question was designed to get the respondent to talk about the meaning and quality of experience of notions of home, identity, and community; in other words, how it related to their life. The second principle of the biographical–interpretative method is that of *eliciting a story*. Again, a question such as "tell me something about your background" is more likely to elicit a story, a narrative, than, for example, "where were you born?" As Hollway and Jefferson note, story-telling shares many things in common with the psychoanalytic method of free association. This principle also allows the researcher to look at various forms of unconscious communication, of transference, counter-transference, and projective identifications that are present in the interview relationship. Why do people tell certain parts of certain stories? Why are they telling them? What form of response are they trying to elicit from the interviewer? It is often the case that the respondent will say at the end of an interview, "Did I give you the 'right' answers?"

The third principle is to try to *avoid using "why" questions*. Hollway and Jefferson note that this may seem counter-intuitive, as people's own explanations of their actions are useful in understanding them. The problem with a "why" question, however, is that you often get a sociological or clichéd answer. This is a more difficult area in fieldwork, because the "why" question tempts an explanation, something we are all looking for. If we ask why someone moved to a particular community, then a respondent will often couch answers in terms of school availability, transport links, or proximity to shops and services. These are all very important, but go no way in explaining what community means to the respondent. If, instead, we couch the question in terms of "how do you feel about living in this particular area?", then the response is more likely to be in the form of a story or narrative, where the respondent attaches meaning to experience.

The final principle is that of *using respondents' ordering and phrasing*. This involves careful listening in order to be able to ask follow-up questions using the respondent's own words and phrases without offering our own interpretations. As Hollway and Jefferson note, although appearing a relatively simple task, "it required discipline and practice to transform ourselves from a highly visible asker of questions, to the almost invisible, facilitating catalyst to their stories" (Hollway & Jefferson, 2000, p. 36). This does not imply the stance of an objective observer; rather, it means not imposing a structure on the narrative. If again I use the example of the recent research project that I have been working on, then we could summarize the psycho-social method in this way: this method uses biography and life history interviews (Chamberlayne, Bornat, & Wengraf, 2000; Hollway & Jefferson, 2000) to situate processes of *identification* within the subject's life history. These identifications include affective attachments to notions of community, nation, and belonging. This will uncover the more subtle psychological dynamics behind identity formation within the context of the in-depth interview. This method is both biographical and systematic, and, crucially, addresses the construction of the research environment and data by both researcher and respondent.

The interviews sought to uncover several ideas and themes around the construction of identity in relation to "otherness". These include the meaning of "home", entitlement, and belonging, and how these ideas relate to the idea of strangeness, nation, and class. In examining the individual's life history, the research team sought to provide systematic empirical evidence about contemporary identity practices and to develop an understanding of the processes of social identification, conflict, and cohesion. The interviews aimed to discover the social and dynamic processes that may link identity construction to privilege and hierarchy.

How reflexive do we need to be to understand the way in which we as researchers have influenced someone else's biographical narrative? This is a central question in the psycho-social method. There is no doubt that we bring our own baggage and agenda to the research interview, not least because we have outlined a fairly detailed account of how we will conduct the research and the questions we intend to address to a government-funded research council and feel obliged in many respects to stick to our promises. As Walkerdine, Lucey and Melody (2001) argue, "no matter how many methodological guarantees we try to put in place, the subjective always intrudes" (p. 84). But, as in all social research, it is unlikely that if we *really* listen to the respondent, indeed give the respondent a voice, we are likely to hear what we expected. Annie Stopford (2004) argues that it is important that researchers include, or give the chance to a respondent to be part of the interpretive process: "Whether or not they are cognisant of psychoanalysis, our participants may offer important challenges or additions to our interpretation and analysis. They may also concur with our analysis" (*ibid.*, p. 18). Stopford argues that whenever a respondent is excluded from the interpretive process for whatever reason, they will always be "other" and their narrative is appropriated for some purpose in which they have no say—no voice.

In the following vignette, written for the ESRC "Identities" psycho-social grouping, I try to demonstrate some of the strengths and weaknesses of a psycho-social approach to research and data analysis. In particular, I examine the complex psychodynamic between researcher and researched and the relationality in the interview environment. I emphasize in this vignette the problem with taking research transcripts at face value, and the way in which we can easily misrepresent the subject if we do not examine our own motivations, projections, and collusions. This is an ethical issue, something that Wendy Hollway takes up in Chapter Seven, where I feel we have a duty of care for the person who has trusted us with their thoughts, often on very contentious issues.

Vignette: two sides of Billy

Billy is one of the respondents that I interviewed several times for the project and it still feels as if he is with me now. It would not be difficult to portray Billy as not a very nice person, but there are many sides to Billy, and many reasons why he holds the views he does. My concern here is about the selective use of interview transcripts, about falling into the trap of not listening to our respondents and making our data fit our preconceived ideas and research questions; in other words, being too quick to judge. We need to know why Billy is the way he is, not just literally say that he is what we want him to appear as. What follows then, is what I term two sides of Billy; in other words, two readings of the interview and material collected.

Literal Billy

On the face of things it would seem that Billy hasn't got a lot going for him. He has a violent past and used to be a semi-professional wrestler, an amateur boxer, and worked as a heavy lifter in industry for many years. He is now retired through ill health and is in his sixties. His way of dealing with things tended to involve force or violence. He gave me several examples of this, which usually involved taking someone outside for "a chat", over the course of the interviews. He had problems with his neighbour for several years. The neighbour's dog had killed Billy's dog, and the neighbour mocked him about it (being mocked or called stupid was usually a catalyst for the violence that I will talk about later). So Billy

> took out my teeth, took off my glasses and bang bang, I went in . . . I made him squeal like a pig in front of the kids who all heard him . . . I just let him go then . . . For months and months the kids were saying hello piggy.

I was confused as to why Billy wanted to convey this impression of toughness to me; I felt both welcomed and intimidated by his presence. I had spent a lot of time with him, going through a rich life history interview using a free association method. I felt quite close to Billy, and when I read the second set of interview transcriptions a few months later I was shocked. The second set of interviews were made of more specific structured questions around British identity, immigration, Europe, and access to welfare, but this did not seem to be the Billy I knew or the interview I conducted. I remembered the emotional feeling around the interview, the anxiety and difficulty, but none of the substantive content.

There are two points to bear in mind here before I discuss some of Billy's responses to the structured interview. First, he felt very uncomfortable, found it difficult to answer the questions, and felt as if he was being tested. Second, I think some of these examples show how we can misrepresent the data and research subject. We started the interview by talking about the previous interview, which Billy had enjoyed; he told me about some of his achievements since I had last seen him and talked about his brother. When I asked some specific questions, Billy started to wander away from the point, but, of course, he was talking about what was important to him. I asked him, "What does being British mean to you?" His reply:

> A lot actually . . . To me, as a, I call meself, a learned historian. The British flag means a lot to me because as you know I study military things, but there again, I study German U-Boats, you see, so when you see a British flag, you look at it and feel a bit proud, I must admit.

Billy continued to tell me how proud he was about being British. I asked him if he thought there was something about the British character. Yes, he replied, it's about the history "it did", it's about British history:

> As I say, being a bit of a historian, maybe that's what it is, I don't know. As was put to me a few years ago, if you study German U-Boats, are you a Nazi? Pardon? You know, it's a complete difference . . . just because you search on German U-Boats, it doesn't mean to say you like Germans, does it?

I remember thinking during the interview—why does he always talk about U-Boats? We continued to talk about what pleased Billy about being British; we couched the questions in terms of positive experiences. Billy liked the food, didn't like the food in other countries, he couldn't buy fish and chips abroad, he would rather stay in England. We went on to talk about things that Billy felt more comfortable with—his childhood, his job, these were in relation to a question around whether he had ever felt like an outsider in his own community. Reading the transcript literally, Billy seemed not to answer questions and frequently go off at a tangent. This was interspersed with very opinionated statements around questions that he found difficult to answer. Billy was a tough guy who had an interest in German U-Boats and didn't particularly like anything foreign. It's hardly surprising that when I asked him about his thoughts on immigration and whether he was afraid of anything in British society he said the following:

> I can go into the question you're going to ask me later . . . I'm not prejudiced, I'm not prejudiced, I wouldn't say it, but I fear at what's coming on this country at the moment. Too many immigrants, they're letting them in, there's far too many, far too many, and obviously the more people you've got, the more quarrelling (?) you've got. I'm not blaming everything on them. Don't get me wrong.

> If they come to this country, I believe they should get rid of their religion. We don't go over there and practise their religion, or take our religion. Wrong again, we did do in the Crusades, we took it over, yeah, all right, but . . . if they want to come to this country, they should start learning, if they are born in this country, the way we live, not to be brought up the way they should be brought up in India or Pakistan or whatever. They're born in England, they're

English, nothing against that at all, but we're getting far too many in. What frightens me is they don't walk around in twos, they always walk around in fours and fives. You never see one on his own, four or five and I've always said, in a car, if there's three blokes in a car, there's a problem. One of them wants to show off, if there's four, two want to show off, so they get mouthy and they do this, that and the other. And it's the same with a lot of these immigrants.

I'm afraid because they're all coming in and we're taking a lot of asylum seekers and God knows what. The British people, I'm just speaking for British now, have lost a lot of things . . . because they're like some people, and always, what do you call, got a social security number or social service number, and they get away with murder. That's what I'm afraid of. Society is going to beat itself.

I'll let you make your own mind up about Billy's feelings on immigration. They seem to be based on some fear of the Other, or the unknown, and they are certainly forthright. Billy seems to slip between issues of immigration and ethnicity. He also seems unaware that when he talks of British people "speaking for the British now" that British people include many different ethnicities and cultural identities. These thoughts are reinforced on the following page of the transcript:

Q: What are your feelings about immigration into the country?

A: Too many.

Q: Have your thoughts changed over time?

A: Put it this way, be blunt, I've never liked coloureds, all my life, I don't know why. I've never liked them.

So, if we read the transcript literally and selectively, then we get one view of Billy that portrays him as a tough man, who doesn't like anything foreign, who could be viewed as a violent racist who has a fairly uncaring approach to others and life. In the next section of this vignette I want to discuss the Billy I knew from the first interview, the Billy that was presented in the free association interview, the Billy that was open and honest with his feelings and entrusted the researcher with them.

The other Billy

I feel that with a psycho-social approach we can get behind the reasons, the "why", of why people say what they do in interviews. I think also that this vignette is a good exercise in why the researcher must conduct all the interviews with a given person as well as do the data analysis. There has to be some continuity to enable a holistic view of the research material and to be able to recognize the co-construction of the data by researcher and researched. There also has to be a certain toleration of uncertainty, to let things go the way the respondent wants to take them. The Billy presented in the previous section was not the Billy I knew; I was shocked when I saw the transcripts, even though I'd conducted both interviews. I was shocked because I could see how someone could be portrayed in a very different light on paper if one is not careful and reflexive about methodological practice.

I liked Billy, I enjoyed interviewing him, and I felt privileged to be part of his life. The other side of Billy is that of a resilient person, someone who can overcome personal tragedy, who is willing to learn and try new things, and of someone who cares deeply about those close to him. Billy seemed to represent something about hope. The life history free association interview reveals many of the dynamics behind Billy's seemingly opinionated and uncaring statements in the structured interview. As I noted earlier, Billy had real problems with the questions in the structured interview, and felt uneasy about answering. He was far more at home in the first interview, where he talked lucidly about his life history for the first time. Indeed, he constantly tried to steer the structured interview back to the subjects he talked about in the first interview. I had to stop talking about immigration with him; he really didn't want to talk about it.

Billy's life history revealed that he was brought up in care, "in homes and boarding schools and God knows what" from the age of six. His father had hanged himself after being torpedoed several times by German U-Boats and losing a lung. Billy had no formal education and was illiterate when he left school. He didn't learn to read and write until he got married—his wife taught him and he also taught himself. He only saw his mother once when he was in care, and wasn't really sure it was his mother, but his brother said it was so he accepted it. He missed his brother and he told me he used to wet the bed because he needed his brother. He moved back in with his mother when he was fifteen and a half and stayed with her until he got married. His working life mainly revolved around heavy labouring. He did the same job for twenty-eight years, then took voluntary retirement. Billy was proud of his job and got a lot of his sense of self-esteem from it. He became a leading person in it and worked his way up, despite not being able to read and write. Because of illiteracy, tests have always been a source of anxiety for Billy, and he also found out recently he is dyslexic—"I do struggle sometimes, but I'm not afraid of it now." Billy found another job after taking voluntary retirement, but suffered a terrible accident while driving to work. He lost the use of one of his arms and suffered serious neurological injuries. He lost his memory, and as a result of the accident he has been unable to work again. Today, Billy cares for his disabled wife, is an active member of a community group, has completed a City and Guilds in computing and now helps to teach new students. He is constantly learning and open to new ideas. His dream is to go to the U-Boat pens in Germany and visit the war graves. His son (whom he never talked of) is supposed to be taking him this year. Despite all predictions from the doctors, he can now use his arm again.

If we go back to some of the issues raised in the first part of this vignette, then we can speculate about some of the reasons behind Billy's ideas and behaviours. It was noticeable that every time Billy talked about something violent, an incident or a feeling, it was always around the issue of his illiteracy, around feeling stupid, around being called stupid, or mocked, as he put it. Billy's obses- sion (his term) with U-Boats, which developed after his accident, seemed not just an extension of his propensity for violence, but more to do with his father, whom he still mourns and still wants to get to know. Billy's childhood in turmoil and uncertainty not only left him incredibly good at adapting to change and resilient in the face of redundancy and ill health, but also, on the other hand, resis- tant and fearful of change. I think this is reflected in his comments about immigrants. In the second interview, he is fearful of them, yet then goes on to say:

> But since I've joined this community thing we run here, I went
> up to a gym meeting with my grandchildren, now all at the gym
> meeting were coloured people, and I have never met such friendly

people in my life as a group. And I came away from there thinking, I enjoyed that. I'm not joking, my view changed overnight. I'll be honest. I wouldn't talk to a coloured man, I don't know why, something may have happened, I don't know, but when I went up there ... my attitude changed, completely changed; now I'll even give them a cup of tea or what, purely because maybe I was ignorant of the fact that they're the same as us. Colour of the skin don't mean ... (?), but I suppose before that, to me, it did.

Although I think Billy is getting confused between recent immigrants and minority ethnic groups, his tone has changed through his own experience. Although he does not like change, he is adaptable to change and learns through experience, something he has had to do because of his lack of formal education. His comments about immigration were constantly peppered with statements like "I'm talking blind because I don't know whether they do it or not"; "I don't know, I'm talking blind you see"; ". . . I wouldn't know. We don't have nothing to do with that. We can only go on what we are told or hearsay." Billy almost admitted that he didn't really know any thing about immigration: "You know, if you lived with them, then fine, you can put your rights and wrongs, but I'm only going on hearsay, people that's lived with them and whatever. There's a difference in that, isn't there . . ."

I think these statements are telling. I think by using the structured interview we pushed Billy into a corner, to talk about things he knew nothing about. I think he felt compelled to comment lest he appear ignorant, something he had been battling all his life. I feel this is a classic example of the researcher co-producing the data. I did not feel comfortable and nor did Billy, and I often colluded with him. Of course, rather than just a typed transcript of the interview, I had the experience of the interview in mind, the emotion, the body language, and the tensions. This has been lost in transcription; part of Billy has been lost in transcription, the identifications and projection do not appear and the very great trust that Billy offered me by inviting me into his life is unwritten.

Discussion and analysis

Thus far, I have tried to illustrate two different readings of the same material. The first a literal reading of the transcripts, the second a subjective reading of the interpretation of the interview and the co-construction of the data by myself and the respondent. The more I think about it, the more I am alarmed. What would happen if I didn't like Billy? I could have portrayed him as a racist bigot without trying to understand some of the underlying dynamics at play. The paradoxical nature of the semi-structured interview is also a problem. On the one hand we need to ask questions, on the other, we are in danger of pushing people into corners. Billy constantly moved away from questions and talked about things that were important to him.

In trying to theorize the dynamics of these interviews, I think it is useful to employ a Kleinian framework. In particular, to think about paranoid–schizoid and depressive functioning (Klein, 1946), processes of identification and projective identification, and the idealization of good objects. I think this holds both for researcher and researched, because in some sense this type of interview makes the researcher confront his or her own racism(s) through identification and countertransference. Why, for example, did I admire Billy and enjoy his company so much? Why did he want to convey this imago of toughness to me?

If we think about the two sides of Billy, then the literal Billy lives in the world of the paranoid–schizoid position. Things are either really good or really bad. Violence pervades this position and bad things are disposed of both metaphorically and, often, physically in Billy's case. Billy is proud to be British, British is good and we don't want anything alien contaminating our goodness, whether that be people, immigrants or that foreign food—fish and chips is best. A lot of this is based in phantasy; by his own admission Billy knew little about immigration or different ethnic groups, and his prejudice stems from a fear of difference and of the unknown. I wonder to what extent Billy's inability to deal with difference and uncertainty—the unknown—is to do with the loss of his parents, the death of his father and not being sure that his mother was really his mother. So, we keep it clear cut. Yes/no, black/white, them/us, good/bad. In the second interview, where we asked difficult questions about immigration, Billy felt cornered and resorted to the paranoid–schizoid defences I have detailed above. The other side of Billy, however, has much more of an air of the depressive position. It is possible to identify with a person who may have some distasteful views and violent ways, but is basically a good person who cares for his family. Billy actually gives us hope, as he has struggled through life and made the most of it; indeed, this is classic depressive functioning: "as good as it gets".

This is only half of the story, though. What gets "lost in transcription" with the account of literal Billy is the relationality between researcher and researched. I, too, bring my own paranoid–schizoid and depressive functioning to the research environment. In particular, my class position(s) that forms a strong identification with Billy's world (see Layton, 2004; Stopford, 2004). A further layer constrains the interview, in which I am aware of the original aims of the research project and feel a great deal of anxiety around "delivering the goods". This makes it difficult to be able to tolerate the uncertainty that a psycho-social method requires. I felt uncomfortable asking certain questions, which Billy then felt uncomfortable answering—we made each other uncomfortable. My own background as a bricklayer who went back to school and became "literate" again has very strong similarities to Billy's story. I found myself identifying with him, seeing myself in him and liking him: indeed, I became fascinated with Billy's story. Billy identified with the "learned" bricklayer: "I call myself a learned historian," he says. There is also an element of the gendered macho world of heavy work. Billy portrayed the impression of toughness to me as a form of identification, because he knew that I would unconsciously understand. I said at the start of this vignette that I was confused about why Billy conveyed this impression of toughness to me, but of course, on reflection, it was a basic point of identification between us. It was, in fact, where we both used to be, and in Billy's case violent feelings return when anyone challenges who he is—he is not stupid!

In some sense this is my PS–D functioning in relation to Billy. On the one hand I am identifying with Billy and projecting things into him, a feeling of a good, almost idealized object whom I strongly identify with, someone who symbolizes hope; someone I want to protect from misinterpretation and misrepresentation. On the other hand, however, I see a reparative Billy, someone who has learnt by experience and changed (like me?) for the better; someone who contains both good and bad, the ambivalent Billy in me. The problem, however, is that these positions often become confused. Because Billy offers hope there is a danger that he becomes an idealized good object and that his blatantly racist views are just whitewashed to preserve him in this state. Billy does not really initiate conversation or communication with other ethnic groups, and indeed is fearful of Others. While we can gain great insights through psycho-social interpretation, we also have to be mindful of the strong countertransference reaction that happens within certain situations.

In this vignette I have tried to demonstrate how we can have two readings of a transcript, one quite literal that will often take the research subject out of context, the other a detailed psycho-social reading by the researcher who conducted the interview and analysis. To add a further level of analysis, I have explored the researcher's own paranoid–schizoid and depressive functioning in relation to a strong identification with the respondent. I think this shows that without careful self reflection we can go too far the other way and start idealizing the subject, whitewashing their views and failing to recognize the relationality in the research situation. This could be just as bad as a literal reading, because, in the process of idealization, or at least preserving the good object, we fail to address the crux of the research. In this case, why Billy is the way he is.

Conclusion

In this chapter, I have described what really has been my own theoretical and practical path to psycho-social research and starting to think about relationality in the context of social science research. My own epistemological and methodological position has developed from an understanding of the early work of the Frankfurt School and later the work of Jurgen Habermas, whose avocation of sustained self reflection on our method and practice is central to a psycho-social position. Going beyond these early applications of Freud's work, I have tried to understand the making of cultural identities within a Kleinian psychoanalytic framework and, more recently, have applied a relational perspective to better understand the psychodynamics of social research. Certainly, from a sociological point of view, this is where psychoanalysis can add an immense quality of understanding and self reflection to the subjects of our research.

In the next chapter, Wendy Hollway discusses relational thinking in the context of her research into becoming a mother for the first time. Hollway understands subjectivity as an ongoing dialectic tension between intersubjectivity and individuality in relational life. Relationality, or unconscious intersubjectivity, is conceptualized as the earliest existential condition of human life, which coexists with bodily and related psychological experiences of the boundary between "me" and the rest of the world. Unconscious intersubjectivity continues throughout life; we learn, after Bion (1962), from experience, using other (than mother) containers for relational thinking dynamics. This container–contained model, argues Hollway, has profound implications for the process of discovery in research in that we use research methods that draw on our whole selves. In other words, we use our subjectivities as a research instrument. Thus, for Hollway, and I think the vignette in this chapter is good example of this, we have to be able to identify with those we research in order to understand their affective states, experiences, and meanings. At the same time, we have to be careful that we do not merge part of our "selves" with the Other. Methodologically, Hollway builds significantly on the free association method with a triangulation of interview, observation, and group analysis in which the researcher has to be able to tolerate uncertainty, relate ethically, and be aware of concern for the object. In this way, Hollway introduces us to the notion of reparative reason as an alternative condition for objectivity.

Acknowledgements

Many thanks to Wendy Hollway and Paul Hoggett for commenting on the vignette used in this chapter. The vignette was developed within the discussions of the ESRC "Identities" psycho-social group and the research was funded by an Economic and Social Research Council grant: RES-148–25–003.

References

Adorno, T., Frenkel-Brunswick, E., Levison, D. J., & Sandford, R. N. (1950). *The Authoritarian Personality*. New York: Harper and Row.

Bauman, Z. (1989). *Modernity and the Holocaust*. Cambridge: Polity Press.

Bion, W. R. (1962). *Learning From Experience*. London: Karnac.

Chamberlayne, P., Bornat, J., & Wengraf, T. (Eds.) (2000). *The Turn to Biographical Methods in Social Science*. London: Routledge.

Clarke, S. (2002). Learning from experience: psycho-social research methods in the social sciences. *Qualitative Research*, 2(2): 173–194.

Clarke, S. (2003). *Social Theory, Psychoanalysis and Racism*. London: Palgrave.

Clarke, S. (2005). *From Enlightenment to Risk: Social Theory and Contemporary Society*. London: Palgrave.

Clarke, S. (2006). Theory and practice: psychoanalytic sociology as psycho-social studies. *Sociology*, 40(6): 1153–1169.

Clarke, S., & Garner, S. (2005). Psychoanalysis, identity and asylum, *Psychoanalysis, Culture & Society*, 10(2):197–206.

Dalal, F. (2002). *Race, Colour and the Processes of Racialization: New Perspectives from Group Analysis, Psychoanalysis and Sociology*. New York: Brunner-Routledge.

Fanon, F. (1968). *Black Skin, White Masks*. London: MacGibbon & Kee.

Foucault, M. (1967). *Madness and Civilisation: A History of Insanity in the Age of Reason*. London: Routledge, 1995.

Foucault, M. (1977). *Discipline and Punish: The Birth of the Prison*. London: Penguin.

Freud, S. (1930a). *Civilization and its Discontents*. S.E.., 21: 59–145. London: Hogarth.

Fromm, E. (1941). *Escape From Freedom*. London: Routledge.

Frosh, S., Phoenix, A., & Pattman, R. (2002). *Young Masculinities: Understanding Boys in Contemporary Society*. London: Palgrave.

Frosh, S., Phoenix, A., & Pattman, R. (2003). Taking a stand: using psychoanalysis to explore the positioning of subjects in discourse. *British Journal of Social Psychology*, 42: 39–53.

Habermas, J. (1968). *Knowledge and Human Interests*. London: Heinemann.

Held, D. (1980). *Introduction to Critical Theory: Horkheimer to Habermas*. London: Polity Press.

Hoggett, P., Beedell, P., Jimenez, L., Mayo, M., & Miller, C. (2006). Identity, life history and commitment to welfare. *Journal of Social Policy*, 35(4): 689–704.

Hollway, W. & Jefferson, T. (2000). *Doing Qualitative Research Differently: Free Association, Narrative and the Interview Method*. London: Sage.

Horkheimer, M., & Adorno, T. (1947). *Dialectic of Enlightenment.* London: Continuum, 1994.

How, A. (2003). *Critical Theory.* London: Palgrave.

Layton, L. (2004). A fork in the royal road: on "defining" the unconscious and its stakes for social theory. *Psychoanalysis, Culture & Society, 9*(1): 33–51.

Lucey, H., Melody, J., & Walkerdine, V. (2003). Transitions to womanhood: developing a psychosocial perspective in one longitudinal study. *International Journal of Social Research Methodology, 6*(3): 279–284.

Macey, D. (2000). *Frantz Fanon: A Life.* London: Granta.

Marcuse, H. (1956). *Eros and Civilisation.* London: Routledge.

Outhwaite, W. (1994). *Habermas: A Critical Introduction.* London: Polity Press.

Stopford, A. (2004). Researching postcolonial subjectivities: the application of relational (postclassical) psychoanalysis methodology. *Critical Psychology, 10*: 13–35.

Walkerdine, V., Lucey, H., & Melody, J. (2001). *Growing Up Girl: Psychosocial Explorations of Gender and Class.* London: Palgrave.

CHAPTER SEVEN

The importance of relational thinking in the practice of psycho-social research: ontology, epistemology, methodology, and ethics

Wendy Hollway

Introduction

The object relations and relational psychoanalytic traditions can have a profound effect on the practices of social science research and, in the UK, this is taking place largely in the tradition that has come to be called "psycho-social". My own research practice has been moving in this direction for some time, and it has become evident to me that the use of psychoanalytic concepts that derive from the object relations and relational traditions have radical effects on every aspect of research. By every aspect, I refer first to the substantive analysis of phenomena that have social and psychological aspects (which surely includes most phenomena of interest to social science). I also refer to the trio of principles informing research that I refer to in the title of this chapter as ontology (how the person as subject of research is theorized), epistemology (how the status of the knowledge generation process is understood), and methodology (how these together inform how the researcher goes about finding out). Not in the title, but also implicated, is the subject of research ethics. After an outline of the project that I use as an illustration, subsequent sections of this chapter deal with ontology, epistemology, methodology, and research ethics.

The reason for calling this research "psycho-social", rather than just psychoanalytic, is to emphasize that the social and societal parts of analysis should be inextricable from the psychoanalytic. Whereas the relational turn has often emphasized just that—relationality (among people in both the external and internal worlds)—psycho-social research attempts also to situate this explicitly in the societal settings involved. Arguably, the object relations tradition has always been capable of casting light on social relations, while concentrating on how they get introjected and projected and the transformations that occur in the internal world.

In this chapter, I illustrate just how I have used concepts from relational and object relations psychoanalysis to inform one research project. It is about becoming a mother for the first time[1] and is part of a large research programme, funded by the British ESRC (Economic and Social Research Council), entitled "Identities and social action". The focus on understanding identities in the context of social action is a relevant context in which to use a psycho-social approach, and the mothering identity is perhaps the most relational of all identities, with intersubjective effects that ripple out into all other relationships and identities.

I explore two interrelated ways in which my current research project engages in relational thinking, largely through the work of Winnicott and Bion. First, I briefly outline my theoretical approach to maternal identity, drawing on relational thinking. Second, my main emphasis, I describe the research practices that follow and what I learn from them.

Becoming mothers: the research project in outline

We wanted to be sure to situate the new mothers that we studied in order to include the social and the "societal". (I am a member of a European network called the International Research group for PsychoSocietal Analysis, which uses "societal" to differentiate its focus from relational; the macro from the micro. Some prefer the term "social formation" to avoid the static and unitary implications of society and societal.) In terms of the sample, this was done in two ways. First, we drew all our mothers from one London borough, Tower Hamlets, which has high levels of deprivation and disadvantage, a history of accommodating waves of immigrants, and a recent surge of policy initiatives concerning children and families. The location of our participant sample in a single Borough, with the same local services on offer (including the same hospital in which babies were delivered), makes it possible for us to become familiar with the environment, including its history in relation to different ethnic and class groups represented in our sample. We expect the research to have relevance for professional maternity and child care services in Tower Hamlets, for example, in relation to the continuing effects of traumatic births, the contradictory professional handling of breast and bottle feeding information, and support.

Second, we aimed to reflect the ethnic and class mix of the borough as best we could with twenty mothers. Tower Hamlets is ethnically mixed, has a high percentage of Bangladeshi Muslim families, many now second or third generation, and a growing number of young professionals, largely white, living in the newly developed areas close to the City, the financial district of London. Because we wanted to conduct all our interviews without translation, we did not include any of the newly arrived groups, for example from Eastern Europe, whose first language was not English. Our research questions reflected the several theoretical frameworks that can inform an understanding of identity processes: we wanted to know about women's experience of becoming mothers, how dimensions of social difference such as ethnicity, religion, culture, age, and class affected their changing identities, and how they were positioned by expert discourses that were available through health and social services and media.

Methodology was a central focus in our research project. Identities have been largely studied in social science through word-based methods. We wanted also to learn about the embodied, unconscious, taken-for-granted and practical aspects of identity formation and change that an interview-based method might not unearth. The choice of these dimensions already indicated the theoretical resources we were drawing on in formulating our research questions, notably psychoanalytic. Specifically, we wanted to see if a method could illuminate what role is played by processes of identification in identity formation.

The fieldwork involves a combination of free association narra-tive interviews and psychoanalytically-informed observation. The combination of these methods was based on the principle that there are conscious aspects of identity that can be articulated verbally in an interview format, and other aspects that operate at less accessi-ble levels, for example, babies' influence on the emotional life and practices of their immediate carers.

With regard to the interviews, each of the twenty women is interviewed three times, first ante-natally, focusing on the story and meanings of the pregnancy as well as anticipations of birth and motherhood, and twice after her baby is born. The second interview takes place between four and six months after the baby's birth. It focuses on the birth, changes and issues since birth, and the moth-ers' evolving identities as their babies do more for themselves. The final interview is held around the baby's first birthday. The inter-view questions are designed to elicit experience-near accounts of specific life events in the sequence and wording of the interviewee, as unimpeded as possible by the structure of the interview agenda. The interview record (listened to as well as read in transcript form) is supplemented by reflexive field notes that record aspects of the research interaction which take place outside the recorded event. They also record the interviewers' subjective responses to the setting and the interview relationship, based on the principle of the value of using the researchers' subjectivities as instruments of understanding. The interviews are analysed using an interpretive methodology that pays attention to the "whole" narrative, to the meanings produced in the researcher–participant relationship, links between parts of the account, to conflicts and tensions within accounts, and the unsaid as well as what is said.

With regard to psychoanalytically-informed observation, trained observers visited six of the sample mothers once a week for one year, and observed them with their babies. This method is closely based on infant observation as it was developed by Esther Bick at the Tavistock clinic for training purposes (Bick, 1964; Briggs, 2002). It involved observers being in touch with their emotional experi-ences and using these, with the help of a weekly seminar group, to process what they observed and its significance. The observers use no mechanical recording device, but after the event write detailed descriptive notes in the tradition of baby observation (Miller, Rustin,

Rustin, & Shuttleworth, 1989; Rustin, 1997). Despite our attempts to select for diversity, the observer group was predominantly white (five out of six) and largely British (four out of six) and all middle-class, less ethnically diverse than our sample mothers. We were not aiming for social matching of researcher and participant (Gunaratnam, 2003), but wanted cultural heterogeneity that would provide diversity in the insights that the seminar group could bring to bear on the observation material.

A child psychotherapist,[2] also experienced in baby observation and developmental research, led a weekly observation seminar group (which included the researchers) to develop understanding of the observations based on their total subjective responses to the presented notes (Urwin, 2007). Notes of the observation seminars provided a further source of data, based on the preliminary and provisional impressions and building up over the year. This seminar also continued for a year. The resulting data illuminate the relational, embodied, and less conscious aspects of identity processes, as well as everyday, relational practices during the transition to motherhood.

In the rest of this chapter, I detail how a psycho-social approach, based on object relational principles informed the research in four key respects: ontology, epistemology, methodology, and ethics.

Ontology

What are the theoretical tenets about maternal subjectivity that informed this research? The understanding of identities in the context of settings, practices, relations, and biographies, as well as intrapsychic, intersubjective, and discursive processes, is the theoretical terrain for this work. By calling this psycho-social, we mean that it reduces to neither individual (internal, intrapsychic) nor social (external, discursive, structural, interpersonal) processes. A psycho-social approach (which draws on psychoanalytic paradigms of subjectivity at the same time as understanding the social construction and situating of identities) has the potential to transcend various troublesome binaries that abound in identity theory: natural–social, universal–particular, freely chosen–heavily regulated. In this context, I focus on the new mother's identity transition:

one in which she experiences herself as primarily responsible for a totally dependent and vulnerable new life, which she grew within herself. It is, therefore, supremely relational.

My approach to understanding subjectivity (Hollway, 2006) is as an ongoing dialectic based on the tension between intersubjectivity and individuality in relational life (and, therefore, in thinking and action). I draw on Thomas Ogden's idea of the analytic third as "a struggle with the complexity of the dialectic of individuality and intersubjectivity" (2001, p. 20). I have brought this out of the clinical situation and used it to think about subjectivity in dynamic movement as a result of the recurrent unconscious identification of the subject with another, which continuously creates a third intersubjective space that potentially transforms that subject. This works as a description of processes involved in moment-by-moment encounters. Identity transitions pose a question at the level of the life course, however: how the dynamic tensions between individuality and intersubjectivity dominate at different times of a person's life and in different circumstances and social positions. This addresses processes that are more solidified and that help define a sense of self. For a first-time mother, both micro-processes of unconscious intersubjectivity and the long-term identity transition none the less start with the relationship with a dependent and vulnerable infant and what is involved in caring for this new life. I developed my theoretical approach to maternal subjectivity through the problematic of the capacity to care (Hollway, 2006), starting with conceptualizing the care involved in mothering and working outwards and forwards in time to think about triangular and serial relationships in families (fathers and other carers and siblings), gender differences, friendship, self care, and caring across difference and distance.

Ogden said that his concept of the analytic third was indebted to Winnicott, specifically his idea that "there is no such thing as an infant", meaning that without maternal care there would be no infant. According to Winnicott (1958), the infant begins to organize a sense of self within the psyche–soma of its mother. This development of self is intersubjective: from early omnipotence to the capacity for concern and its expression through reparative action. The mother is ruthlessly used as an extension of itself. This is bound to change her. The baby's emerging sense of self is achieved in dynamic relation with mothers who—each according to her own idiom—will oscillate between identifications with her baby/her own infancy and experiences of herself as a subject in her own right. In the intersubjective space with her baby, she is confronted with the conflicts between ruthless use and care, omnipotence and reality, facing good and bad in the same object, tolerating frustrations, wanting to merge and needing to be separate, which have continuing and profound effects on her identity. The power of these effects can be partially explained by the way the baby's experiences chime with aspects of her own subjectivity, in which these conflicts, while not new, may remain and re-emerge shockingly in her intersubjective experience of her baby. Cathy Urwin sums this up as follows:

> Not only do babies by definition make mothers, but our assumption is that the strong emotional reactions stirred up in the mother by the baby, feelings of anxiety, euphoria, pleasure, entrapment, rivalry, loss, helplessness, terror of dependency, rage and so on, have to be housed and worked upon within the adult personality, and that the result contributes to a new sense of the self, or identity, as a partial consequence of finding a modus vivendi in relation to these feelings. From a psychoanalytic point of view, we assume that some of the intensity of the feeling results from the mother's identification with the baby, and his or her successful projection of emotional states into the mother . . . and that processes of the mother's own infancy, at a deep level, may be replayed in this process. [Urwin, 2006, p. 4]

The baby has little option but to depend on its mother (or other maternal figure) to hold itself together, and the resultant demands are likely to precipitate the mother into conflicts between her own needs and desires and those of her baby. The mothers in our sample expressed these in different ways, and they changed over the course of a year. They can be understood as being situated on a continuum. At one end, they could embrace being mothers with fervour, building up the attributes of being a certain kind of mother like an identity project, and, at the other end, being desperate to get their lives back, while feeling responsible, sometimes painfully so, for their babies' welfare. Their positions in relation to this continuum were not singular, however. It seemed that these extremes represented a conflict present in all the new mothers, even though the strength of the various feelings varied across the sample and over time.

I came to see the identity processes involved in becoming a mother as revealing a fundamental tension that is more opaque in other relational identities; that is, between the pleasures and frustrations on the one hand of putting oneself and the satisfaction of one's desires and ego needs at the centre of one's actions and, on the other hand, care for others based on identification with the needs and wishes of another or others. I summarized the challenge to maternal subjectivity as follows:

> The mother–infant relationship is paradigmatically characteristic of the dialectical relationship between individuality and intersubjectivity which characterises all post-infant subjectivity, but with a different accent. This is because the infantile experience of the intersubjective space shared with the mother is not expunged with the development of psychological separation and differentiation but coexists in dialectical tension with it. The demands of new babies . . . ensure that new mothers are challenged to re-experience the intersubjective state of her baby in an intensified way, in parallel with whatever state of differentiation she has achieved as an adult. At the same time this will involve identifying with her mother through the vestigial experience of her own infantile and child state. Thus the demands on the new mother call up a doubly intersubjective dynamic, from both sides of the mother–infant couple. The infant's self development will have to be paralleled by maternal development (Parker, 1995), involving recognition of its need to differentiate. All this adds up to a picture of maternal subjectivity as unique amongst adult subjectivities. [Hollway, 2006, p. 65]

It is possible that there will be systematic differences in how new mothers from different cultural groups experience this tension. Such an expectation is based on a sociological and social anthropological literature that sees Western societies as continuing to go through changes that lead to individualization, for example, in family forms and women's roles (Beck-Gernsheim, 1983). In terms of Tower Hamlets, we are looking to see if and how this is played out differently in the Bangladeshi mothers and the African mother in our sample, in contrast to the white and black British and other "Western" mothers, and if it varies with class. While the examples of some of our Bangladeshi mothers who live with extended families in cramped conditions suggest in some cases a lack of individuation (Woograsingh, 2007), in others this can encourage the kind of reserve that led another Bangladeshi mother to describe herself as "a very private person" even (or perhaps especially) within her husband's family, where she lived. Psychological boundaries cannot be read directly off social arrangements.

As part of a psycho-social perspective, it is helpful to use positioning theory (Skeggs, 1997) to analyse our data. It helps us to notice the multiple ways in which the women in our sample are repositioned when they become mothers for the first time. In their extended families they remain the daughters of their parents and the sisters of their siblings, but the new baby is now the "baby" of the family (displacing some who were youngest daughters). Many of them appear to get access to a new cluster of identifications with their own mothers. If we use this concept of identification together with positioning theory, it helps to go beyond the static character of post-structuralist theory of identity that has no account of internalization at all. We can infer the dynamic changes effected by intergenerational identifications. For example, Liyanna, a London-born Bangladeshi, at the second interview had ensured that she showed some family photos to the interviewer. One photo is of her mother with her older sister. She and her sister, whom she describes as having "always been pretty close", have a difficult relationship with their mother, who has been chronically depressed. She says:

It's this picture, it's so strange. [Baby cries.] I was showing it to my sister the other day, and I said to her that when I used to look at this before it was like "Oh, there's Mum and Amina" [her sister] . . . and you just sort of flick through it, you know, and I never really stopped to analyse it. But I said to her, since I've had Maryam, I look at that picture and I know exactly what my Mum was feeling when she was looking down at my sister. [Interviewer: Really?] 'Cos I know how I feel when I look down at her, and when I play with her, and it's just taken on a whole new meaning, you know, it's like there's my Mum and that's her first-born child, it's a little girl, same as me, you know, and I can just see the love and the emotion that she's feeling when she—when she—when that picture was taken.

There is a lot at stake here for Liyanna: the identification, made possible by herself becoming a mother, enables her to recognize that she was loved by her mother. In this case, Liyanna's identification as her mother's baby ("same as me") passes through her close older sister, to enable the parallel with her first-born daughter. Through this, she acquires an emotional understanding that was not accessible before she became a mother herself.

In the above analysis, positioning theory has been rendered psycho-social by the use of the concept of identification. It goes beyond identification as used in social theory, which usually refers to the process (untheorized) by which an individual identifies with a social group, to draw on the Kleinian tradition of psychoanalytic theory to emphasize processes of unconscious identification, introjective and projective. In object relations psychoanalysis, identification is a central concept because our relations to objects are understood as made possible by identifications. Conversely, it is by introjecting parts of objects, or, more precisely, our relationship to these, that the self is made up. This is how central introjective identification is to subjectivity. Projective identification, by contrast, can result in depletion of the self, because it involves ridding oneself of unwanted parts and lodging them outside in objects. However, Bion (1962, and see Hinshelwood, 1991) uses the concept of projective identification, which he bases on mother–infant unconscious intersubjectivity, to refer to normal, primitive processes of emotional communication. This is my basis for understanding relational thinking. It also forms the basis of how I understand the intersubjectivity at the core of all subjectivity—more or less overlaid by the separation processes involved in the development of a differentiated self (Hollway, 2006).

The claim that all subjectivity is underpinned by relationality (or intersubjectivity) attained through identifications with objects is complicated by a set of theoretical problems concerning the relatedness and defensiveness or otherwise of differentiated individuals (for example, see Layton, 2004 on defensive autonomy in young North American women) and the mergedness or otherwise of relationality. This issue remained mired in theoretical disagreement in the ethics of care literature that characterized the 1980s and early 1990s, starting with Carol Gilligan's *In a Different Voice* (1982). I have discussed this in detail elsewhere (Hollway, 2006, Chapter Two).

Here, I want to clarify the difference between the Kleinian concept of identification and that used less precisely to imply "over-identification". In the latter, identification assumes that, in order to identify with another, one has to feel their feelings (like empathy) and that this involves losing the boundaries between oneself and the other. In contrast, Hinshelwood defines identification as follows: "Identification concerns the relating to an object on the basis of perceived similarities with the ego". He goes on to comment that "The simple recognition of a similarity with some other external object that is recognised as having its own separate existence is a sophisticated achievement" (Hinshelwood, 1991, p. 319). Developmentally speaking, it involves recognizing the other (mother) as a whole object, and is a product of the same dynamics that enable differentiation from the mother. Liyanna's identification with her mother ("I know exactly what my Mum was feeling") perhaps illustrates that identification often falls in between these two ends of a continuum, perfect separation and total merger, and oscillates along it. Jessica Benjamin's problematic of identification with/across difference (1998) also reflects the fact that this is no mean achievement. This achievement is never full or final, however, more a question of merger and separation oscillating constantly to produce different kinds of knowing. This seems particularly evident in early motherhood.

Bion (1962) takes the mother–baby relationship as the prototype for unconscious intersubjective communication in his theory of the container–contained relationship and how it provides the capacity for thinking and learning by experience. The mother's capacity to receive, via projective identification, the states that the baby is incapable of processing itself, is a crucial resource for the development of the baby's self. She is faced with her baby's need for her to contain and metabolize or detoxify the projected anxieties and desires of the infant and return them in bearable form, having been able to do the thinking that the baby cannot do for itself. She is plunged back into an identification with the vulnerability of infancy and, at the same time, needs recourse to her differentiated subjectivity, which enables her to think about what her baby needs so as not to return the projection in an unmodified form. (Of course, depending on her own state of mind, this is not always possible.) It is possible, I think, to infer such relational dynamics from our data and thus begin to theorize the changes this requires in the new mother.

For example, Zelda, a white South African, is here described in an observation record as she goes in to see if her son, Tom (at three months old) is ready to wake from his daytime sleep:

> Tom is at first still but slowly begins to wake, wave his arms, lift his legs, and cry out, one single cry . . . Zelda talks gently to Tom as he wakes up and sits on the edge of the bed, waiting until he is ready, she strokes his tummy and his chin, talks and brings her face close to his, she kisses him. She strokes her fingers gently down his torso, asking him if he is ready yet to be awake. Tom doesn't seem sure, his eyes flicker open as he begins to wriggle and stretch and rub his face, but they quickly shut again. Zelda talks to him about not being sure . . . "Are you ready? Are you still sleepy?"
>
> Slowly Tom's eyes open more and he looks first towards the light of the window and then towards the cupboard, which is on the opposite side of the room from the window. His eyes seem to fix here and he looks intently. Zelda continues to talk to him, and he turns to look at her; fixing her with his gaze. She tickles him gently and strokes his mouth and chin, encouraging him to smile. He yawns several times but then smiles and is greeted by Zelda's warm delight. Zelda now picks him up, he wriggles slightly and seems uncertain, she holds him at her shoulder and he yawns and crashes into her and then cries out a weary irritable moan. Zelda asks him, "What is the trouble, are you still tired, perhaps you are not quite decided?" She rocks him gently and pats his back and he begins to smile and hold his head up and look around. "That's better," says Zelda, "now you feel better."

This fully awake mother is capable of identifying with the uncomfortable transition between sleeping and waking that she has come to know in her baby. She is therefore capable of attuning to the subtleties of his changing state. Yet, the boundary between her and Tom is clear: "Are you ready, are you still sleepy?"

In summary, identification is a valuable concept for conceptualizing the constant psychic traffic between psyche–somas (to use a phrase from Winnicott that does not split minds and bodies). Through this process, people have the capacity to identify with another person's affective states, experiences, and meanings. This is a core principle of my relational ontology. The use of Ogden's dialectical notion of the third tries to ensure that the ensuing subjectivity is understood to be in constant dynamic, and often conflictual, tension. In the following section, I discuss how it informs the epistemological principles on which the research is based.

Epistemology

Bion's concept of the container–contained relationship not only affords a powerful tool for understanding the tension and mobilization of intersubjectivity and individuality in new mothers, it also provides a radical foundation for a psycho-social research epistemology. We learn through identifications with objects. This is at the core of the idea that researchers can use their subjectivity as an instrument of knowing. Applied thus, it is not about mothers identifying with their babies, but about researchers identifying with the mothers and babies participating in the research. This can work at both levels mentioned earlier: the life–historical transferences involved, because we all have our infantile experiences that can be replayed, and the here and now relating to the material produced through identification with the experience conveyed emotionally by another person. Thinking in this paradigm is based in intersubjective, not intrapsychic, processes; moreover, it does not split the cognitive and affective (for Bion, the capacity to think depends on the processing of emotions). Bion's phrase "learning from experience" refers to this kind of thinking:

> The capacity to know through the process of learning from one's own experience is a function that has to be acquired and it comes about from introjecting an external object (mother) who can understand the infant's experiences for him and then gradually introduce him to himself. [Hinshelwood, 1991, p. 298]

The container–contained relation provides an explanation for the affective development of our capacity for thought and it does so, not from the perspective of a unitary rational subject, but through unconscious, intersubjective dynamics, initially in the relation of mother and infant, where the mother functions as a container and the baby's projections are contained. This kind of unconscious intersubjectivity continues throughout life as we learn to use other containers (and parts of ourselves) to help us to think. Links between the containing mind and its content are of three kinds: love, hate, and the wish to know (L, H, and K). The same goes for research (see below). The resulting principle is that we, as researchers, are exploring methods that draw on our whole selves —our subjectivities—as the research instrument. I understand these responses through the concept of identification.

To talk of using subjectivity as an instrument of knowing is to contest received ideas about objectivity. Although the possibility of objectivity in the positivist sense has been comprehensively dismantled, an understanding of what takes its place has become mired in the dualism of realism and relativism that underpins a similar binary between objectivity and subjectivity. I find the non-dualistic treatment of objectivity and subjectivity in the psychoanalytic literature helpful in conceptualizing subjectivity in a way that does not get mired in relativism. By objective, I mean, following Winnicott, when an object "is discovered to be beyond omnipotent control" (Phillips, 1988, p. 114), which is when it becomes "an object objectively perceived". This usage can accommodate the critique of objectivity enabled by the constructivist turn, which is widely recognized as establishing that reality is, none the less, always mediated through the constructions that are involved in comprehending it. Objectivity conceptualized thus can be pursued through the use of oneself (the researcher) as an instrument of subjective knowing.

Bion's understanding of the difference between learning from experience and needing to know is one example (1962). He is sceptical of the kinds of knowledge that are stripped of emotional experience, whose *raison d'être* is to substitute rigid control of the world that can be thought ($-K$) for the uncertainty of being open to new experiences through thinking ($+K$). In pursuing the goal of a kind of knowing stripped of affect, the protocols of positivist science when applied to the human sciences resemble "the aim of the lie" more than they resemble "the aim of the truth" (*ibid.*, p. 48). This description resembles Horkheimer's and Adorno's critique of "instrumental reason", which defines objects according to "how they may best be manipulated or controlled" (Alford, 1989, p. 139). Instrumental reason stems from a failure to transcend narcissistic omnipotence, so that it is pursued defensively through symbolic activity. According to Alford (*ibid.*), it robs the thinker of the possibility of "concern for the object qua object". The importance of concern here echoes that under discussion in the earlier section on ontology, where two forms of identification were distinguished: that which subsumes the object (in Winnicott's terms "pre-routh", prior to concern) and that which has concern for the object as a whole person. This kind of concern, which Alford links with "reparative" as opposed to "instrumental" reason, provides a way of thinking about an alternative condition for objectivity that is also the basis for a research ethics. In this mode, care or concern for the object will involve laying oneself open to the new experience and using the resources of one's mind as the instrument of learning, as free as possible of the defences against finding out something that could pose a threat to one's self and the beliefs that form a carapace around it. The poet Keats made a similar distinction in his notion of negative capability (which is actually very positive). As Keats saw it, there is an "irritable reaching after fact and reason" (letter to his brothers written in 1817), which, for negative capability, needs to be countered by tolerating uncertainty.

In summary, the psychoanalytic understanding of objectivity is helpful in recognizing that the objective use of subjectivity is a challenge involving knowing the difference between myself and the person or situation I am trying to understand. I have said that this is unlikely ever to be a complete achievement. Projective identification often refers to relational dynamics where this is not achieved, where it suits one or other party to lodge unwanted aspects of self in the other. Once this is recognized, it is possible to build safeguards into research to help awareness of these threats to objectivity, as I describe below in the section on ethics.

Methodology

So, how does one design a piece of empirical research on the identity processes involved in the first-time transition to being a mother that is based, ontologically and epistemologically, on the principles of psycho-social subjectivity, including the unconscious intersubjectivity of the baby–mother pair? The methodology must take into account this way of approaching identities both between the participants and in the research relationships. Relational thinking should inform the learning by experience of researchers, in ethics, data production, and data analysis. I am going to focus on data analysis.

I will not dwell on the interview method used in the "Becoming a mother" project—the Free Association Narrative Interview—since that has been documented elsewhere (Hollway & Jefferson, 2000). Suffice to say that it depends on eliciting the kind of experience-near accounts based on free associations, on the basis of which the subsequent interview questions and data analysis can suggest interpretations about the affective content and meaning of various parts of a person's narration. Its limitations inhere in the way that this method depends on an individual's narrative, based in language. This means that it may only partially bring out unconscious intersubjectivity, being most likely to miss how this works through embodied communication. We addressed this limitation in two ways. Our field notes around interviews became increasingly influenced by the genre of psychoanalytic observation, and these feed in to our analysis in important ways. For example, the researcher who interviewed Sylvia wrote in her field note after the second interview, "At the end of the first interview I felt quite bored, ready to leave. This time I am fascinated . . . I am keen for her to keep talking." Another member of the team, having listened to both the interviews in succession, noted how she warmed to Sylvia much more in the second interview. By discussing these responses in the group, we got some clues as to what kinds of dramatic changes were taking place in this new mother, which informed our further thinking about the data.

The second way was the use of the "infant observation" method, adapted for research purposes, alongside the interviewing to provide us with data that were not dependent on participants' accounts. Significantly, the form of learning that it offers the researchers and observers is based on the very same processes that it assumes to be the basis of mother–infant communication: projective identification. In terms of a clinical psychoanalytic methodology, we are therefore borrowing a data analytic method based initially on transference dynamics.

We have adapted the Esther Bick infant observation method as little as possible, which means an emphasis on the baby, on being in touch with emotional experience, and avoiding the move to judgement or theorizing, based inevitably on an adult viewpoint. This is the method in which our six observers and their group leader have been trained, one that allows observers and researchers to be, at least to some extent, in touch with infantile states of mind, as new mothers are faced with being. For example, although our research focus is mothers, not—as has traditionally been the case in the observation method—the infant or child, if the mother and baby are in different rooms, the observer sits with the baby (as in the original method). Because of the relational principle concerning the infant's and mother's intersubjectivity (described above), we proceed on the basis that we can learn about the mother by observing the baby (and of course, observing the baby with the mother). There are also often other family members around—notably the mother's partner and her mother and father and siblings. By observing their relationships with the mother and with the baby, we can ensure that the mother is multiply placed in her relational settings.

This attention to the setting is a part of what makes the method psycho-social, as opposed to relational–psychoanalytic. (Clinical relational psychoanalysts would perhaps point out that the setting of the clinical session is very well-defined and provides a strong frame in which to understand what takes place in the more general social context. In this light, perhaps 'psycho-social' simply refers to non-clinical settings; the kind that inevitably characterize research, as opposed to clinical, practice.) Observers can often observe the new mother as daughter, sibling, and wife/partner as well. Additionally, there is a fair bit of movement between homes in our sample: both white working-class and Bangladeshi women move between parents' (or parents-in-laws') home and a home they are often just in the process of establishing with their husband/partner or on their own with the baby. This aspect of the setting also brings out different aspects of their relation to the baby and their maternal identity. For example, the interviewer and the observer both first encountered Azra, a British-born Bangladeshi new mother, in her father's house, where she lived until after her baby was born. For several years previously she had been primarily responsible for the care of her nephew, while her older sister went to work. The house had the feel of a nursery, since Azra's father's new wife also had two young children and other grandchildren spent time there. There was a great deal of action and liveliness, in contrast to the fifteenth-floor flat to which she moved with her husband after the baby was born and where she was often alone with her baby. She frequently returned to her father's house and the observer often visited her there. Her behaviour came across very differently in these two locations, with implications for the consequent inferences that could be drawn about her changing identity as a new mother.

Observers take no notes in the session, but have been trained to write up notes afterwards. This method is based on detailed, often microscopic, observation of embodied relations (see Zelda and Tom, above), including those with the observer herself. Her aim is to defer analysis and privilege description. A valuable source of data is her own emotional responses to what she is observing and these are duly written down. Taking her turn with the other observers over a cycle of a few weeks, her notes are read out to the group, which met for ninety minutes weekly. After the notes are read, the group spends some time thinking about the emotional atmosphere that results: "This is one way of beginning to think about the emotional work that the baby is requiring the mother to do, in the sense described by Bion in his account of containment and the role of unconscious communication" (Urwin, 2006, p. 3). The group's task is likewise to use members' subjective responses to the case, which the group can reflect upon and help the metabolization of observers' experiences. Urwin points out (*ibid.*) that it is particularly useful to pay attention to shock as an emotional reaction to the material under discussion. Identifications with any or all of the participants who have been observed will be present in this material. The different identifications in the group provide a kind of triangulation and contribute to the analysis of the material. An example of the first is when the observer was wondering what the significance of the mother's home culture in West Africa was for Martina when her mother visited and wanted to take the baby back with her. In this case, group members could contribute their varying knowledges of that culture and together think about what the maternal grandmother's offer might signify in that context. An example of the second is when one observer, who was treated in very inconsistent and careless ways by the mother she was observing, "was able to process my hurt and angry feelings and to think about them as belonging to Azra who had no other way of communicating them. Azra lost her mother when she was fifteen and was denied the opportunity to work through some of her conflictual feelings towards her mother" (S. Layton, 2007, p. 260).

A different group member acts as *rapporteur* for each session that deals with a particular case. These notes are also read out at the beginning of the session when a particular mother and baby are next heard about, probably six weeks later. These notes "provide a record of the group's attempts to find meanings in the observation that go beyond the viewpoint of the singular observer noting alternative possibilities" (Urwin, 2006, p. 3). In this way, they help to validate, through a kind of triangulation, the emerging organization imposed on the data. Both sets of notes (individual observation and seminar discussion) constitute the data set for each observed mother. The three researchers attended most of these sessions, but absented themselves when the case was one of a mother they had interviewed. This is because the observation group did not wish to mix the data derived from the two methods until the seminars were concluded. The research team, who conducted between them all the interviews, chose, by contrast, to bring together the two sources of data, while remaining clear about which method produced which information.

The observation method was intended to enable us to see identities that are less the product of conscious, intentional production through narrative, more sensitive to affect, to unconscious intersubjectivity, and to embodied aspects of identity. This has broadly turned out to be the case. Two further aspects are striking, however. First is the way that the method captures the mundane practices (and the emotions that are inextricable from these) involved in the going on being of mother and baby over time. This is generally not what is expressed in words. Second, a weekly visit succeeds in recording the ups and downs involved in identity change processes. Becoming a mother involves conflictual dynamics that are not necessarily represented in words. The way that identity is understood is, not surprisingly therefore, more in line with psychoanalytic theory: recognizing of unconscious conflict, changing over time, and fluid and more embodied. Its concept of relationship is different (not two separate individuals interacting but two selves engaged unconsciously in communication, holding and transforming parts of each other). In summary, although this is a generalization that does not apply across all cases, this method was more likely to show us the emotional upheaval involved in becoming a mother.

The method also produced data that are richly descriptive, situated in space and time, particularly within the family, and, more broadly, in Tower Hamlets. I have already referred to the fact that several mothers moved a lot between the family home of their parents or parents-in-law and their own flat (either shared with their husband or occupied on their own). The change in settings—which would probably have been missed over the course of only three interviews in a year—was informative because we saw them situated differently as daughters, sisters, aunts, wives, at the same time as being new mothers.

Ethics and the use of subjectivity as an instrument of knowing

The quarrel about objectivity and subjectivity in research has always had an ethical dimension: what kinds of research methods of data production, data analysis, and interpretation are safe? Positivist science operationalized this question by concentrating on reliability and validity. Critics of psychoanalysis argue that the power relations that are inextricable from interpretation render its use for research unethical. In post-positivist circles, ethics of interpretation have been restricted to a social perspective: the power relations between researcher and researched and how to equalize them or minimize the power of the researcher. Despite widespread uptake of post-structuralist theory, power is almost always assumed to be negative and thus to be avoided, unlike in Foucault's idea of the positivity of power, which suggests that the beneficial and harmful effects of power are questions to assess empirically. I am bringing into qualitative empirical social science research two principles that are commonly regarded as unsafe: the use of researcher subjectivity and the use of interpretation (according to some, rendered all the more unsafe because it is outside the testing ground of the ongoing analytic relationship [Frosh & Emerson, 2005]).

Identification also provides a useful starting point for conceptualizing ethical relating, which should involve recognizing others for what they are (not for what you want or need them to be, or for how they might want to be recognized). As I have shown, psychoanalytic theorizing of identification problematizes how we can differentiate between ourselves and others in ways that enable us to identify with their experiences without confusing their situation with our own. In research ethics, this applies to how the researcher construes what she experiences and whether it is a fair and respectful way of knowing participants.

The following extract from an observation raises ethical questions. Azra had started to feed Zamir (who is ten weeks old) with his bottle.

There was a knock at the door and Azra put Zamir in his chair and followed her husband to see who had called. Zamir looked at his mother as she was retreating. I could hear someone talking to them. Zamir was sick and a distressed look came over his face and he began to cry. [I wanted Azra to return.] Azra returned and told me it was someone selling rugs. . . . Azra noticed that Zamir had been sick and said that he was naughty. She reached down and held on to one of Zamir's legs. She pulled his leg and he came out of the chair and his head went towards the floor. He hung upside down for a few seconds before she turned him the right way up and put him on her knee. He was moving about, his legs agitating back and forth and his body was writhing around. Azra said he is always moving about like this and she had to hold him firmly. She handled him a bit roughly. She wiped the sick from around his mouth two or three times and then removed his top. Azra tried to give him the bottle and he refused to take it [I found this painful to watch because she seemed to be forcing him to feed and he was struggling to prevent her]. She tried again, but this time by putting the teat at the corner of his mouth and at an angle to find a way of his accepting the teat. Zamir gyrated his body in protest. Azra tried again and Zamir cried. I commented on his having more to drink this week as I noticed the bottle was bigger. Azra said yes it was a 6oz bottle. I said that must be because he is getting bigger. Azra said that her Dad thinks that he is too small. She told me that her cousin has a really big boy of four months . . . Azra tried again to make Zamir, who was now clearly upset and distressed, feed. Azra stopped trying to feed him and sat him up and he calmed down and looked around the room. Azra tried again to feed him and he accepted the bottle.

The infant observation training method is based on a recognition that observers will powerfully identify with the vulnerability of the new baby (we have all been one) and that these emotions must be carefully managed on behalf of ensuring an ethical relationship to the family. Here, the observer is witnessing a distressing scene and she is not meant to intervene to try and change the mother's behaviour or make recommendations. However, she does make a more subtle intervention, which arguably has positive effects. By commenting on the larger size of the bottle, she elicits a story that conveys the pressure on Azra from her family to get Zamir to grow faster. Even before the story, she says something very helpful: "that must be because he is getting bigger". By witnessing the scene of the struggle with the bottle, by not getting agitated as Azra is, and by noticing the increase in the bottle size and Zamir's weight, the observer seems to be enabling Azra's anxiety to be processed by containing it. It is possible that this changes Azra's state of mind sufficiently to enable Zamir to feed, which he does soon after. This is an example of ethical relating in a research setting that goes beyond the formal ethics strictures of informed consent, doing no harm and not leaving a participant in an upset state (see also Hollway & Jefferson 2000, Chapter Five).

The sensitivity to her own emotional reaction to the baby's unhappy state, recorded in square brackets to differentiate it from the main focus of the observation, which is outward looking, indicates that she is remaining capable of processing her own discomfort, which will make her a more containing and more accurately recognizing presence, as her intervention demonstrates. This also enables subsequent data analysis to benefit by this processing and produce an understanding of Azra that is not blinded by unease into making inappropriate judgements about her mothering. Earlier, I gave an example of the seminar group's role in helping the observer process her difficult feelings about Azra. Urwin provides another example, this time of Zelda and Tom:

> The first observation had a powerful and subduing effect on the group; we felt shaken. The baby emerged as very still, frozen. Mother was describing a traumatic birth, but she appeared detached from the affect. The group discussed the impact on themselves and concluded that both baby and mother were still traumatised by the event. [Urwin, 2006]

The group provides a mental space for relational thinking that is containing and helps symbolization of these reactions. Group data analysis of interview material fulfils a similar function.

In recognizing that the (inevitable) use of researcher's subjectivity runs the risk of not achieving good enough objectivity (in the psychoanalytic sense), we have built three sets of safeguards into the research, all based on the relational principle that it is unprocessed, uncontained, intersubjective dynamics that are liable to compromise objective knowing of external reality. First, as I have already described, the observation seminar provides some shared thinking to help the group process elements of emotional experience generated in the observers (and shared by other group members on hearing the observation notes read aloud). The seminar notes provide a record of this process. Second, we are increasingly using a group form of data analysis because of how fruitful this has proven to be in generating insight that combines and goes beyond the understanding of individual researchers. Third, the research fellow—herself a mother living in Tower Hamlets—has access to a consultant who is trained as a psychotherapist, whom she can use in the manner of clinical supervision to support her in articulating and working through dilemmas, difficulties, and blind spots in relation to her potential identifications with the mothers and babies.

The relationship between interviewer or observer and participant (or the relationship, mediated by a transcript or a tape recording, between researcher and participant) can be conceptualized in terms of the containment and recognition provided (Hollway & Jefferson, 2000). The observation seminar goes further, however, to provide observers with a kind of supervisory and group containment for their experiences with mothering and family relationships. In this way, there is structured, formal support that is regular and reliable.

Conclusions

My purpose in this chapter has been to use the example of a research project on becoming a mother for the first time to illustrate how psycho-social principles can systematically inform the ontology, epistemology, methodology, design, and ethics of research. I have shown how psycho-social principles are defined in practice, drawing on object relations psychoanalysis alongside positioning theory and close attention to the wider social and societal setting, to understand the processes involved in identity transitions. At the time of writing, the fieldwork is only just complete, but it is clear that this paradigm has radical implications for social research. First, this approach is capable of delivering a different understanding of identities: less dualistic and taking account of emotions, their embodiment, and the effect of past experiences on present identity conflicts and change. Second, it can go beyond the binary of realism and relativism by working rigorously through the implications of the principle of using researcher subjectivity as an instrument of knowing. This involves putting into practice a different conceptu-alization of objectivity. Third, this use of subjectivity and the safe-guards put in place to help objective knowing illustrate an extended treatment of research ethics.

Notes

1. "Identities in process: becoming African Caribbean, Bangladeshi, and White mothers in Tower Hamlets". Wendy Hollway (PI), Ann Phoenix, Heather Elliott, and Cathy Urwin. ESRC-funded grant number RES 148-25-0058.
2. Dr Cathy Urwin acted in this role and led the observation side of the fieldwork, taking considerable responsibility for the transformation of this method from a training into a research method and from a focus on babies' development to one on the identity processes involved in becoming a mother.

References

Alford, F. (1989). *Melanie Klein and Critical Social Theory*. New Haven, CT: Yale University Press.
Beck-Gernsheim, E. (1983). From "living for others" to "a life of one's own". In: U. Beck & E. Beck-Gernsheim (Eds.), *Individualization* (pp. 54–84). London: Sage, 2002.
Benjamin, J. (1998). *Shadow of the Other: Intersubjectivity and Gender in Psychoanalysis*. New York: Routledge.

THE IMPORTANCE OF RELATIONAL THINKING 161

Bick, E. (1964). Notes on infant observation in psycho-analytic training, *International Journal of Psychoanalysis*, 45: 558–566.
Bion, W. R. (1962). *Learning From Experience*. London: Karnac.
Briggs, A. (Ed.) (2002). *Surviving Space: Papers on Infant Observation*. London: Karnac.
Frosh, S., & Emerson, P. (2005). Interpretation and over-interpretation: disputing the meaning of texts. *Qualitative Research*, 5: 307–324.
Gilligan, C. (1982). *In a Different Voice*. Cambridge, MA: Harvard University Press.
Gunaratnam, Y. (2003). *Researching "Race" and Ethnicity: Methods, Knowledge and Power*. London: Sage.
Hinshelwood, R. D. (1991). *Dictionary of Kleinian Thought*. London: Free Association.
Hollway, W. (2006). *The Capacity to Care: Gender and Ethical Subjectivity*. London: Routledge.
Hollway, W., & Jefferson, T. (2000). *Doing Qualitative Research Differently: Free Association, Narrative and the Interview Method*. London: Sage.
Layton, L. (2004). Relational no more. In: J. A. Winer, J. W. Anderson, & C. C. Kieffer (Eds.), *The Annual of Psychoanalysis, Volume XXXII, Psychoanalysis and Women*. Hillsdale, NJ: Analytic Press.
Layton, S. (2007). Left alone to hold the baby. *Infant Observation*, 10(3): 253–266.
Ogden, T. (2001). *Conversations at the Frontier of Dreaming*. Northvale, NJ: Jason Aronson.
Phillips, A. (1988). *Winnicott*. London: Fontana.
Rustin, M. R. (1997). What do we see in the nursery? Infant observation as laboratory work. *Infant Observation*, 1: 93–110.
Skeggs, B. (1997). *Formations of Class and Gender*. London: Sage.
Urwin, C. (2006). Changing identity in becoming a mother: infant observation as a research methodology. Unpublished paper, "Inner parents and actual parents", given at the annual conference of the European Society of Psychoanalytic Psychotherapy, Berlin, May.
Urwin, C. (2007). Doing infant observation differently? Researching the formation of mothering identities in an inner London borough. *Infant Observation*, 10(3): 239–252.
Winnicott, D. W. (1958). *Collected Papers. Through Paediatrics to Psychoanalysis*. London: Hogarth.
Woograsingh, S. (2007). A single flavour of motherhood: an emerging identity in a young Bangladeshi woman. *Infant Observation*, 10(3): 267–280.

CHAPTER EIGHT

How does a turn towards relational thinking influence consulting practice in organizations and groups?

Karen Izod

Enter . . .

I am writing this chapter as an attempt to convey the kind of thinking that goes on in me as I work with individuals, groups, and organizations in challenging situations. It is a contribution from consulting practice that links with pieces of theory that have found some resonance with how I conceptualize my role as an organizational consultant. It is also a practice that resonates with my inner and outer worlds, which babble away in me as I am involved in making sense of the experiences of my client systems, the tasks they are engaged in, and myself in relation to them.

I see this as an opportunity to stimulate an exploration of issues arising from relational thinking, as it applies to working in, or consulting with, groups and organizations. I will outline what I understand to be "the Relational Turn", and how I conceptualize it as a set of ideas that can address a capacity for negotiating the meaning and organization of relations while taking a position as an engaged individual.

Drawing on contributions from psychoanalysis, attachment theory and social theory, I outline some features that I consider to be core to working from a relational perspective. These include the capacity to expose and manage polarized tensions in group and organizational life, subject-to-subject relations, and the dynamics involved in recognizing "the other". I will illustrate how issues arising in my current consulting practice are shaped by working with relational concepts; in particular, for those individuals and organizations working with the challenges posed by risk, creativity, and orthodoxy.

The chapter is intended to contribute to the conceptual and practical range of consultancy interventions in the field of human process and human relations through the linking of theoretical strands. It should have specific relevance for those working in situations with multiple stakeholders, and in inter-group and inter-organizational partnerships and alliances.

Painting the backdrop . . .

Theories that have had major resonance in my work belong to times and contexts. They include a socio-political perspective arising from a 1970s training in social work, which optimistically emphasized the capacity to confront oppressive and exploitative systems. A 1980s Tavistock Clinic training in clinical social work and group relations emphasized an object-relations approach to individuals and groups through the theories of Klein (1976) and Bion (1961). Seemingly two ends of a spectrum, these two approaches were equally concerned with the liberating of the individual from either restrictive external or internal authorities. Consultancy training with the Tavistock Institute in the 1990s brought together a systems psychodynamics approach with organizational theories, emphasizing the relatedness between individuals and their working environments, and the dynamics of intervening in organizational systems.

Most recently, relational thinking has become one of those strands of theory that has been exciting to encounter, and that speaks to some of the consulting dilemmas that I faced. As an organizational consultant, I work with both organizations and in a number of project groups, partnerships, and alliances of varying degrees of permanence. Inter-agency and inter-sector alliances have become a preferred organizational structure for delivering public service agendas (see, for instance, the Crime and Disorder Act 1998, which sees partnership with communities as central to contemporary policing) and for creating knowledge that cannot exist or arise from one discipline alone, as in Child Protection. In the private sector, interrelations between business units are seen as a principal means by which value is created (Galbraith, 1995), for instance, the responsiveness between technological development and customer service in relation to corporate social responsibility. Inter-agency alliances are recognized as creating knowledge that leads to competitive advantage (Dyer & Singh, 1998), and indeed are often required in joint tendering proposals, for instance.

Yet, my experiences tell me that maintaining these organizational structures is hard work, that individuals and agencies find it difficult to sustain these partnerships over time, without recourse to contracts that lock in outputs and intellectual property. Finding ways of working together that can address the dynamics of collaboration, and manage difficult feelings and behaviours that arise (rivalry, envy, withholding, and so on), need both exploring and recognizing as entities with their own particular needs for governance. (Learning that emerged from the Tavistock Institute's conference, "The ties that bind: partnership and collaboration", October 2003, indicated that partnerships are rarely thought of as entities with their own needs for management, primarily because this has resource implications. See www.tavinstitute.org archive.)

At the same time, the issues that my client systems and I are currently exploring are indicating a tension between a need to stay close to one's central, or traditional, organizational task and identity and the need to innovate and bring about change. A university department struggles with attracting numbers: how might it improve the quality of its work by doing things better and more efficiently and how might it find entirely new, as yet un-thought of ways of conceptualizing vocational education? A multi-national company needs to maintain its brand sufficiently to attract and retain leading edge thinkers, but has to make huge strides in its business culture so as to continue to maintain market share. And, in group relations work itself, dilemmas occur around a need to work at the cutting edge of organizational dynamics, while maintaining a rigorous design and methodology.

These kinds of tension, between recognizing and making the most of what the organization is and does (the brand) and yet leaving space for change and growth, often erupt as crises and generate strategic conflicts in which individuals and departments can be pulled and pushed into polarities. Dynamics can swing between helplessness and withdrawal on one extreme, and over-activity and relentless optimism on the other. Departments that task themselves with making the best of what they have—legal and financial functions, for instance—and those who innovate, the creatives and research and development departments, often find such a "split" helpful. However, directorates and internal staff responsible for generating conditions for change, or who manage developmental agendas, tend to hold these polarities, either in small working groups, or as individuals. Not unusually they often ask for consultation on strategy formulation for their units or for individual coaching.

Working in the face of these structural and strategic dilemmas involves me in a consideration of positioning—that of working with the images of what one is engaged to do as an individual, and the images of the organization as to what it is there for, in relation to the range of tasks being undertaken. Both involve a recognition of how polarities can emerge, and how personal and organizational meaning has to be negotiated in order to create a sufficiently solid platform for work. Recognition of these multiple elements and appreciation of one's self and one's working group in relation to the other is central. In this sense, Mitchell's (1993) description of relational psychoanalysis as "involving a reclamation and revitalization" of a sense of self sets an inspiring tone.

Building the stage . . .

Relational thinking in psychoanalysis takes its place on a stage that, since the 1960s, is located in a movement away from modernity, with its emphasis on the ideals of the Enlightment, towards postmodernity as a way of thinking and being in the world. Modernity emphasizes a need for progress as rational, coherent, and linear, predicated on a notion of the autonomous and differentiated individual. Postmodernity, in contrast, acknowledges multiplicities—of meanings, of perspectives, of identities, and of experiences that are fragmented and temporary. (For further reading on the postmodern turn, see Best & Kellner, 1997; Loewenthal & Snell, 2003.)

These shifts over time, which can be experienced as existential tensions, challenge the notion of the scientific knowing observer, and allow for a more engaged, participative, and fallible stance. Behaviourally, this might be conveyed as an inclination towards, a blurring and merging, in contrast to a drawing away and separation from.

A relational approach to psychoanalysis has emerged predominantly in the USA, in the works of Stephen Mitchell (1988, 1993), Jessica Benjamin (1998), Lew Aron (1996), and their colleagues (see, for instance, contributors to *Psychoanalytic Dialogues: A Journal of Relational Perspectives*).

It represents a way of conceptualizing the individual as existing in, and having developed in, a social world, and offers a framework for therapy that speaks from an inter-subjective stance. Often described as a "two-person psychology", relational psychoanalytic theories recognize that the therapeutic alliance involves two individuals with two separate states of mind, who together can create meaning, and renegotiate meaning.

Its origins are associated with the British Independent Group of Psychoanalysts, and the works of Fairbairn (1958) and Winnicott (1992) in particular, as building on a socially orientated object-relations theory. Recent developments in the field of attachment theory continue to bring a social and interactive development of the self to bear, predicated upon mother–infant observations (Beebe & Lachmann, 1988; Stern, 1985), and developmental theory and clinical research (Fonagy, Gergely, Jurist, & Target, 2004). Huge developments in neuroscience and biology (Damasio, 1994) add to these perspectives in attachment theories; they provide a picture of how the infant brain develops in response to the help it has to regulate feelings through the comfort and mirroring of the parent (Diamond & Marrone, 2003; Gerhardt, 2004). All of these strengthen the notion of a social relationship in which the mood of the infant can be noticed, mirrored, and given words to. In other words, that regulation of affect and the patterns of behaviour that arise from how this is achieved, rely on some form of mutual feedback, a reciprocity, a negotiation, the one influencing and being influenced by the other.

These relational theories tend to be described in contrast to a "one-person psychology" arising from a Kleinian object-relations theory. Here, primacy is traditionally given to the state(s) of mind of the patient, as she is encountered and experienced by the therapist. With its concentration on the nature of the relationship between the mother and the infant and the development of part-object and whole-object relationships, the focus of analysis is upon the creation of an inner world, in relation to inner anxieties and fantasies, particularly those arising from a fear of annihilation, and the defensive structures that arise to manage or suppress them.

With such a focus on the inner world, the nature of lived experience between real babies and real parents in the contexts of families and communities is secondary. Symington (1986) suggests that the personal encounter is under-emphasized, so that all that is encompassed in the mother–baby relationship is impersonalized in the construct of mother as object. He considers that a Kleinian technique can lead the patient into experiencing the analyst as a part-object, tending to reinforce a paranoid–schizoid position. This has a significance, which I will return to, in thinking about approaches to consulting with groups in relation to difference.

"Multi-person" psychologies, the networks of familial, social, and cultural relationships that the individual inhabits, are most often associated with group analysis and the works of Foulkes (1990) and Elias (1998), and more recently Dalal (1998). Here a concept of a social unconscious is developed as both an automatic and learned means of social behaviour, and as an intricate weaving of the social—the "structure and the content of the psyche being profoundly informed by experience rather than inheritance" (*ibid.*). Elias's contribution from sociology prefigures the postmodern in indicating a distrust of static expression, boundaries, structures, and stratified systems as suggesting unchanged conditions, rather than a continuous flux of social life.

In the concept of relationship psychology, Stacey (2000) brings together elements of the social unconscious, and relational thinking, to understand behaviours in organizations as emergent and self-organizing. Decentring the individual, he emphasizes that relationship is the means through which individuals communicate and around which power relations form in complex adaptive systems.

What emerges from these different strands of relational theories as they help understand human and organizational process is that of a capacity for negotiating and renegotiating patterns of meaning and the organization of relations. This is how I conceptualize the core of the Relational Turn.

Act 1: the relational landscape, central considerations

I work out of a relational landscape, because it speaks to some issues of common sense and experience for me. I know that I work better when I am able to discuss and create things with others, and when there is a sense of fun and life in what I am doing, when I can be connected to my own sense of agency.

My conceptual ground makes a distinction that to work from a relational perspective is to work out of a different paradigm from that offered by the classic psychoanalytic and Kleinian positions. Significant differences arise from models that observe infants developing with internal structures created through intrapsychic phenomena, and those that develop through social interaction (Orbach, 1999). Corresponding differences arise in analytic styles that emphasize one or two person psychologies. The one maintains a separateness, something distinct and knowable informed by a grand narrative, the other involves inclusion, something blurred and ultimately emergent and unknowable. This is not to suggest immovable positions. Within these different schemas, huge variations of practice exist in relation to provisional structures and knowledge, and the meaning of the countertransference and enactment in particular (Ellman & Moskowitz, 1998; Izod, 2003).

At the same time, is the acknowledgement that working with relational theories as an organizational consultant goes hand in hand with a postmodern sensibility and contemporary constructs of organizations in which role, task, boundary, and authority are reconsidered, together with the dynamics and artefacts of power (Gertler & Izod, 2004; Hatch, 2006).

I want to outline now three strands from a relational approach.

The capacity to surface and manage tensions which present themselves as polarities

Perhaps not surprisingly, an approach that draws from a developmental perspective values a sense of space, and the creation and holding of a space as a means by which new learning can emerge, and in which affect can be moderated. Described in the psychoanalytic literature as the creation of the analytic third, it suggests a space in which it is possible for either subject to recognize the difference of the other (Benjamin, 1998), and provides a mode of containment for the interacting pair (Ogden, 1989). The analytic stance moves away from that of a distant and knowing observer, in relation to a fallible, unknowing object, to one that acknowledges that knowledge and fallibility have a place in each. In doing so, it implies a capacity to move between the either/or, and to hold them in tension as a complementarity. To use Benjamin's words, to move in and out of "entanglements", the emotional experiences that hold the mind to a position, and that limit options and the actions needed to realize them.

This space, which is both "in-between" and created by two subjectivities, becomes the unit of analysis, and as with system psychodynamics, becomes the field of engagement, the *what happens in the space between* inner and outer worlds, the individual and the group, the group and the institution. A central analytic element will be that of bringing to the surface what it is that entangles, that ties up individuals and groups to their orthodoxies, and their preferred patterns of relating. Holding a space for inner conversation, and actual dialogue has the capacity to create movement and to negotiate new positions from which to think. In doing so, the negotiation is not about trading, giving up an either for an or, but is about grasping something of the both as existing in a set of images and identities that create the platform for action. Being aware of this, both at a cognitive and insightful level, has been helpful for a director of planning who found herself separating out quality-of-life issues from performance metrics. With staff who divide around competing ways of working, and apportion different values to their activities, holding a mental space where both exist in relation to the other, and, indeed, where both can only progress in relation to the other, has provided a clearer base to work from.

Working with this concept of complementarity at a group level offers an alternative to Bion's (1961) basic assumptions and the notion of relinquishing or trading a part of the self in an anxious response to the task. Rather than suggest that an individual splits off their capacity for leadership, in a basic assumption dependency, for instance, behaviour might be thought of, instead, as a way in which the emotional life of the group has become entangled around issues of leadership and the anxiety of making choices. Consulting to this scenario might involve trying to open up the capacity to mediate positions, in the face of the emotions being activated or suppressed.

Subject-to-subject relations

A subject-to-subject relationship in organizational work requires some sense of what it means to be a subject, how one comes to be, think, and act in the world. This for me links to a political aware- ness, and a view of organizations as political entities, holding multi- ple views and perspectives that need to surface and be worked out in the context of the enterprise itself, and the power relations that are inherent.

McAfee (2000), writing on links between subjectivity and citi- zenship, makes a comparison between the experiences of a political subjectivity in the ancient Greek city-state, or *polis*, with that of a modern, post-Cartesian view. She equates a modern position of an individual as having a unique core being and a substantial endur- ing sense of self with political models that divide interests and that are inevitably conflictual and competitive. This is in contrast to the Aristotelian view, with the city-state functioning as a whole entity; the needs of the city inseparable from the thoughts and actions of the individual, and where to be an individual (if this is indeed feasi- ble) is to be political, public, and co-operative.

This is not to suggest an absence of conflict, or to deny that different social identities with different, and possibly totaliz- ing, social ambitions pertained. Rather that there is a co-creation between individuals and societies, working towards shared values. Being political connotes acting in the general interest, being open to deliberation, and to voices from the margins. Of course, decisions have to be made, and in this schema decision-making is essentially rational, but the interest here is that of the holding of difference in the moment before decision, rather than the competition of preformed ideas.

I mention this not to enter the debate about the primacy of either individual or society (Dalal, 1998; Stacey, 2000), but more to link with these different political frameworks as to how one thinks and acts in the world: the tension between politics as a set of opposi- tional power relations arising from the self-interests of a liberal individual, and politics as a deliberative process, where power is located with others, rather than between others.

This modern, self-interested individual embodies a notion of autonomy, something that is to be strived for, in ways that liberate from both internal and external oppressors. Group relations, when it is conceptualized within a modern paradigm, links with this notion through an emphasis on the movement of the individual from dependency to autonomy (Miller, 1993) with an increasingly personal and organizational authority.

In contrast is a postmodern notion of the self, which arises as more fluid and provisional rather than enduring. Kristeva (1984) proposes the subject as an open system, a subject in process, which is entirely social and contextual, and where the self is an assembly of heterogeneous parts. Subjects in process are those who need others in order to know and act in the world, who are open to ideas and vulnerable to their implications. This implies a concept of open systems (Miller & Rice, 1967) as one that has both active and passive complementarities, emphasizing the active in the transfor- mational as much as the passive in the process of conversion.

Organizational change, whether it is planned or not, interrupts this ability to know and act in the world; power relations shift, and new patterns of relating in the organization are constructed. An example follows.

Against the background of a merger, I recently consulted to two indi- viduals whose working relationship was conflictual to the extent that a grievance procedure had been initiated by one against the other. It was possible to negotiate a consulting role that was less to do with a reso- lution of the conflict, and more to create conditions for dialogue by which the working relationship might be reinstated. Consulting in this scenario focused upon exploring how the relationship breakdown had arisen from situations in which both participants had different percep- tions of their encounters, and consequently how misinterpreted and misunderstood they felt their actions to be. Involving myself as a stakeholder in their conflict, with feelings and views that came both from my experience of being with them and from my own inner response to their conflict, it was possible to acknowledge that there was no truth, or one version of reality, through which one might triumph and the other accede. The learning, rather, was one of being able to acknowledge that different realities could pertain, and could be held in a complementarity, allowing for a renegotiation of relations between them.

What might this shift involve for these individuals? Again, it is important to stress that this renegotiation is not a trading, is not giving up one angry and hurt experience for another, and therefore does not imply reciprocity. More, it illustrates an extent to which these individuals are able to be open to new possibility, to be subjects in process. An intervention like this is itself fluid, and unlikely to be sustained in the face of continuing environmental conditions that give rise to conflict. In such a merger, a transitional relatedness might need to be encouraged through symbols and metaphors, such as the creation of new logos and other artefacts through which connections can be made, before the detail of how to work together in new structures can be agreed (Cartright, 2000).

The dynamics involved in recognition of the "other"

The example above, of conflict arising out of the experience of a merger, requires a capacity to appreciate the other (individual and organization) as being outside the self, and in relatedness to one's self. This is not only as a subject who can evoke one's own emotions and coping patterns, or internal working models (Bowlby, 1969), but also as a subject with his own desires and coping patterns.

Internal working models, or patterns of interactions that become generalized, to use Stern's (1985) language, arise in relation to an attachment to a parental figure, founded on the need to form close affectional bonds. Unable to relieve his own disorganization, the infant finds his emotional ups and downs understood and responded to in a constant interplay with his parent (Fonagy, 1999). Based on sensitive interactions, in which the infant's mood is noticed and responded to, the infant reaches a state of organization where emotions can be stabilized or regulated. Where these inter-actions are more intrusive, or less attentive, then a different kind of negotiation occurs. Responses to stressful situations become more disorganized, and the infant's ability to regulate his emotions is impaired.

At the same time, the infant is developing his sense of self as thinking and feeling, and interactions with the parent provide a mirroring or reflection of the infant's states of mind in actual and symbolic exchanges. Being held in mind by the parent as a thinking and feeling being allows for the internalization of these representations of the self, and of the other, in a way that will lead to establishing a reflective part of the self. This forms the basis of intentionality that can ultimately lead to action (Fonagy & Target, 1998).

In consulting to processes occurring between the individual and the group, group dynamics can relate to how this capacity to recognize otherness plays out, and what conditions might be needed to support that recognition. I see this as linked to processes of identification, an ability to see one's self in the other, and mirrored by the other, while recognizing that the other exists with their own capacities and needs for identification. Without this process of connection, experiences of working together can become isolating and alienating. Finding a level of recognition inevitably means encountering difference, which in turn will necessitate a negotiation of relations, of who, or what one can be for the other (Pizer, 1992).

Part of this negotiation will be that of working with one's own, and the group's, patterns of response to difference. One tendency is that of incorporation (Benjamin, 1998), to minimize, and in extreme, to consume and obliterate. Group relations' work powerfully illuminates the way social identities and viewpoints become invisible, denying citizenship or subjectivity in silent voices. In contrast is the tendency to keep difference at arm's length, to an extent that any cathexis, or emotional involvement, is impossible, and the potential for meaning and multiplicity of meaning is lost. This tends to a more disinterested, even nihilistic, position where connection is interrupted and the capacity to influence through relatedness breaks down. The task for the consultant here is to recognize her own proclivities towards either of these tendencies and to attempt to hold them in tension. Consequently, a feature of organizational consulting from this position is to find ways for silent voices to have a platform, and to minimize isolation through opportunity for interaction between individuals and groups.

Recent work to look at the nature of shared leadership between managerial and political leaders in local government (Aram,

Abraham, Hadjivassiliou, & Izod, 2006) showed just this tendency to blur and minimize difference. These relationships encompass different power bases for work, through election or appointment, and in the face of these differences we often saw seemingly united and cordial leaderships that diminished the political cut and thrust. At the same time, this paired leadership tended to co-create an "other" in the mind, i.e., the electorate, a central government department, against whom they could position themselves in terms of power differentials. From a classic psychoanalytic perspective, this might be seen as a split-off part of the pairing that had to be projected into an "object" other. However, thinking about this relationally, we might suppose that these leadership pairs were so far unable to face the interdependent nature of their relationships and how they might continually (re)negotiate the inherent power in both their positions.

Intermission . . .

Bringing relational thinking to the context of organizational life seems to me to speak of how constant change provides a challenge to continuity and to any sense of self as an enduring, autonomous, and knowing being. This position exists alongside experiences that are inevitably temporary, and where any continuity of meaning is rare. Grasping meaning, which is then partial, can be experienced as a constant series of bursting bubbles, against which one has to face loss, amd adjust and reposition. In the face of such emotional tasks, creating new meanings and new connections can be to encounter significant risk. Preferred ways of doing things can take on the flavour of orthodoxy, gathering up all the boundary or regulatory elements of the organization to keep things as they are. In contrast, innovation can appear boundaryless and unregulated, and working in this domain can create an agony of not knowing how and where to focus attention. Consulting in these situations is often a question of keeping these elements in tension, until a point of desire can be identified, which might then leverage structures and processes to create better conditions for change. Organizational development interventions that encourage boundary spanning and the linking of key people and functions at critical moments can provide such leverage often, bringing a quick shift in regulatory behaviours in favour of risk-taking and innovation.

Act 2: the relational landscape and groups

I want to turn my attention now to the understanding of process as it might be worked with in educational and consultative interventions. Working at interfaces of individuals, groups, and organizations is to be involved in the way individuals who work together are able to construct sufficient meaning from their experiences and manage sufficient of the feelings involved to be purposeful. It involves a capacity to recognize who one is and what one is there to do, along with identifying assets and resources and generating knowledge and skill to undertake the tasks required. All this is within an environmental context in which boundaries, to varying degrees of permeability, will exist.

Process attends to connections at interfaces between individuals and working groups that are related, through task, for a period of time, together with the felt and observed dynamics that occur in the behaviour between them. The concept of relatedness comes in here as a central focus for study, as one of mutually created imagery and enacted behaviours between individuals and groups as particular subjectivities. It becomes a concept of activity, attending to patterns of personal and group engagement in the work, within its organizational and social context.

These activities link with the concepts of representation and regulation, which I have outlined earlier. With a primary need to find some connection, dynamics occurring in groups can both support and interrupt one's sense of self, evoking feelings that need testing out for their applicability and relevance, either internally or in dialogue with others. An activity for the individual, then, is to find ways to manage these interruptions to the self, and to find some recognition for these processes in relation to others. This is a transitional representational space, where images and metaphors and play can create the material for reflection.

At the same time, the individual is working to regulate her emotions in a process of negotiation with herself and others so as to find ways of keeping on an even keel. The group is working in ways that either relieve or accentuate those emotions through its management of difference. These might be at the political level of holding difference as complementarities, or in adversarial ways that place ideas and identities in competition.

I am suggesting the term "governance" as a way of thinking about how the group as a whole manages these dynamics in relation to itself and other groups. By this, I am thinking of how patterns of interactions emerge over time, in ways which support or limit opportunities, and which are unconscious. Examples might include the way task groups can be exceptionally busy, but not achieve any significant outputs, or how a group might appoint a leader, but withhold authority. Tensions will exist in relation to how the group can govern itself and deal with very real disruptions to the task and to expected behaviours, or with the necessity to create additional authority through the use of contract or external regulation.

These elements, task, representation, regulation, and governance, form a backcloth against which process might be illuminated and understood. An attempt to formulate this is outlined in Table 1.

The consultancy stance

Making sense of these processes and their accompanying emotions and behaviours is a task for both participants in groups and consultants working in and with them. I realize that I have not so far given much attention to emotions and the irrational. So I want to describe a group that I worked with briefly in a group relations event that was consumed with competition.

The group, at the time that I joined it, had returned from a meeting with another group, where the members had been seen as withholding and unwilling to share their experiences, and they were preparing for their next encounter. Their own desires for the forthcoming meeting were unformulated, and the mood was one of indignation and disbelief. Comments in the room about how to behave in any forthcoming meeting used words like *go get . . .em*, *let's trip them up*, and showed an intention to be devious and disruptive. I repeated these words back to them, asking if this was the perception of themselves that they wanted to perpetuate. They realized then that a wish they had shared as a group, but not spoken, was

Table 1. A framework for conceptualizing groups from a relational perspective.

Task	Process	Representation	Regulation	Governance
To work together to find, share, and create meaning with others	Relates to task, representation, regulation, and governance	Tests emotional states for applicability, relevance, or modification	How does the group relieve or accentuate the individual's early patterns of relating?	Indicates patterns of interactions that become generalized
Involves recognition of desires and creating actions to fulfil them	Relates to developmental attributes and deficits of the group emerging over time	Attempts to find connections to mediate between temporary and enduring sense of self	How does the group manage patterns of response to identifications—bridging/blurring?	Supports or limits opportunities for surfacing desires and agency
Involves recognition of collective assets, knowledge and capabilities	Involves exploration of the ways that interests intersect	Relates to recognition of self/other dynamics	What are the approaches to difference—holding complementarities, adversarial either/or?	Mediates between internal self-governing and external authorities
Involves a relatedness to the broader environment	Might need supporting through symbols or play	Creates images, metaphors as the material for reflection	How does the group actualize its desires in relation to boundaries and governance?	Seen in shared or dispersed ownerships

that they were primarily interested in what they could learn of themselves in the behaviours of the other group towards them. In other words, they had objectified the group as existing only for their benefit, rather than as a group with its own needs and desires. It seemed likely that this was in the absence of finding sufficient connection with each other in the face of their own competitiveness, and being unable, at that time, to explore their own assets. A shift was enabled whereby the group could give its own previously withheld authority to their leader to bring about a more generous kind of interchange, both between themselves and with their "rival" group.

It seems to me that the way individuals managed their emotional states about performing well in this event created an unconscious pattern of interaction characterized in withholding, both internally in the group and in their external relations. This had manifested in the appointment of a leader who was not given authority. The desires of individual members, which might have the capacity to create connections, had been lost in a style of governance that was limited to asking questions of each other. I was also able to recognize that the way I framed my responses to the group conveyed that I found their intentions devious and might wish for a more collaborative response.

To work as a consultant who is engaged in the process is primarily to acknowledge oneself as a stakeholder in the system, and to allow oneself a voice and a position to speak from. With an emphasis on working with complementarities, rather than polarities, the role of the consultant is more on filtering, framing, rendering the subjective into something more tangible, to use Weick's sensemaking language (1995). This is in contrast to an interpretive mode, particularly from the Kleinian position I touched on earlier, which has the capacity to objectify difference and concentrate attention on the tensions between splits (Symington, 1986). The unconscious here can then be seen as relating to developmental deficits that arise from actual lived relations at interfaces, rather than arising from internal structural conflicts.

Ending . . .

I have been attempting to describe how strands of relational theory link with my practice as a consultant, in thinking about the way theory helps to shape organizational interventions and in providing a framework for understanding group process.

I am often asked what a group relations event might look like from a relational perspective. Some of these ideas, in particular an approach to group relations conceptualized as collaborative enquiry and advocating a more visible, self-disclosing consultancy stance, are outlined elsewhere (Gertler & Izod, 2004).

At another level, relational thinking has been seeping into practice through a number of channels. It is not unusual to hear talk of behaviours linked to developmental tasks in groups, or to challenge the expectation that staff teams are infallible when they have so little time to form and generate a *modus operandi*. All interactions are social, convey meaning, and require capacities to negotiate, whether this is explicit or not.

However, the door is open for innovation. Ideas emanating from citizen subjects, which I have touched on in terms of the communitarianism of the polis, and the holding of political debate as complementarities, lend themselves to development in conceptualizing the large group, where examining core/periphery and polycentric relations with voices from the margins continues to be an important element.

I will, though, describe a piece of work that a colleague and I are planning (an event that is a collaborative enterprise between Anjet van Linge and Karen Izod, undertaken through the auspices of the Tavistock Institute's Advanced Organisational Consultation Society), which will bring together some of these elements from relational thinking in the context of a learning event. Drawing on our consulting experiences in large systems, we have observed the difficulties that our clients face in making rapid adjustments in their perception of role in the face of changing centre–periphery relations. We are interested to know more about how to work with these client systems when perceptions of the organization and how it operates in relation to its constituent parts can change so rapidly.

We are approaching this scenario from a perspective that will emphasize a collaborative approach to enquiry, by designing an event for an open audience whom we know to be affected by these issues, through the formulation of a set of research questions. We will shape the event around data gathered from individuals in a pre-event phase, and work with a design that has pre-planned and emergent elements. We are interested in how we and these participants together can work as resources to each other, both in the transfer of existing and tacit knowledge and in the creation of new perspectives. How, as individuals and as groups, we create and make adjustments to shifts within the system as a temporary organization will become the focus for experiential learning. In a post-event phase, we expect to extend the member/participant role to produce some form of artefact to distil the learning that has emerged.

The way we position ourselves as both co-enquirers and convenors will challenge us and others to work from a both/and perspective, and will invite us to construct our own meanings from that relationship in relation to the research question we are asking. Holding the research element of group relations in tension with the learning that can emerge from a temporary organization seems to us to have potential in illuminating dynamics of knowledge transfer and knowledge generation in a shifting environment.

Finally, I want to raise the idea of reciprocity, which has emerged here in different guises, as central to the negotiating capacity, and which invokes the position of being a subject *for* others, with the delights and wounds that that necessitates. It seems to me that being such a subject poses a question about where one places a boundary, about where is the cutting edge of a relational approach. If negotiation is at the core of relational thinking, then this is where the boundary is, at what one can own and take responsibility for. This involves, as Daniel Barenboim (2006) has recently been illustrating, the curiosity, and the courage, "to listen to the narrative of the other, and at the very least accept its legitimacy".

Enter . . .

I welcome hearing your ideas on, and associations to, this chapter. Since writing it, I have used the design methodology described here with an organization wanting to explore its practices in relation to executive coaching. Working with organizational partners as co-enquirers and convenors has made it possible to offer this kind of experiential, research-orientated event to an in-house audience and enabled internal staff members to take up authentic and participating roles alongside their colleagues.

Acknowledgements

I would like to thank my clients at KIzod Consulting and The Tavistock Institute, with whom I think and learn. I am appreciative of enduring conversations with Evelyn Cleavely. Also Veronika Greuneisen, Bernie Gertler, and Jane Thorp for her understanding of Ancient Greek city-states.

References

Aram, E., Abraham, F., Hadjivassiliou, K., & Izod, K. (2006). The political meets managerial: towards an understanding of the dynamics of council top teams. Unpublished paper, The Tavistock Institute.

Aron, L. (1996). *A Meeting of Minds. Mutuality in Psychoanalysis.* Hillsdale, NJ: The Analytic Press.

Barenboim, D. (2006). *The Reith Lectures.* www.bbc.co.uk/radio4/reith2006/lecture4.

Beebe, B., & Lachmann, F. M. (1988). The contribution of mother–infant mutual influence to the origins of self and object representations. *Psychoanalytic Psychology, 5*(4): 305–337.

Benjamin, J. (1998). *Shadow of the Other: Intersubjectivity and Gender in Psychoanalysis.* New York: Routledge.

Best, S., & Kellner, D. (1997). *The Postmodern Turn.* New York: Guilford.

Bion, W. R. (1961). *Experiences in Groups.* London: Tavistock.

Bowlby, J. (1969). *Attachment and Loss, Vol 1. Attachment.* London: Hogarth.

Cartright, S. (2000). *HR Know How in Mergers and Acquisitions.* London: CIPD.

Dalal, F. (1998). *Taking the Group Seriously: Towards a Post-Foulkesian Group Analytic Theory.* London: Jessica Kingsley.

Damasio, A. R. (1994). *Descartes' Error.* New York: Grosset/Putnam.

Diamond, N., & Maronne, M. (2003). *Attachment and Intersubjectivity.* London: Whurr.

Dyer, J. H., & Singh, H. (1998). The relational view: cooperative strategy and sources of interorganizational competitive advantage. *Academy of Management Review, 23*(4): 660–679.

Elias, N. (1998). *On Civilization, Power, and Knowledge.* Chicago, IL: University of Chicago Press.

Ellman, S. J., & Moskowitz, M. (Eds.) (1998). *Enactment: Toward a New Approach to the Therapeutic Relationship.* Jason Aronson.

Fairbairn, W. R. B. (1958). On the nature and aims of psychoanalytic treatment. *International Journal of Psychoanalysis*, *39*: 374–385.

Fonagy, P. (1999). Transgenerational consistencies of attachment: a new theory. Paper presented to the Developmental and Psychoanalytic Discussion Group, American Psychoanalytic Association Meeting, Washington, DC. www.pscychematters.com.

Fonagy, P., & Target, M. (1998). Mentalization and the changing aims of child psychoanalysis. In: L. Aron & A. Harris (Eds.), *Relational Psychoanalysis Vol.2: Innovation and Expansion* (Chapter Nine). Hillside, NJ: Analytic Press, 2005.

Fonagy, P., Gergely, G., Jurist, E. L., & Target, M. (2004). *Affect Regulation, Mentalization, and the Development of the Self*. London: Karnac.

Foulkes, S. H. (1990). *Selected Papers*. London: Karnac.

Galbraith, J. R. (1995). *Designing Organisations: An Executive Briefing on Strategy, Structure, and Process*. San Franscico, CA: Jossey-Bass.

Gerhardt, S. (2004). *Why Love Matters: How Affection Shapes a Baby's Brain*. Hove: Brunner/Routledge.

Gertler, B., & Izod, K. (2004). Modernism and postmodernism in group relations: a confusion of tongues. In: S. Cytrynbaum & D. A. Noumair (Eds.), *Group Dynamics, Organizational Irrationality, and Social Complexity: Group Relations Reader 3* (Chapter Four). Jupiter, FL: A. K. Rice Institute.

Hatch, M. J. (2006). *Organizational Theory, Modern, Symbolic and Postmodern Perspectives*. Oxford: Oxford University Press.

Izod, K. (2003). Book review. *Enactment: Toward a New Approach to the Therapeutic Relationship. Organisational and Social Dynamics*, *3*(1): 170–174.

Klein, M. (1976). *The Writings of Melanie Klein, Vol 3*. London: Hogarth.

Kristeva, J. (1984). *Revolution in Poetic Language*. L. S Roudiez (Trans.). New York: Columbia University Press.

Loewenthal, D., & Snell, R. (2003). *Post-modernism for Psychotherapists: A Critical Reader*. Hove: Brunner-Routledge.

McAfee, N. (2000). *Habermas, Kristeva and Citizenship*. New York: Cornell University Press.

Miller, E. (1993). *From Dependency to Autonomy*. London: Free Association.

Miller, E., & Rice, A. K. (1967). *Systems of Organisation: Task and Sentient Systems and their Boundary Control*. London: Tavistock.

Mitchell, S. A. (1988). *Relational Concepts in Psychoanalysis: An Integration*. Cambridge, MA: Harvard University Press.

Mitchell, S. A. (1993). *Hope and Dread in Psychoanalysis*. New York: Basic Books.

Ogden, T. H. (1989). *The Primitive Edge of Experience*. Northvale, NJ: Jason Aronson.

Orbach, S. (1999). Why is attachment in the air? *Psychoanalytic Dialogues*, 9(1): 73–83.

Pizer, S. A. (1992). The negotiation of paradox in the analytic process. *Psychoanalytic Dialogues*, 2: 215–240.

Stacey, R. (2000). *Strategic Management and Organisational Dynamics* (3rd edn). London: Prentice Hall.

Stern, D. N. (1985). *The Interpersonal World of the Infant*. New York: Basic Books.

Symington, N. (1986). *The Analytic Experience: Lectures from the Tavistock*. P274. London: Free Association.

Weick, K. E. (1995). *Sensemaking in Organizations*. Thousand Oaks, CA: Sage.

Winnicott, D. W. (1992). *Collected Papers: Through Paediatrics to Psychoanalysis*. London: Karnac.

CHAPTER NINE

Inquiry as relational practice: thinking relationally about the practice of teaching and learning

Margaret L. Page

Introduction

What conditions are needed and what conceptual tools required in order for the consultant/educator to enable clients and students to creatively explore tensions that present themselves as polarities? What might relational thinking offer to educators and consultants who wish to develop this capacity? This chapter takes up these questions and explores them through examples drawn from experiences of teaching and learning within management education. Taking up the themes explored by Karen Izod, it draws from the work of Jessica Benjamin and from current research on experiential teaching and learning to explore difficulties and opportunities of inquiry-based teaching and learning within contexts where instrumental approaches predominate. Finally, it returns to the question: so what is special or radical about relational thinking? What is its potential or actual contribution to teaching and learning in university-based management education programmes?

In the first section, I offer an introduction to relational theory and practice, as an application of inquiry-based learning and teaching.

This is developed in the three illustrations that follow. The first of these is a co-mentoring relationship that enabled teaching staff to sustain an inquiring stance in relation to Masters level students, and to resist institutional pressures to adopt a more instrumental approach. The second and third sections also relate to Masters level students, this time in the context of a programme that is experiential and based on peer learning. Two vignettes are offered that explore how relational thinking offered a way of making sense, in reflection after the event, of the challenges of sustaining inquiry in the context described. The final section draws together reflections on these experiences to consider what relational thinking might offer to inquiry practice. More specifically, it explores its potential contribution to working with the difficulties and opportunities of management learning in the current UK context, where pressure is intense to stick to instrumental approaches.

Relational theory, inquiry practice

The relational perspective has been important to me in my practice as a management educator on a number of levels. First and foremost, it has offered a way of thinking creatively about seemingly irreconcilable polarities encountered in my teaching and consultancy practice. The strongest of these is the apparent contradiction between expectations brought by clients or students to be told how to do things, to be given answers, and the approach to learning and teaching that I offer, based on student-led inquiry. These different expectations bring about inevitable clashes that have to be negotiated in how we take up our roles as teachers or consultants and students or clients. These negotiations are carried out between the individuals concerned, each of whom carries expectations from their respective organizations, communities of practice, and cultural backgrounds. Thus, how we take up our roles as teachers and learners, clients and consultants, becomes the subject of negotiation, as does the relationship between each of us and our respective organizations and communities. These negotiations raise powerful emotions and strongly held opinions, and can lead to clashes in the teaching and learning encounter (Case & Selvester, 2000, 2002). A strong conceptual framework can offer a container for negotiating the conflicts that are likely to be experienced. The relational perspective offers, in my view, a conceptual framework that can present an effective container for inquiry in this context.

On a deeper level, my interest in relational theory and practice stems from a need to work across boundaries, to hold together seemingly irreconcilable tensions in my own ontological stance as a feminist, and as a university-based management educator. I was first attracted to relational theory through the writings of Jessica Benjamin, who introduces her approach to relational theory as a project of bringing into dialogue clashing discourses: feminism and psychoanalysis. The experience of living with apparently irreconcilable discourses and values, without allying oneself exclusively with either one, has been described by Meyerson and Scully as the experience of being a "tempered radical" (1995). The tempered radical is an identity instantly recognized by public sector managers with whom I work in leadership and management development and with which they strongly identify. Moreover, this experience and the associated skills of working across boundaries, of holding together identities that belong to communities that have historically been in conflict, and defined themselves against negative images of each other, has been widely conceptualized in feminist and post-colonialist management literature (Anzaldúa, 1987; Lugones, 1997; Stanley, 1997). Benjamin's work offers concepts that speak directly to the practice of working across these boundaries of conflicting identities, of community, of cultures for the purposes of bringing opposing voices into dialogue. As a feminist management educator, working in university-based business schools that are predominantly positivist and managerialist in culture and pedagogy, I have found this conceptual frame useful as a sense-making framework to support the introduction of inquiry into my teaching practice.

Inquiry-led learning and teaching is illustrated in the approach developed by Reason and Marshall in their teaching of graduate students (1987, 2001). They describe one of its key features as enabling students to tap into their passion for learning and to access the root of their interest in the subject they are studying. Inquiry offers opportunities to rework distress that may be evoked during this process and to move through and beyond self limiting patterns and defences. Reason and Marshall refer to the disciplines and practices of inquiry as including a capacity to "bracket", or loosen, attachment to an individually held perspective sufficiently to be open to new possibilities. Similarly, they refer to critical subjectivity as a capacity to be aware of one's inner world without being ruled by it (Reason & Marshall, 2001, p. 414). Benjamin's work offers four key concepts that I have found useful to support these disciplines and practices of inquiry within my pedagogical and consultancy practice. These will be elaborated more fully in the illustrations that follow. The first of these is the concept of "inter-subjectivity", and the oscillation between subject-to-subject and subject-to-object relating. Related to intersubjectivity is the concept of desire and need for "recognition" and its associated powerful destructive and generative emotional dynamics. Third, the inevitability of breakdown of subject-to-subject into subject-to-object relating, and refocusing away from a normative state of dialogue towards the inevitability of breakdown and the need for skills of repair as an arena for leadership and change. Finally, the concept of "thirdness" offers a means of conceptualizing the psychodynamics of thinking together, and the difference between a dialogue in which each advocates a single perspective and a dialogue in which new thinking arises within the interaction between two independent subjects (Figure 1).

These relational concepts speak directly to the challenges and opportunities of facilitating learning between individuals who

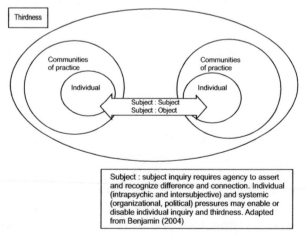

Figure 1. Conceptualizing the psychodynamics of thinking together.

carry different sectoral and organizational and, indeed, gender and national cultures, and to travellers between cultures. They offer potential for making sense of the psychosocial challenges of working across boundaries and for keeping at the edge of inquiry, resisting pressures to assimilate to a single hegemonic view when the going gets tough. Acceptance that subject-to-subject relating will be achieved in moments and inevitably break down moves the focus of inquiry to skills of repair and seems a liberating alternative to setting dialogue as a standard for learning.

The illustrations that follow explore how these concepts were useful to illumine the challenges and opportunities within the practice of inquiry in two contrasting educational contexts. In each illustration the students were mid-career managers, on Masters level university-based management education programmes. While the context of the first is a modular programme in a business school, with no specific ideological or practice affiliation, the second and third are set in a programme with a strong alternative culture, where pedagogic practices are based on experiential learning and peer learning community.

Illustration 1: Sustaining vitality through co-inquiry/mentoring—a relational perspective

> The creation of a space in which new learning can emerge, and in which affect can be moderated . . . The creation of the analytic 3rd . . . a space in which either subject can recognise the difference of the other (Benjamin, 1998) and provides a mode of containment for the interacting pair (Ogden, 1989). [Izod, 2006, p. 6]

The illustration that follows describes the co-inquiry developed in the context of mentoring and co-teaching (Page & Kirk, 2006). In it, mentor and mentee explore how inquiry enabled mentor and mentee to access and sustain their capacity for learning and curiosity. The concepts of intersubjectivity, recognition, and thirdness enabled them to make sense of and develop their teaching and learning practice

> Mentee
>
> A major issue for me in taking up a role as a "teacher" was grappling with theory as the perceived knowledge base that legitimizes

and lends authority to university-based teaching. While experienced as an agent of change, I could not find any of the qualities of my experience of doing change in the organizational literature about change leadership or management. I felt lost within a territory within which I expected to be a guide. If I owned up to disorientation and difficulty, I seemed to give away my legitimacy as an academic. Yet when I tried to engage with the theory, I seemed to lose touch with my own knowledge and sense of competency, grounded in experience of the territory of actually doing workplace change and change leadership.

Mentor

As I read the chapters in the main text for my preparation for these sessions, I felt that I was stuck inside the book. I couldn't find my way out. It was as if I was made invisible by the theory and yet I had to come out of the book so that I could communicate what was in it to the students, and do it in a way that was effective and demonstrate my effectiveness as a teacher to my new colleague and mentee. I shared my feeling of being stuck in the book with Margaret. The conversation helped me to work my way out of the book, and into my role as a teacher.

Confronted by the reality of undertaking tasks that present risk and uncertainty, I had escaped the anxiety by stepping out of the role and into the book (Hirschhorn, 1988, p. 47). I had buried myself in the text as if the theory would be a substitute for creating a worthwhile educational experience for the students. The uncertainty was because I was unfamiliar with some of the theory, and the risk was that I would expose my inadequacies and this would threaten my identity as a teacher in the eyes of the students and my new colleague, who was also my mentee.

What is revealing about this incident is that it spoke to the teaching dilemma that we were facing in our teaching. [Adapted from Page & Kirk, 2006]

In common with students, mentor and mentee were experiencing the difficulties and anxieties of engaging with the work of integrating theory with experience and making meaning of it. They began to reflect on how they might use this experience as a basis for helping students to critically engage with the theory alongside reflection on their experiences in the workplace.

In conceptualizing their inquiry processes, they drew from the concepts of intersubjectivity and of recognition, developed by feminist relational psychoanalyst Jessica Benjamin. In her practice and research, Benjamin explores the centrality of recognition between individuals, and the difficulties that each individual subject has in recognising the other as an equivalent centre of experience (Benjamin, 1990). In her concept of intersubjectivity, she speaks of an oscillation between mutual recognition, in which individuals relate to each other as subject to subject, and moments where this sense of separateness is lost, and subject-to-object replaces subject-to-subject relating. In such moments, mutual recognition as two equal subjects may turn to a form of misrecognition, a failure to appreciate the individuality of the other and loss of contact with their subjectivity (*ibid.*, p. 12). From her perspective, this oscillation between subject-to-subject and subject-to-object relating is part of the human condition, and skills of repair replace an idealized concept of dialogue in which subject-to-object relating does not occur.

These concepts of recognition and intersubjectivity proved useful in thinking about the struggle to sustain inquiry in the classroom, and for confronting expectations carried by students that tutors "perform" as holders of knowledge. These expectations were embedded in the culture of the business school as well as in their own internalized ideas of what it meant to be a "good teacher". In their roles as mentor and mentee, they discovered that they shared the value of inquiry as a way of being, and this mutual recognition became the ground that enabled each of them, from our different histories and positions, to find a place and purpose in taking up their roles as teachers in the current reality of the business school.

Co-inquiry became a means of revealing and bridging different sets of expectations about how to take up teaching and student roles. At the core of the inquiry process was the constant effort to find agency, and in enacting agency to enable students to find their own vitality. This effort to find "vitality" was cyclical, needing times together for joint thinking and times apart to develop our own thoughts. The liberating effect of inquiry conversations, their qualities of subject-to-subject interaction, was related to maintaining the distinctive qualities of their individual voices each speaking from their own purpose and passion. Figure 2 represents this process.

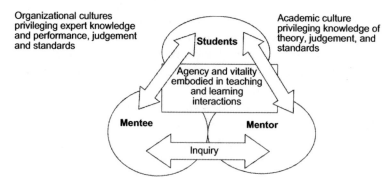

Figure 2.   The qualities of subject-to-subject interaction in inquiry conversations.

Theory is the knowledge base of academic learning. Yet theory can be both a ritualistic defence against thinking and a provocation to thinking, an enabler to thinking one's own thoughts. In order for the teacher to enable learners to access their own thinking in relation to theory, she must first find her own thoughts in relation to the theory: take it inside herself, make her own meaning from it, and develop her capacity to use it or to reject it as a way of making sense of the world. But then, there is a danger that she will reproduce the same relatedness to theory that she has struggled against, asserting or advocating her version rather than the other.

So, teaching is not concerned only with transfer of knowledge from teacher or text to student, but with a quality of relationship to knowledge. This quality of relationship, or "relatedness", has emotional as well as intellectual qualities (Armstrong, 2005, p. 15). From this perspective, the idea of "knowledge transfer" or knowledge exchange evokes a fantasy, a belief that learning can take place without the work of engagement with ideas, and without the agency of the individual as s/he accesses and makes meaning of ideas in her own context.

Yet this fantasy is a seductive one that is embedded in the teaching and learning environments of business schools and organizations today. Both staff and students are likely to "carry" these expectations into the teaching and learning encounter. Powerful emotions, desires, and frustrations are likely to be triggered in this encounter, and choices have to be made about how to work with them. The choices made will follow from the sense of purpose held by staff about their role as academics, and their assessment of what might be possible in the context of each programme (Simpson, French, & Vince, 2000). This will be shaped in part by their inner world and individual predilections, and in part by the culture and purpose of the organisation of which they are a part (Page, 2006).

The authors of this co-inquiry found that the qualities of relatedness that developed within the co-mentoring relationship enabled both to create a space with students within which new learning could emerge. The co-mentoring was itself a space within which affect was moderated and learning took place. But it was more than this. It seemed to embody qualities of thirdness that then became available to be offered in the teaching context. This process was not smooth or consistent. It involved challenge, confrontation, and conflict, and a capacity to engage in the political environment in which these struggles took place. Crucially, it involved mutual recognition as individuals struggling to take up a role as educators in a context where the meaning of teaching and of learning was, and will continue to be, contested.

The following two illustrations explore challenges that arose in a very different context. While the previous context was a single, time-limited module in which students met each other for the first time, this programme was nurtured by dedicated academic staff who protected it from modularization or the introduction of teaching practices inconsistent with the programme philosophy. While students were not subjected to the pressures of a modular teaching environment, similar dynamics came into play as staff and students had to negotiate clashes between students' desire for answers and inquiry-based learning and teaching introduced by staff.

Illustration 2: Holding open a space for inquiry between conflicting realities

> The learning was one of being able to acknowledge that different realities could pertain, and could be held as complementary, allowing for renegotiation of relations between them. [Izod, 2006, p. 8]

Allowing different realities to be held as complementary requires both will and capacity to moderate considerable pressure, arising from history of conflict, and loyalties to ideologies mediated through relationships embedded in systems and cultures. In the following vignette, I illustrate how I stumbled upon the capacity to hold in tension two complementary realities, and in doing so discovered a way of taking up my role as an educator with authority that I had previously been unable to take up.

The group of students sat in a circle, checking in. My attempts to discuss the purpose of this were interpreted by some of them as evidence of my lack of knowledge of programme practice and culture, by others as simple incompetence. Check-in was self facilitated time; attempts to modify the process were experienced as intrusive, and encroachment on their territory. I found them hard to bear. Drawn out, some students assumed meditative posture, eyes closed. Contributions bore no apparent relation to each other, yet this space offered opportunity for students to express thoughts and preoccupations without invitation for comment and outside the boundary of the taught programme. I felt de-authorized, deprived of a role, as the skills and conceptual frame from which I was working was not only unfamiliar to students, but seen as off limits, inappropriate to programme culture and ideology.

Working with this group a year later, a breakthrough occurred. Students repeatedly asked what had been the basis of my interpretations of their group process. Instead of holding myself apart, maintaining an interpretive stance, I found myself able to articulate to them how I felt and the sense that I made of this. I felt tearful, and able to both speak from this place, and to suspend from it sufficiently to speak to it. I felt a surge of relief as, far from dissolving and losing authority, as I had feared, I felt more "myself", as if I had entered my own body at last, and come truly alive in my relatedness to the students, to have entered my role in a different way in the context of the programme. This sense of relief at no longer holding myself apart, and of release of tension, seemed to mirror something of the student's experience. Students expressed this later by congratulating me on "joining" the programme—and we entered into a more dialogic and less defended way interacting from this point on. It felt as if a visceral shift had taken place, as a result of which I had found a way of taking up my role with a different kind of authority. I was able to experience "authority" and "peer relating" in a way consistent with the qualities of relatedness on the programme. [Adapted from Page & Sanger, 2006.]

Working at the time with a systems psychodynamics approach to experiential learning and group work (Gould, Stapley, & Stein, 2004), I wondered whether I should have held out and sustained a consultant role that was separate from the student group. Was it right to hold to the disciplines of the group relations tradition, in order to give students the opportunity of this specific form of experiential learning, or was it time to adapt method to context, and take up my role as tutor in a way more adapted to the course culture (Gertler & Izod, 2004)? From the group relations' perspective, I experienced the invitation from students to "share what I was feeling" as tremendous pressure to give up my authority as a member of staff and assimilate to a culture that was dysfunctional, and to succumb to being pulled out of role. Intuitively, however, I sensed that the shift that had occurred was a healthy one, in which I had found a different kind of authority within the programme that was more consistent with its culture. Moreover, that this resolved what had previously felt to be an impossible tension arising from holding to a conceptual frame and pedagogy inconsistent with the humanistic philosophy on which the programme was based. From the perspective to which I adhered, I could "see" and experience group defences against learning, namely, Bion's basic assumptions (Bion, 1961). I could feel in my body the buzz of fight–flight, the seduction of the invitation to merge into oneness with the group, or indeed to deny its existence and insist on my individuality. I also felt frustration rising as students seemed mired in incapacity to think clearly for themselves, and the pressure was on me as facilitator to provide answers and think for them. I could also see that they could not "see" any of this, and had expectations of me as academic staff member that were entirely at odds with how I was taking up my role in this context. I was not on a group relations programme, where participants had contracted to join an event of this kind, but on a programme where students expected the facilitator to be part of the group, and a focus on individual development. I needed to find a way of making my reading of events available to them that made sense within the culture of the programme as it was. To do this, I needed to let go of a sense of the "rightness" of my approach, to "hold it more lightly" in order to introduce it as one possible reading among many possibilities (Reason & Marshall, 1987). In other words, to model inquiry at a level that could engage with the conceptual frames and paradigms within which we were operating. In time, I discovered ways of doing this that honoured the programme culture while inviting students to discover its norms and to make them available for inquiry.

Significantly, and perhaps the key to holding these different realities, was finding the capacity to let go of affiliation to one or the other and to hold both in equal esteem. This was a process, and needed a length of time. Once I was able to acknowledge that different realities could pertain, and could be held as complementary, I could make inquiry within this territory available for students. However, as previous illustrations show, this carries risks for the consultant or educator, and responses to such invitations will be shaped by the context in which they are made. Subject-to-subject relating may be achieved in moments, but will inevitably break down in contexts where anxieties are likely to be high and pressures will be experienced and enacted by students and staff to abandon inquiry in favour of more instrumental approaches. It is to the skills of repair that I will turn in the next illustration.

Illustration 3: The dynamics involved in recognizing the "other"

> A capacity to appreciate the other (individual and organisation) as outside the self, and in relatedness to one's self . . . a subject with his own desires and coping patterns. [Izod, 2006, p. 9]
>
> . . . finding a level of recognition inevitably means encountering difference—working with one's own and the group's patterns of response to difference. [*ibid.*]

On management education programmes, the idea of learning community has become fashionable. Research literature explores the tendency for the "community" to be experienced and constructed as "alternative", better than workplaces, and the challenges this raises for learning from reflection on experience (Reynolds, 2000; Reynolds & Trehan, 2003). Introducing inquiry within such a context can be a risky affair, as defences are likely to be tightly held and anxieties intense where they are called into question (Page, 2006; Reynolds, 2000; Reynolds & Trehan, 2003). In this situation, the teacher will need to make a judgement about how much anxiety can be held by students within the context, and at what point it may become undermining to the learning task (Simpson, French, & Vince, 2000). The concepts of intersubjectivity and of oscillation between subject-to-subject and subject-to-object relating offer a useful holding frame to support inquiry in this context.

The context of the vignette that follows is a teaching session on gender in organizations. In it, I explore a situation in which inquiry offered a frame within which students were able to move into subject-to-subject relating momentarily, through exploration of gender difference. At a later stage, however, subject-to-subject relating broke down, as students experienced levels of anxiety that made it difficult to sustain inquiry.

Discussion in the teaching session had a flat, start–stop quality, and students had expressed frustration at feeling stuck, unable to see the relevance of what we were exploring. In the previous session, an external speaker had presented her work on gender in organizations, and, while students had engaged with it, once she had gone seemed to disown their interest in it, some making reference to corporate clients who were unlikely to be interested in either inquiry as an approach or in gender. As a way of enabling students to explore the relevance of the issues, they were invited to take part in a co-operative inquiry into their own experiences of being men or women on the programme (Reason, 1988). Parallels and contrasts could then be explored between their experiences of interactions on the programme and in their practice as managers in their organizations.

The students took up this invitation with enthusiasm. They formed single sex groups that then came together to report their findings. The experience of the opportunity to work in single sex groups was very different. While the experience of the male students was of energetic release and excitement, the female students experienced ambivalence and loss, and a wish to claim their identity as "human beings". In discussion, the male students expressed a sense of being constrained by female students and the course culture, and of reclaiming attributes that they had to suppress on the programme; the female students felt that being asked to identify as women was equivalent to being asked to collude with being somehow lacking, being somehow less than "human beings".

This contrast was reflected in the painful and conflictual nature of the discussion when they came together. During this discussion, both male and female students stated that only certain ways of being men or women were acceptable on the programme. For some of the female students, being with the male students offered a heightened sense of femininity that was fun, powerful and subversive. Both male and female students spoke of their desire to be recognized by each other as sexed and gendered, and of feeling that the androgynous and asexual culture of the programme was preventing this from happening. Yet, the qualities and politics of gender were not explored, and this resulted in an unproblematized assertion of heterosexual norms and conventional ideas of sexuality and sexual attraction. Thus, while some of the more vocal male students shared this sense of fun, a gay student voiced a sense of being negatively judged by the women for not living up to their ideal of how men should be. One of the female students, the only lesbian, stated that her femininity had not been "seen" by the other women, while others stated that they could and would not compete and did not wish to relate to "the boys" in this way.

As the session was drawing to a close, male and female students seemed to achieve a synthesis by reworking an interaction that had taken place during the group discussions, now recounted with great hilarity by one of the male students. He told his story of arriving at the door of the room where the group of female students were working in order to get some flipchart paper for his group. He had been so caught up in his group's "testosterone fuelled" exchange that he had forgotten there would be "another group" in the room until he arrived at the closed door. He knocked loudly. It was, he insisted, "a big knock". At this point, female students interrupted to protest that they had not heard his knock. Continuing his story, he said he opened the door and saw what looked like "people bending over papers, reverentially", and thought defiantly, "I live here too!" At this point, a chorus of women interrupted again and described his entrance variously as "feeling tentative" or "a burst of testosterone through the door". Associations were made between the reverential figures and "nuns in a convent". The exchange between the male storyteller and female audience seemed to go back and forth several times and become a joint performance. As hilarity rose, the story was told again and again with zest and gusto; both male and female narrators seemed to take up exaggerated roles with enthusiasm and irony.

It seemed that through their inquiry some of the capacity to own and to play with the meanings attributed to sex difference had been restored to the room. Revealing and naming these qualities that had previously been repressed seemed to restore energy and playfulness within their interactions, and some of their lost capacity for creative interaction was recovered. A sense of agency, and a capacity to take up authority was one of these lost qualities, identified by both male and female students. However, there was also a sense of danger, of ambivalence, that was difficult to contain. It was difficult to develop a discussion of the event and, in subsequent sessions, students again seemed to disown the discussion that had developed during the inquiry and expressed hostility towards the tutor. While a substantial proportion of the students took up gender relations as a theme in their written assignments, it was as if, in the group, defences against anxieties raised acted as a powerful block to learning. The subject-to-subject interaction that was achieved was achieved momentarily, but could not be sustained. Repair took place subsequently in individual interactions and discussions with the tutor, but could not be managed within the group.

In subsequent discussion, some students spoke of their sense of insufficient containment for the anxiety they experienced in "not knowing". What they wished for was not inquiry, but an expert-led approach that would tell them how to apply their learning within their organizational roles. Related to this was a sense of academic staff having underestimated the difficulty they experienced of doing inquiry. Yet, in their reflections, they also showed that they had a wish to break free of dependency on expertise and in assignments that they were able to be inquiring.

In the words of one student:

> I am left with the sense that the group has missed something "gritty", probably in the cause of "community" or however you describe it, but certainly because we haven't lived our differences. Our still emerging inquiry skills also put undue onus on the facilitator to "make things right for us", which is a fine fractal of the very tension you highlight, of an organization wanting an "expert" facilitator with the answers, which the facilitator resists. Of course

as a consultant you can simply agree that you are not the right person for the job, but as a tutor, what do you do????

Relational thinking as inquiry practice

To work as a consultant who is engaged in the process, is primarily to acknowledge oneself as stakeholder in the system, and to allow oneself a voice and a position from which to speak. With an emphasis on working with complementarities, rather than polarities, the role of the consultant is more on filtering, framing, rendering the subjective more tangible. [Weick, 1995, cited in Izod, 2006, p. 13]

Learning in management education has the potential to be co-inquiry, a contract between the educator and students. Yet, pressures are intense to adopt a more instrumental, knowledge transfer based approach to teaching and learning. These pressures come from the increasingly business led priorities of academic institutions and from the aspirations of students and their organizational sponsors from local and international markets. Teaching and learning thus does not take place in a vacuum, but in organizational and social contexts that shape and give meaning to interactions within the class room. Readiness to relate in subject-to-subject mode is determined as much by externally given meanings and values that have to be negotiated as by organizations in the mind.

"Thirdness" is not a new concept in psychoanalytic thinking, yet I have argued and demonstrated in the illustrations above how the concepts of intersubjectivity and of thirdness developed by Benjamin can offer a means to develop and enrich the disciplines and practices of inquiry that are needed to sustain it. Keys to this are the concepts of holding difference *and* connection; of holding the intrapsychic "organization in the mind" brought by each individual *and* the specific qualities of relationship experienced *between* subjects as a separate domain to the intrapsychic. These relational and psychodynamic concepts offer a language that facilitates understanding of how the political and social domains permeate the psychodynamics enacted in teaching and learning contexts. Moreover, they offer a conceptual framework that supports inquiry practices through the inevitability of breakdown of subject–subject dialogue, and offer a means for subject–object relating not to be pathologized, or seen as a failure of inquiry, but accepted and incorporated into inquiry practice. I have illustrated how this oscillation between modes of intersubjectivity was a central feature of staff–student interactions in each of the three examples above. From a psychodynamic relational perspective, skills of repair replace an idealized concept of dialogue in which subject–object relating does not occur. The focus of inquiry practice can then move to moments of reparation. In all three illustrations, skills of repair, and the dynamics of recognition and misrecognition, were played out over a period of time, which allowed an understanding of inquiry processes to develop. The concept of "thirdness", I have suggested, captures the qualities of relatedness needed for the long haul and the ups and downs of sustaining inquiry with others.

Final reflections

The illustrations above are primarily concerned with how relational thinking can support inquiry-based teaching in management educational contexts. I have shown that the students carried with and within them instrumental pressures from their organizational contexts, and that the practice of inquiry proved valuable to sustain their learning and capacity for critical thinking. Many subsequently introduced inquiry practices to sustain themselves in work contexts, and some have introduced the methods within their practice with peers and teams that they manage. The impact of the inquiry practice thus went beyond the classroom, into organizations where some students attempted to become change agents, resisting the pressures towards instrumentalization and introducing inquiry practices to sustain more reflective and reflexive approaches with peers.

Reason and Marshall speak of working with students to discover purpose in their inquiry in three interrelated arenas: inquiry for me, for us, and for them (1987, pp. 112–113, 2001, p. 413). Each domain contains potential for finding or losing agency and vital connection. In each domain, competing narratives jostle and collide. These may be carried from previous contexts or be embedded or enacted in current contexts. They must be negotiated by members of organizations as they enter or leave and as their context changes. The process is anxiety provoking and destabilizing. Both educators and students may become stuck in defensive or ritualistic behaviours that lead to a loss of agency, or be overwhelmed by pressures to conform to powerful sets of expectations and projections. In these circumstances, educators and members of organizations need a protected space to recover their thinking capacity and retain a sense of agency.

Co-inquiry, supported by an understanding of the psychodynamics of relational thinking, can offer disciplines and practices for sustaining agency in role taking. However, inquiry cannot replace instrumental pressures and cultures, but can and must take root in forms and in spaces that already exist and be held alongside existing cultures and practices. Relational thinking offers a conceptual frame that can sustain individuals who seek to introduce inquiring relationships and to sustain vitality within organizational as well as educational contexts.

References

Anzaldúa, G. (1987). *Borderlands/La Frontera: The New Mestiza*. San Francisco, CA: Aunt Lute Books.

Armstrong, D. (2005). *Organization in the Mind: Psychoanalysis, Group Relations and Organizational Consultancy*. London: Karnac.

Benjamin, J. (1990). *The Bonds of Love: Psychoanalysis, Feminism and the Problem of Domination*. London: Virago.

Benjamin, J. (2004). Beyond doer and done to: an intersubjective view of thirdness. *Physchoanalytic Quarterly, XXIII*(1).

Bion, W. R. (1961). *Experiences in Groups*. London: Tavistock.

Case, P., & Selvester, K. (2000). Close encounters: ideological invasion and complicity on an "International Management Master's Programme". *Management Learning, 31*(1): 11–23.

Case, P., & Selvester, K. (2002). Watch your back: reflections on trust and mistrust in management education. *Management Learning, 33*(2): 231–247.

Gertler, B., & Izod, K. (2004). Modernism and postmodernism in group relations: a confusion of tongues. In: S. Cytrynbaum & D. A. Noumair (Eds.), *Group Dynamics, Organizational Irrationality, and Social Complexity: Group Relations Reader 3* (pp. 89–108). Jupiter, FL: A. K. Rice Institute.

Gould, L. J., Stapley, L. F., & Stein, M. (Eds) (2004). *Experiential Learning in Organizations: Applications of the Tavistock Group Relations Approach*. London: Karnac.

Hirschhorn, L. (1988). *The Workplace Within: The Psychodynamics of Organizational Life.* Cambridge, MA: MIT Press.

Izod, K. (2006). How does a turn towards relational thinking influence consulting practice in organisations and groups? Conference paper presented to Relational Thinking, Linking Psychoanalysis, Organisations and Society, UWE, Centre for Psycho Social Studies, June.

Lugones, M. (1997). Playfulness, "world"-travelling, and loving perception. In: D. T. Meyers (Ed.), *Feminist Social Thought: A Reader* (pp. 275–290). London: Routledge.

Meyerson, D., & Scully, M. (1995). Tempered radicalism and the politics of ambivalence and change. *Organization Science*, 6(5): 585–600.

Page, M. (2006). A traveller's tale: on joining a peer learning community; moments of passionate dis/connection in a quest for inquiry. In: S. Gherardi & D. Nicolini (Eds.), *The Passion for Learning and Knowing. Proceedings of the 6th International Conference on Organizational Learning and Knowledge* (pp. 628–648). Trento: University of Trento e-books.

Page, M., & Kirk, P. (2006). Worker as researcher, researcher as worker. Paper given at Teaching and Learning as Inquiry: International Work Based Learning Conference. Northampton, March.

Page, M., & Sanger, C. (2006). Subverting Utopias/Dangerous Dialogue: can humanistic and systems psychodynamics be bridged in experiential teaching and learning? *OPUS Conference Paper*, London, November.

Reason, P. (1988). *Human Inquiry in Action.* London: Sage

Reason, P., & Marshall, J. (1987). Research as personal process. In: D. Boud & V. Griffin (Eds.), *Appreciating Adult Learning* (pp. 112–126). London: Kegan Page.

Reason, P., & Marshall, J. (2001). On working with graduate research students. In: P. Reason & H. Bradbury (Eds.), *Handbook of Action Research, Participative Inquiry and Practice* (pp. 413–419). London: Sage.

Reynolds, M. (2000). Bright lights and the pastoral idyll. *Management Learning*, 3(1): 57–73.

Reynolds, M., & Trehan, K. (2003). Learning from difference? *Management Learning*, 34(2): 163–180.

Simpson, P., French, R., & Vince, R. (2000). The upside of the downside; how utilizing defensive dynamics can support learning in groups. *Management Learning*, 31(4): 457–470.

Stanley, L. (Ed.) (1997). *Knowing Feminisms, On Academic Borders, Territories, Tribes.* London: Sage.

INDEX

Abraham, F., 174–175, 182
addiction, 45, 49–51, 54, 56, 61–62, 81
Adorno, T., 114–115, 133, 135, 150
Alford, F., 150–151, 160
Altman, N., 6, 12, 22
anxiety, 7, 9, 17, 19, 21, 28, 72, 90–91, 100, 103, 124, 128, 131, 143, 147, 158, 168, 170–171, 190, 196–197, 199, 202
Anzaldùa, G., 187, 202
Aram, E., 174–175, 182
Armstrong, D., 192, 202
Aron, L., xiv, 5–6, 22, 27, 44, 167, 182
attachment, 30–31, 40–42, 121, 173, 188
    theory, xx, 7, 25, 47, 163, 167
attunement, xv, 6, 10–11, 18, 20, 94, 98, 100–101, 105–107
autonomy, 10, 14, 18, 21, 41, 65–66, 68, 77, 102, 146, 166, 172, 175

Bacal, H., 59, 63
Banton, R., 90, 109

Barenboim, D., 181–182
Bateson, G., 58, 63
Bauman, Z., 106, 109, 115, 134
Beck-Gernsheim, E., 144, 160
Beebe, B., 25–26, 167, 182
Beedell, P., 119, 134
Benhabib, S., 75, 83
Benjamin, J., xiv–xv, xx–xxii, 6, 10–13, 15, 18–22, 40, 73–74, 76, 83, 89, 91, 94, 100–102, 104, 109, 147, 160, 167, 170, 174, 182, 185, 187–189, 191, 200, 202
Best, S., 167, 182
Bick, E., 140, 152, 161
Bion, W. R., xv, xx, 8, 75, 83, 107, 109, 133–134, 138, 146–147, 149–150, 154, 161, 164, 170, 182, 195, 202
Blather, C., 89, 109
Boal, A., 107, 109
Bollas, C., xviii, 25, 73–74, 83, 94, 105–106, 109
Bornat, J., 121, 134
Boston Change Process Study Group, 2, 10, 22

205